CHRISTIAN

FAITH

COMPENDIUM

McDougal & Associates
Servants of Christ and Stewards of the
Mysteries of God

CHRISTIAN

FAITH

COMPENDIUM

Sundry Sermon Substance

BY

GANI CORUÑA

Published by:

McDougal & Associates

18896 Greenwell Springs Road

Greenwell Springs, Louisiana 70739

www.ThePublishedWord.com

McDougal & Associates is an organization dedicated to the spreading of the Gospel of Jesus Christ to as many people as possible in the shortest time possible.

ISBN 978-1-940461-68-7

Printed on demand in the US, the UK, and Australia

For Worldwide Distribution

DEDICATION

I dedicate this book:

To my beloved wife, Liling Cortes Coruña, who stood by me
and did not leave me when I was poor.

To our children, Norman, Noemi, Gabriel (Garry), Joseph and
Atty. Gani (Jay jay) Coruña.

To the memory of Erik Gunnar Eriksson and his wife Karin,
Founders of Tentmission and Star of Hope in Sweden, who
trusted us as partners of Star of Hope mission and work
in the Philippines.

To the Eriksson siblings, Lennart, Maria and Ulrika, who continue to advance the work and legacy of their parents, the
Star of Hope International mission around the world.

ACKNOWLEDGMENTS

I must acknowledge the impact of these individuals upon my life and ministry:

Rev. Harold McDougal, Founder of Christ to the Philippines and our father in the faith, whose missionary life inspired and encouraged us to continually serve our Lord Jesus Christ until now. He helped edit this book through his technical and literary expertise.

Rev. Robert (Bobby) Robinson and his wife Rita, who were kind and gracious enough to restore me as Pastor of Murphy Pentecostal Church after I came back from the United States.

All the American missionaries and families who served under Christ to the Philippines here in our country

CONTENTS

FOREWORD BY HAROLD McDOUGAL

The years I spent teaching in Bible training centers in the Philippines, Ecuador and West Africa were among the most enjoyable times of my life. I had loved pioneer evangelism and had endured pastoral work, but teaching was my delight. I imagined myself doing it the rest of my life. It not only gave me the chance to duplicate my efforts through inspiring others, but I always learned much more than my students.

Little did I know that those early ministries were but preparation for what I do now — publishing God's Word. The fact that several of my former students, Gani among them, are now authors that I publish makes it all the more wonderful.

As a young man, Gani's situation was very unusual. We usually did not accept married students into the program. They had a responsibility to their family first, and we had no proper facilities to house families. But Gani and Liling were willing to sacrifice to prepare themselves for the ministry. And sacrifice they did. I rejoice with them over their victories for the Kingdom.

Harold McDougal

Introduction

This book is a compilation of my select, various messages and teachings during our Sunday and midweek services at the Christian Faith Church in West Crame, San Juan City, Philippines, where I have now served as pastor for many years.

There are different subjects on Christian Faith in this book, which cover the origin and nature of man, sin and its effects, divine providence, interesting and exemplary Bible characters, the Gospel of Jesus Christ, faith, hope, love, prayers and eschatology, just to name a few.

Our personal testimonies and experiences regarding the modern miracles of God of healing and divine provisions are also included here. We trust that these testimonies will inspire and challenge the readers to trust and believe God for His promises.

Besides the aforementioned, the messages in this book are aimed at fostering beneficial biblical doctrine, reproof, correction and instruction in righteousness, so that the Christian might be without blame, exemplary and prepared to answer the question of hope that is in him.

Let me warn the reader that the teachings are in no particular order, and there is some overlap from one to another. Each one was intended to stand on its own, so we have not bothered to remove any duplication or to combine those of a similar theme. Let me also say that I know some of my teachings are rather unorthodox and many may disagree with them. If you have accepted the Lord Jesus Christ as your personal Savior, you are my brother, and I respect your views on these and other subjects.

Gani Coruña

൦ **1** ൬

EXPECT THE UNEXPECTED!

Text: Hebrews 11:7

Man's life has many expectations. These expectations are particular events, or occurrences, that he will experience which are yet future. There are three categories of expectations. They are (1) the expected, (2) the least expected and (3) the unexpected. These may be either good news or bad, depending on the information received or whether or not one is totally unaware or uninformed of the coming events, especially when such an event is unfavorable and destructive. The feeling accompanying good events is great anticipation and excitement, but the bad ones may come as an utter surprise and shock. The keys to overcoming these expectations are information, knowledge, understanding and preparation.

When a woman is pregnant, they say that she is "expecting." Expecting what? She is expecting a baby. In that case, she needs knowledge, information, understanding and preparation in order to take care of herself and the baby. She needs to constantly consult her mother or the gynecologist regarding the matter of her pregnancy. Perhaps, if she is smoking, drinking or engaged in substance abuse, she will be advised to quit all these vices for the welfare and benefit of her baby. She must also avoid stress because this can also adversely affect the baby. She and her husband must also prepare financially because having a baby costs money. There are women, however, who are pregnant but they don't have husbands. That will be an added financial burden to her parents or other members of the family.

The farmer who expects a bumper harvest of his crop must also prepare. Besides the physical preparation of ploughing his field for the sowing and planting of the seed, he needs vital information, knowledge and understanding on modern farming techniques. Modern farm implements, irrigation and fertilizers will certainly help to bring about the farmer's expected bumper harvest.

An athlete who expects to win in any athletic competition that he engages in must also prepare through rigorous discipline of physical and mental training. He must focus and consider strategies and styles of the game needed for his goal of winning.

Today, those who are in charge of dealing with calamities and disasters are talking about "the big one." What is this "big one"? It is the big earthquake that will surely hit mega cities like Los Angeles, San Francisco or Metro Manila. Scientists predict that because of the fault lines traversing these cities (the San Andreas Fault in California and the Valley Fault in Metro Manila), tens of thousands and, perhaps, even hundreds of thousands of people will die when such an earthquake will occur. This is not to mention the devastating effect on properties.

Even if the epicenter of an earthquake is out in the sea, still the devastating effect of a tsunami are equally catastrophic. Do you remember the "Ache" Indonesia earthquake and the resulting tsunami of 2004? More than two hundred thousand lives were lost, including many in Thailand and neighboring Sri Lanka. In

2011, a powerful tsunami caused by an earthquake out in the sea hit eastern Japan and killed more than ten thousand people, plus the serious damages done to properties. This included breaching the integrity of the Fukushima nuclear power plant. The resulting radiation leak caused the displacement of many thousands of Japanese families.

These are nothing compared with the catastrophe that happened during the Great Flood at the time of Noah. This flood was of such a cataclysmic magnitude that only eight people were saved. The rest of the people of the world perished in a watery grave. How did that happen? Why were only Noah and his family saved? How did they survive the flood? Our text says that Noah *"was warned by God concerning events as yet unseen."* Noah and his family believed God, and that was why they were saved. Noah prepared an ark to the saving of himself and his family. The circumstances surrounding these events are narrated in Genesis 6 through 9.

Many sceptics dismiss the story of the Great Flood during the time of Noah as being a fable and hence fictitious. Christians, however, believe that it is a true story. This Bible story was narrated by Moses, confirmed by the apostle Paul and validated by Jesus Himself. What does this mean? It means that the flood during the time of Noah was a historical fact.

But as the days of Noah were, so will be the coming of the Son of man. For as in those days before the flood they were eating and drinking, marrying and giving in marriage, until the day that Noah entered the ark. And they did not know until the flood came and swept them all away, so will be the coming of the Son of Man. Matthew 24:37-39

Another translation of this phrase *"and they did not know"* is *"people wouldn't believe."* Yes, people refused to believe what was going to happen until the flood actually arrived and took them all away.

The Bible says:

> *Then the LORD saw that the wickedness of man was great in the earth, and that every intent of the thoughts of his heart was only evil continually. And the LORD was sorry that He had made man on the earth, and He was grieved in His heart. So the LORD said, "I will destroy man whom I have created from the face of the earth, both man and beast, creeping thing and birds of the air, for I am sorry that I have made them." But Noah found grace in the eyes of the LORD.* Genesis 6:5-8

Verses 9 says of Noah:

> *Noah was a just man, perfect in his generations. Noah walked with God.*

So it was that God spoke to Noah:

> *And God said to Noah, "The end of all flesh has come before Me, for the earth is filled with violence through them; and behold, I will destroy them with the earth. Make yourself an ark of gopherwood."* Genesis 6:13-14

Again the Lord spoke to Noah:

Then the Lord said to Noah, "Come into the ark, you and all your household, because I have seen that you are righteous before Me in this generation."   Genesis 7:1

Noah obeyed both commands:

So Noah, with his sons, his wife, and his sons' wives, went into the ark because of the waters of the flood.   Genesis 7:7

Very quickly, what God had warned about came to pass exactly as He had said:

On that day all the fountains of the great deep were broken up, and the windows of heaven were opened. And the rain was on the earth forty days and forty nights.   Genesis 7:11-12

The rains kept coming until ...

And the waters prevailed exceedingly on the earth, and all the high hills under the whole heaven were covered.   Genesis 7:19

And all flesh died that moved on the earth: birds and cattle and beasts and every creeping thing that creeps on the earth, and every man.   Genesis 7:21

Only Noah and those who were with him in the ark remained alive.   Genesis 7:23

Why did God decide to wipe out all mankind and spare only Noah and his family? The answer to this question is in the preceding paragraphs. It was God's divine prerogative, as a sovereign Lord, to impose this judgment upon mankind. If Noah was warned by God concerning this cataclysmic event which was to happen and was instructed to build an ark to the saving of himself and his family, were not the other people of his generation also informed or warned of this coming catastrophic event? I believe they were, and it was done through Noah.

Noah had a double task, and it was great and challenging. He had to build an ark, as God had commanded him, but he was also to preach to the people of his generation and warn them to turn away from wickedness and violence and to embrace righteousness.

Noah would need enormous resources to build such a gigantic seaworthy vessel. A group of people in America made it a project to build an exact replica of Noah's ark, and it cost them more than $400 million to complete it.

Preaching to the people of his generation was, for Noah, against all odds, but he did it faithfully for about a hundred years. Still, the people did not believe him. Why didn't the people believe Noah? What was his message to them? His message was that God would bring a flood of waters upon the earth so great that it would *destroy all flesh.* Every living creature wold die. He preached that rain would come down in mighty torrents from the sky, and the subterranean waters would burst forth upon the earth. The people did not believe this because there was no rain in those days. The earth was watered by a mist or vapor. And there was a canopy of water above the earth's atmosphere. The earth was a paradise, with a perfect environment—perfect humidity and perfect temperature. No wonder people lived for hundreds of years in those days!

Did the people expect such a flood to come? The answer is clearly no. But were they informed of the coming of this cataclysmic event? Yes, they were, by Noah himself, through his persevering, patient and persistent preaching. So, why then did the people perish? The people of Noah's day perished because they did not believe his preaching. Otherwise, they would have prepared to be saved too.

Thankfully, today we don't have to build an ark to be saved. Salvation is now free! It is not expensive. It has already been paid for by Jesus Christ on the cross of Calvary. It is also easy! The only requirement is that we repent and believe the Gospel. Whoever believes in Jesus Christ will not perish, but will have eternal life! ✄

 C3 **2** EO

THE GOSPEL TO THE POOR

Text: Luke 4:18

After He had fasted for forty days in the wilderness and then was tempted by the devil, Jesus returned to Galilee in the power of the Spirit. The first message He preached when He commenced His public ministry, according to the gospel account of Luke, was *"the gospel to the poor."* This took place in His own hometown of Nazareth.

It happened in this way:

And as His custom was, He went into the synagogue on the Sabbath day, and stood up to read. And He was handed the book of the prophet Isaiah. And when He had opened the book, He found the place where it was written:
"The Spirit of the Lord is upon Me,
Because He has anointed Me
To preach the gospel to the poor ... ".   Luke 4:16-18

22

Then He closed the book, and gave it back to the attendant and sat down. And the eyes of all who were in the synagogue were fixed on Him. And He began to say to them, "Today this Scripture is fulfilled in your hearing." So all bore witness to Him, and marveled at the gracious words which proceeded out of His mouth. And they said, "Is this not Joseph's son?" Luke 4:20-22

Jesus discerned the doubts of the people concerning His person, so, He responded by giving them a rebuke:

"Assuredly, I say to you, no prophet is accepted in his own country." Luke 4:24

After hearing Jesus cite two historical incidents which suggested that God is no respecter of person when it comes to miraculous benefits, the people became furious. They seized Jesus and took Him to the edge of the city where they attempted to throw Him down headfirst over the cliff. He somehow escaped.

This rejection on the part of His hometown folks did not deter Jesus from continuing His mission. Now He went to other Galilean cities like Capernaum and spoke in their synagogues and He continued to conduct His deliverance and healing ministries for those who were possessed by demons and those who were afflicted with sickness:

And He came down with them and stood on a level place with a crowd of His disciples and a great multitude of people from all Judea and Jerusalem, and from the seacoast of Tyre and Sidon,

23

who came to hear Him and be healed of their diseases, as well as those who were tormented with unclean spirits. And they were healed. And the whole multitude sought to touch Him, for power went out from Him and healed them all.

Then He lifted up His eyes toward His disciples, and said:

"Blessed are you poor,
For yours is the kingdom of God.   Luke 6:17-20

What is the Gospel relative to the poor? Will the Gospel make the poor rich? First of all, the fundamental message of the Gospel is the Good News of salvation in Jesus Christ. It is the saving work of God through His Son Jesus and the call to faith in Him. It has been said that Jesus is more than the messenger of the Gospel; He is the Gospel! The Good News of God was present in His life and teachings and also in His atoning death and resurrection. Therefore the Gospel is both a historical event and a personal relationship.

Who were (and who are) the poor Jesus referred to? Perhaps we could categorize the poor as economically poor people, physically poor people, socially or emotionally poor people and also those who are spiritually poor. People who are economically poor are destitute of the basic necessities of life, like food, water, clothing and shelter. Those who are physically poor are suffering and languishing in sickness and affliction. The socially and emotionally poor believe that they are alone and no one cares for them. This leaves them fearful, hopeless and feeling unloved. Those who are spiritually poor are actually spiritually dead.

What are the indicators that these groups of people can be considered poor? First, they beg from others, and second, they depend on the good will of others. That's why children are included in

24

the Kingdom of Heaven because they depend on their parents. Jesus said:

Let the little children come to Me, and do not forbid them; for of such is the kingdom of heaven. Matthew 19:14

Poor people beg because their survival and existence depend on the kindness and generosity of their benefactors. Such was the case of Lazarus, who begged at the rich man's gate. Unfortunately, the rich man was greedy and unwilling to share, so Lazarus died. Children depend on their parents to sustain them, and without support from their parents, they will also perish.

Actually, all people—whether physically poor or rich—are spiritually poor in the eyes of God, even though most of them don't realize their spiritual condition. When Jesus said, *"Blessed are the poor,"* He was not implying just the spiritual, physical or economic poverty, and the blessedness of these poor was in begging and depending on the grace and mercy of God.

True Christians adopt this kind of dependant attitude from the time they are saved and continue to maintain it because they are still very much dependent on God for spiritual sustainability. So, the spiritually poor who beg and children have one thing in common: they are both heirs of the Kingdom of Heaven. Jesus said:

Assuredly, I say to you, unless you are converted and become as little children, you will by no means enter the kingdom of heaven.

Matthew 18:3

As to the question of whether the Gospel will make the poor rich, the answer is yes. The riches of the poor, when the Gospel is responded to positively, is in the promise of blessing: *"Blessed are the poor."* This promised blessing has a wide range of implications. There are many promises in the Bible concerning how the poor can become rich. For example:

For you know the grace of our Lord Jesus Christ, that though He was rich, yet for your sakes He became poor, that you through His poverty might become rich.   2 Corinthians 8:9

The blessing of the Lord makes one rich,
And He adds no sorrow with it.   Proverbs 10:22

Being rich is not just the accumulation and possession of wealth and material things, but it is in how one utilizes his resources. There are wealthy people who do not want to help the poor and needy. Them there are those who are not so wealthy but find a way to help those who are poor and needy.

It is interesting that while the super-rich Middle East, Arab states like Saudi Arabia, United Arab Emirates and Oman, have more than enough resources to help the refugees from Syria and other Muslim countries that are being displaced by civil war, they offer little or no help at all. Saudi Arabia, for example, has hundreds of thousands of air-conditioned tents sitting empty tents which could provided shelter for the refugees, but, for some reason, they ignore the dire need of their brothers. Instead, it is the United States, Canada, Australia and the Christians of Europe who have responded to this crisis and opened their hearts and homes to help these desperate people. It is Christians who are providing emergency relief assistance to the thousands of families displaced by the war between the government forces of the Philippines and the Muslim extremists and terrorists, Maute group and Abbu Sayyaf in Marawi City, Mindanao.

One thing is for sure: If poor people choose to follow Christ, they will always be provided for. One of the names of our Lord, Jehovah-Jireh, shows us that He will provide.

When Jesus was walking on the earth, thousands of poor people followed Him, and when they were hungry, He miraculously provided, feeding them with bread and fish until they were all satisfied. The sick and afflicted who came to Jesus, were healed, and those who suffered demon possession were set free.

Is this Gospel message to the poor still relevant and effective today? Oh, yes, for *"Jesus Christ is the same yesterday today and forever."* How does He do it today? He does it through His Church.

Even today, different ministry gifts are manifest in and through the Church to heal and comfort the poor. Social and charitable programs are part of the ministry outreaches of the Church. In our church, besides the Gospel message being broadcast every church service, we also feed and otherwise help our poor members. If we really want our life to be blessed and we really want to be rich, it can only be accomplished through Jesus Christ. The challenge for each of us is to follow Jesus Christ the rest of our lives. In order to do that, it is indispensable that we repent of our sins and receive Jesus Christ into our lives as our Lord and Savior.

BESIDES FAITH

Text: 2 Peter 1:5-9

Faith is very important in our lives. Why? And just how important is it? If there is one thing that pleases God, it is faith. His Word declares:

> *But without faith it is impossible to please Him, for he who comes to God must believe that He is, and that He is a rewarder of those who diligently seek Him.* Hebrews 11:6

It is through faith that we come to know and understand God, and if we diligently seek Him, He rewards us. It is by faith that we understand Creation:

> *By faith we understand that the worlds were framed by the word of God, so that the things which are seen were not made of things which are visible.* Hebrews 11:3

The Bible also says:

For by grace you have been saved through faith, and that not of yourselves; it is the gift of God. Ephesians 2:8

But what is faith? Hebrews says:

Now faith is the substance of things hoped for, the evidence of things not seen. Hebrews 11:1

Here we see four important words that constitute faith. First, there is the *"substance."* Next there are *"things hoped for"* relative to the substance. Then, there is the *"evidence,"* which is related to the phrase *"things not seen."*

What is a substance? A substance is "an essential nature or form of a matter."

What are the things that we have hoped for? Things that we have hoped for is something which is yet in the future. It has not happened yet. We each have several or many hopes. Let us categorize them in two: There are temporary hopes, and there are eternal hopes. We hope to have a better life here in this world, and, of course, we hope to be saved and live forever in Heaven with God!

What is evidence? Evidence is "something that indicates or furnishes proof." It is also "a testimony by one who bears witness to the fact and the truth of a matter." The objects of this evidence are "things not seen." When convincing someone of "things not seen" in a particular matter, it is necessary to offer evidence or proof.

What are *"things not seen"* relative to the question of evidence in faith? Most of us don't see God or Heaven (where He dwells and where He promised to take us who are saved to live with Him forever. It is faith that gives us evidence of God and Heaven, although they are unseen.

So, what are the substance and evidence of the things hoped for and the things unseen? It is the Word of God, the Bible, the promises of God that it contains, the testimonies of God's saints then and now relative to the future, to God, to Heaven and to all the things unseen and future.

So, how do we get faith or how can we receive faith? The Scriptures teach:

So then faith comes by hearing, and hearing by the word of God.   Romans 10:17

That is why it is necessary to disseminate the Gospel of our Lord Jesus Christ through preaching and teaching:

How then shall they call on Him in whom they have not be-lieved? And how shall they believe in Him of whom they have not heard? And how shall they hear without a preacher?

Romans 10:14

And He said to them, "Go into all the world and preach the gospel to every creature. He who believes and is baptized will be saved; but he who does not believe will be condemned."

Mark 16:15-16

How do we appropriate faith in our lives so that we may receive the benefits of the promises of God? It is through the process of believing. Believing is being persuaded with conviction that what God said is true and that He will fulfill His promises:

Believe on the Lord Jesus Christ, and you will be saved, you and your household.   Acts 16:31

Jesus said to him, "If you can believe, all things are possible to him who believes."   Mark 9:23

Jesus said to her, "Did I not say to you that if you would believe you would see the glory of God?"   John 11:40

This is also true with healing and miracles. When a woman who had been bleeding for twelve years approached Jesus, she said to herself: *"If only I may touch His clothes, I shall be made well"* (Mark 5:28). Jesus said to her, *"Daughter, your faith has made you whole"* (Mark 5:34).

Two blind men came begging Jesus for healing. He asked them, " *'Do you believe that I am able to do this?' They said to Him, 'Yes, Lord.' Then He touched their eyes, saying, 'According to your faith let it be to you.' And their eyes were opened"* (Matthew 9:29-30). Have faith in God! Praise God! Hallelujah!

There are two kinds of faith. They are the right faith and the wrong faith. What is right faith? This is faith or belief based on the Word of God, the Bible. What is wrong faith? This is faith or belief based on words or things other than the Word of God or on false gods. Those who are in the wrong faith also believe. They are sincere but sincerely wrong. The gods they worship are man-made, idols of stone, wood or plaster of paris. Of them the Bible says:

They have mouths, but they do not speak;
Eyes they have, but they do not see;
They have ears, but they do not hear;
Noses they have, but they do not smell;
They have hands, but they do not handle;
Feet they have, but they do not walk;
Nor do they mutter through their throat.
Those who make them are like them;
So is everyone who trusts in them.   Psalm 115:5-8

Faith is only the beginning of our spiritual experiences and relationship with our true God, Jesus Christ. There is much more to it, so that the apostle Peter encouraged followers of Christ to add to their faith:

Add to your faith virtue, to virtue knowledge, 6 to knowledge self-control, to self-control perseverance, to perseverance godliness, 7 to godliness brotherly kindness, and to brotherly kindness love. 8 For if these things are yours and abound, you will be neither barren nor unfruitful in the knowledge of our Lord Jesus Christ. 9 For he who lacks these things is shortsighted, even to blindness, and has forgotten that he was cleansed from his old sins.   2 Peter 1:5-9

It is apparent that there is lack of other Christian characteristics, such as goodness or virtue, in the lives of many Christians.

That is why the apostle said that these must be added to their faith.

What is goodness or virtue? It is good manners and right conduct for Christians. Many Christians have faith but they lack manners, good manners and right conduct. I have a missionary friend who scolded and shouted at his wife in front of us. Of course, the poor wife was extremely embarrassed. So I privately advised him not to do that again because it was not right. Unfortunately, after offering my advice, I lost him as a friend.

Christians must also add knowledge to their faith. What kind of knowledge? Well, general knowledge, but, most importantly, knowledge of the Word of God. God does not want His people to be ignorant. He said:

My people are destroyed for lack of knowledge.   Hosea 4:6

That's why the apostle Paul wrote:

Study to shew thyself approved unto God, a workman that needeth not to be ashamed, rightly dividing the word of truth.
                                        2 Timothy 2:15

Because of the lack of this knowledge, many people today are deceived by the words and doctrines of man. They cannot discern what is true faith from what is false faith.

Other Christian characteristics that must be added to our faith are temperance, patience, godliness, brotherly kindness and love or charity. This passage, in 2 Peter 1:5-9, is the apostle Peter's version of 1 Corinthians 13. It is time to examine ourselves as Christians and be sure that, besides our faith we have added these other important Christian characteristics. If not, we may be in danger of being weighed in the balances and are found wanting. ✄

cs **4** so

THE SHREWD STEWARD

Text: Luke 16:1-9

Many consider this to be one of the most puzzling parables of our Lord Jesus Christ, but if we can begin to understand it, we will find that the message of it is a profound perspective and preparation for our everlasting future.

One of the hallmarks of our Lord's parables is the presence of the element of comparison. Often we have to study these parables seriously, with prayer, seeking the guidance of the Holy Spirit, so that we can discover the truths of their message. What is the comparison in this parable? It is quite obvious. It is the comparison that *"the children of this world are wiser in their generation than the children of light."* Let us ask God to reveal His Word to us.

What or who is a steward? A steward is "one who is employed in a large household or estate to manage domestic concerns, including the supervision of servants, the collection of rents, and keeping accounts." A steward is also "a manager and or a finance officer in a business." So, what kind of a steward do we have in this story? How should we characterize him? Was he a good steward?

35

First of all, we must notice that this man was accused of wasting his master's goods, and when he was summoned by his master to give an account, he did not deny the accusation. Next, he prejudiced his master's business gains by granting discounts to his debtors on their obligations to gain their friendship. He issued a discount of 50% to one and of 20% to another. And he did this, not for his master's business benefit, but, rather, for his own benefit so that when his master put him out of stewardship, he could expect that his master's debtors would accept him into their houses.

Why did the steward do this? He has his personal reasons. He said, *"I cannot dig"* and *"I am ashamed to beg."* The strange thing about this parable is this line in verse 8: *"So the master commended the unjust steward because he had dealt shrewdly."* Does this mean that the Lord Jesus commended the unjust steward in this story? The answer is a resounding no. It was his master who commended him.

So why did this master commend the man who had wasted his goods and given uncalled-for discounts? The text clearly states that the master commended the dishonest steward for his *"shrewdness."* And does this mean that Christians should emulate this shrewd steward? Absolutely not! His methods, deceiving others for personal gain, is the way of the world, not the way of God's Kingdom.

It is sad to say that there is so much graft and corruption in all sectors of our society today that such illegal and immoral acts are all easily justified under the maxim, "the end justifies the means." In other words, to the worldly, it doesn't matter how the money or goods are procured, as long as the money is there. For example, the peddlers of illegal and prohibited drug have no pity or concern for those who became drug addicts because of their menacing, destructive and deadly activity.

What crime, if any, had the dishonest steward committed? He had committed the crime of qualified theft, and he deserved to lose his job.

So, what did Jesus mean when He said, *"for the children of this world are in their generation wiser than the children of light"*? I see two meanings in this pronouncement of our Lord. First, it is a rebuke to Christians (the children of light). Second, it is a challenge to Christians. Why a rebuke? It is a rebuke because Christians ought to be wiser in their performance and producing results of their affairs in this world, whether spiritual or practical, compared with the worldly people. Christians should excel in this world in all their endeavors and achievements. Why? Because we are the children of light, and as children of light, we have more than sufficient resources from God to excel and to be wiser than the children of this world. Far too many Christians, however, remain naïve to this reality.

Now, what is the challenge? The challenge is that Christians around the world today can reverse their situation and they can be wiser than the children of this world! How? God has already given us renewed minds and other available spiritual resources. We must appropriate and utilize these with our renewed minds. We must pray for knowledge and understanding. We must be ingenious, creative, productive and daring in all our endeavors and exploits, especially those which are directly for Christ and for the cause of His Kingdom. We have the promises of God to back us up and ensure our success and prosperity.

Remember, we are all stewards of God. Our life, our time, our resources, our money and everything else we have are in trust to us as God's stewards. He has appointed all Christians to be His representatives (stewards) on earth, and He wants us all to

37

be good, honest, diligent, loyal and faithful stewards (unlike the one in this story, who was wasteful and dishonest). Yes, we can be wiser than the children of this world in conducting our affairs under the principle and the conviction of our Christian integrity.

The challenge is becoming clearer: Make friends, Jesus was saying and not enemies. Christianity and the Church are friendship organizations. Jesus had an inner circle of friends, His disciples. He had other very close friends, some not so close friends and at least one friend who betrayed Him.

How are we to make friends? According to Jesus, we are to do it by means of unrighteous mammon. What does this mean? *Mammon* is a word that speaks of "wealth, riches or earthly goods," especially wealth that is used in opposition to God. The modern version of it is "money, gold and material possessions." Now, why did Jesus call money *"unrighteous"*? It is because money is pernicious. It has the tendency to corrupt people, especially when one loves it:

> *For the love of money is a root of all kinds of evil, for which some have strayed from the faith in their greediness, and pierced themselves through with many sorrows.*   1 Timothy 6:10

Not so very long ago thirty-eight lives perished in a Resorts World Casino attack in Manila, all because of money.

Whereas the dishonest steward use the money for his temporary benefit and future, Christians should use their money and whatever valuable resources they have for everlasting purposes and benefits. This is what it means for Christians to be wiser compared with the people of this world. Christians should never turn their money into wastage, but, rather, invest it in the Kingdom of God by making friends now and in the world to come.

We should be investing in evangelism, church planting, mission work, charitable, educational and social actions to help people, especially the poor, and all the name of Christ. Sometimes Christians also fail, but when we give priorities to these challenges before we fail, those people whom we make friends with our money now will become our friends forever in Heaven. I am sure that Heaven will be full of friendship when we go there.

While it is true that we cannot serve God and mammon, we can serve God with our mammon.

I cannot forget our very good friend Peter Ek who became one of our benefactors for the poor children at Star of Hope in the Philippines. Before he died, his family and his business company had sponsored and sent hundreds of poor children through school until they finished. Some even finished their college degrees and are now gainfully employed, helping themselves and supporting their families.

Peter's family, his wife Lena and their children—Lisa, Rasmus and Johanna—continued their father's legacy of helping the poor here in the Philippines, especially in the Taytay, Rizal area. They also built modest houses for very poor families. They practically saved our school in Taytay by donating a substantial amount of money to save the school property. Every year the Ek siblings come and visit the Philippines and make poor children very happy by taking them to a mall shopping for their needs and treating them to good food. I am sure that the Ek Family made lot of friends here and now, but also friends forever in Heaven.

Rev. Harold McDougal and his family came as missionaries to the Philippines in the mid 1960s. They were joined by Pastor Bobby Robinson and his wife Rita followed by John Chappell and his wife Pattie, together with other couples: Robbie and Bonnie Ridenour and Lauren Sr. and Pat Yost. Later, Etta Hampton came from Kentucky.

Rev. McDougal founded Christ to the Philippines, a religious organization established for the purpose of training and sending Filipino missionaries throughout the islands of the Philippines. My wife and I were among the many Filipinos who were saved by the grace of God through their missionary endeavors. We may never know the sacrifices they made when they decided to come to the Philippines and do their mission work, but they invested their lives and resources here with everlasting returns. We are ever grateful to them. With their sacrificial mission work, they made many lasting friends among us, and they are our friends forever—even when we get to Heaven.

Only one life, 'twill soon be past,
Only what's done for Christ will last. [1]

The things of this world will soon pass away, but there is coming a judgment day.   ✂

---

1. From the poem by C.T. Studd

ɕ **5** ɜ

Son, Remember …

Text: Luke 16:25

The story of the rich man and Lazarus is a revelation, a revelation of man's transition from what is visible in this life to that which is invisible beyond death and in the afterlife. Jesus revealed in this story the invisible and ultimate destiny of man.

Is this a true story? My answer to this question is no, this is not a true story. This is a story all right, but this story is expressed within a parable, and parables don't have factual reality. In other words, this story did not happen. This is fiction, a product of Jesus' imagination.

A parable is designed to convey, or communicate, spiritual truths or moral lessons. This was one of the teaching methods often used by our Lord Jesus Christ during His earthly ministry.

Although this parable has no factual reality, it is replete with truths, and truth transcends factual reality.

What are the truths that we can see in this story? There is the truth that in this life, there is social inequality. There are rich people, and there are poor people. While the rich people are enjoying their riches, the poor people are languishing in their poverty, in hunger, in sickness and in desperation.

Another truth is that whether one is rich or poor, we will all die. Death, however, is not the end of man. There is the truth of the afterlife and the different destinations, the ultimate destinations. There are those who are found in the place of comfort, and there are those who are found in the place of torment called Hell.

Many among the mainstream Christians, including pastors, use this story as a reference to their belief and doctrine of the intermediate afterlife. They say that based on this story, when a man dies, his soul survives death and immediately is ushered into Heaven (if he is a righteous man) or into Hell (if he is an unrepentant sinner). They usually used this doctrine in their homilies, especially during funeral services. They say that their departed loved ones are in a much better place and state than we are because they are already in Heaven. Those Christians and pastors who believe and teach this doctrine, that there is an intermediate afterlife, put themselves in a doctrinal conundrum, having totally misconstrued the meaning and the interpretation of this story.

There is no intermediate afterlife in the Bible, and the human soul does not survive death. The Bible says, *"The soul who sins shall die"* (Ezekiel 18:4 and 20). When a man dies, his soul dies as well because man is a living soul. A dead man is nonexistent, so those who teach otherwise could be liable of ignorance of the Scriptures or worse, they could be liable of lying because they are not telling the truth.

What's the truth of the matter? One way to find out the truth in any biblical matter is to criticize or exegete the passages. One mode of criticism, in order to extract the truth, is by way of asking questions. So, let's ask some questions.

What was *"Abraham's bosom?"* It was part of Jewish folklore. The Jews believe that when they died they would join their fathers, and Abraham was regarded as the Father of the Jews. At death, therefore, the Jews believed that they would join father Abraham.

Why was it that after the rich man died and was buried, he found himself in Hell and in torment? He could even see, talk and feel. This is exactly the point that I am driving at, that this story is fiction. After a man dies, he no longer exists. How can a dead man see, talk and feel? He cannot because he's dead.

Abraham was also talking to the rich man in Hell here. Was it really Abraham talking? No, Abraham had long been dead, so how could he talk? Let us remember that a parable is sometimes like a riddle. We have to find and then understand the missing links in order to see the truth.

Who was the main protagonist in this story? Was it really Abraham talking to the rich man? Or was it really the rich man responding to Abraham? The main and the sole protagonist in this story is Jesus Himself. He was the One who put the words into the mouths of Abraham and the rich man.

Let's ask some more questions. Could this story become a factual reality? The answer is yes. But we have to interpolate other essential and complementary eschatological doctrines in order to make this story a factual reality. These are the missing links in this story, if we want it to become a doctrine on the afterlife.

What are these essential and complementary eschatological doctrines? They are resurrection and judgment. The only time that those who died will be conscious again and with complete human faculty is when they are resurrected. Those who are resurrected will possess a body in order to express their human personality. It is only during this time that those who died and have been resurrected can See, talk and feel.

Resurrection is the raising up of those who died, never to die again. In other words, those who are resurrected will possess immortality. The main purpose of resurrection is for those evil and wicked people who died to face judgment. Man cannot escape judgment. There will be a day of reckoning for evil and wicked people. This is what Jesus revealed in the latter part of the story, the invisible. This is what He meant also when He said, " *For what will it profit a man if he gains the whole world, and loses his own soul?*" (Mark 8:36).

Why was the rich man in Hell? What was his sin? Is it a sin to be rich? I will leave that for you to answer.

While the rich man was in torment in Hell, he saw Abraham afar off and Lazarus in his bosom. Then he cried out, "Father Abraham, have mercy on me and send Lazarus that he may dip the tip of his finger in water, and cool my tongue for I am tormented in this flame."

Why did the rich man call Abraham father? He was a Jew, and the Jews believed that Abraham was their father. This parable was addressed to Jews, especially to the Pharisees. The answer of Abraham to his appeal was a denial and an aggravating circumstance. Abraham said, *"Son, remember ... ."* So, the rich man in Hell had his full faculties. He had memory, in addition to sight, speech and sensation, which was one element of his soul.

What did the man remember? He remembered that in his lifetime on earth, he received good things. He remembered that he was a rich man who was clothed in purple and fine linen. He remembered that he feasted on good food every day.

What else did the rich man remember in Hell? He remembered that while he was feasting on sumptuous food, there was a poor beggar named Lazarus, full of sores, lying at his gate, desiring to be fed with what fell from his table. He remembered that the dogs came and licked Lazarus' sores. He remembered his five brothers who, like him, were now bound to Hell.

The rich man had all the capacity, the power and the resources to help Lazarus, but he failed to do it. He missed his opportunity to help the poor and needy, and God is sympathetic to the poor and the needy.

Jesus repeatedly pronounced His sympathy toward the poor in His Sermon on the Mount by saying, *"Blessed are the poor in spirit, for theirs is the Kingdom of Heaven"* (Matthew 5:3). The Gospel contains the message of social justice, and that means helping the poor.

The rich man made a second appeal because he remembered his five brothers, and he did not want them to join him in Hell. He begged Father Abraham to send Lazarus to his brothers to testify to them. But his second appeal was denied as well. Father Abraham gave an alternative, and that was hearing Moses and the prophets. The rich man considered that if one went to the brothers from the dead, they would repent. Father Abraham knew that if they would not listen to Moses and the prophets, they would not be persuaded even if someone rose from the dead.

What did Abraham mean when he said to the rich man, regarding his appeal for his five brothers, *"They have Moses and the prophets; let them hear them"* (Luke 16:29)? Moses and the prophets have had long been dead, so when he referred them to Moses and the prophets, he was referring them to the laws of God. These laws were established by God through direct revelation to His people, and they were to govern His people in their worship and in their relationship to Him, as well as in their social relationships with each other. The laws of God were broadcast in the Jewish synagogues during times of worship, and the people studied them at home as well. Were the rich man and his five brothers perhaps absent from worship in their synagogue? And, if so, did this account for their spiritual ignorance of their divine and social obligations. That wouldn't be surprising, would it? Many Christians are also neglectful of attending regular church services. That's why Jesus said:

Assuredly, I say to you that it is hard for a rich man to enter the kingdom of heaven. Matthew 19:23

In the New Testament, the Law of God was condensed into a twin compendium of divine and human obligation:

"You shall love the Lord your God with all your heart, with all your soul, with all your strength, and with all your mind," and "your neighbor as yourself." Luke 10:27

In Hell, the rich man was suffering torment externally and internally. Outwardly, he was tormented by the flames and an unquenchable thirst. Internally, although he had some good and memories of his lifetime on earth, he would be haunted forever by regrets and remorse because of his failure to hear Moses and the prophets and the missed opportunity for helping the poor, sick and begging Lazarus. So, to all rich people, including rich Christians, I say:

1. Don't absent yourselves from church services because that's where you will hear the Word of God and know His will for your life!

2. Do what you can to help the poor and the needy, thereby validating your salvation!

3. Don't allow your memories to haunt you forever in Hell because of remorse and regrets!

4. Make sure you will have good memories in Heaven!

✄

A MOTHER TO MIMIC
(A TRIBUTE TO MOTHERS EVERYWHERE)

Text: Genesis 3:20

After nine months, more or less, from conception to giving birth to their babies, mothers bear them with tender loving care in their wombs. At the time of giving birth to their babies, their lives are also at risk. It has been said that one of the feet of a mother is in the grave while she delivers her child.

Then, a mother's sacrificial responsibilities continue long after that child is born. With love, care, patience and perseverance, she nurtures her child until it is grown and able to fend for itself.

Besides delivering to us physical nourishment, our mothers are our first teachers, with regards to literacy, tradition and culture. Their influence becomes part and parcel of our human personality, which will largely determine our success or failure in life. Therefore, it is only fitting and proper that we should honor and appreciate our mothers and all mothers.

In the Bible, we have ideal and exemplary mothers whose godly lives and influence raised great men of God. Jochebed, for instance, the mother of Moses, was one among the many mothers of the Bible. Although she was an obscure person in history, her faith and Godly influence on the life of her son became evident and obvious when Moses became a man. Truly, when mothers teach their children in the way they should go, they will not depart from it when they grow up (see Proverbs 22:6). The story of the mother and son relationship between Moses and his mother is extraordinary and amazing.

Before the birth of Moses, there was a king (known as a pharaoh) who rose to power in Egypt who did not know Joseph. This new king was suspicious and afraid of the unprecedented growth of the population of the Israelites in Egypt. He was afraid that the Israelites might connive and join the enemies of Egypt, if war broke out, and fight against them. So, the Egyptians oppressed the Israelites through hard labor and service. But the more they were oppressed, the more God's people multiplied and spread abroad.

Alarmed, Pharaoh, King of Egypt, commanded his people to kill every baby boy born to the Hebrews and to allow only the girls to live. After the birth of Moses, his mother hid him to save his life. This went on for three months. Then, when she could no longer hide him, she put him into a reed basket one day, a basket which she had daubed with asphalt and pitch to waterproof it. Imagine what she must have been feeling as she tucked that child into the basket and then set it among the reeds near the bank of the mighty River Nile. Nearby she positioned her daughter, Moses' sister, to keep watch and see what would happen to him.

Soon enough the daughter of Pharaoh came down to bathe at the river. She saw the basket among the reeds and immediately sent one of her maidens to get it. When she opened it, she was amazed to find saw the child (who just happened to be crying at that moment). She couldn't help but feel pity for the child, even though it was obvious that he was one of the hated Hebrew.

In that moment, Moses' sister approached and offered to go find a nurse from the Hebrew women to nurse the child for her, and this pleased Pharaoh's daughter. Naturally, the girl went and called her own mother, and when she had come, Pharaoh's daughter told her to take the child and nurse him for her, and she would pay her a suitable wage for doing it. How amazing is that?

> *And the child grew, and she brought him to Pharaoh's daughter, and he became her son. So she called his name Moses, saying, "Because I drew him out of the water."* Exodus 2:10

Moses grew up in the palaces of Egypt, but the Bible shows that when he was a grown man he refused to be called the son of Pharaoh's daughter. He chose to share ill-treatment with the people of God rather than to enjoy the short-lived pleasures of sin. He considered abuse suffered for Christ greater wealth than the treasures of Egypt, for he looked for the reward (see Hebrews 11:24-26).

> *By faith he forsook Egypt, not fearing the wrath of the king; for he endured as seeing Him who is invisible. By faith he kept the Passover and the sprinkling of blood, lest he who destroyed the firstborn should touch them.* Hebrews 11:27-28

If you are thinking, "Why?" you are not alone. Why did Moses refuse to be called the son of Pharaoh's daughter? That title was equivalent to a prince, and it would have made him the heir apparent to the throne of Egypt.

Why did Moses choose to suffer with God's people? Most people don't like to suffer. Why did he consider abuse suffered for Christ greater wealth than the treasures of Egypt? Why did he leave Egypt? Egypt during this time was the center of world civilization. And why did he keep the Passover? The answer to all those questions, according to the Bible, is *"by faith!"* How and where did he get that faith? The Bible says that faith comes by hearing and hearing the Word of God.

Did Moses get his faith from Pharaoh's daughter? I don't think so. There is no doubt that he got his faith from his mother, Jochebed, who, through a miracle, raised him and nurtured him. Yes, it was the faith received from his mother that made him the leader of the Israelites and delivered them from their Egyptian bondage of some four hundred years. Moses became one of the greatest, if not *the* greatest, of leaders the world has ever known.

They say that there is a woman behind every man's success or great achievements. Who was the woman behind Moses' success and achievements? It was his mother, Jochebed. Kudos to all mothers around the world, from Eve, the mother of all living then, and to all mothers alive today. Without you, this world will be void of people. Happy Mother's Day!

A FRUITFUL CHRISTIAN LIFE

Text: Matthew 13:3-8

When a great multitude of people gathered around Jesus, He got into a boat and from there, spoke many things to them in parables. One of the parables He gave that day is known as the "Parable of the Sower." A *sower* is another word for a husbandman or a farmer. What Jesus was telling in this story was a familiar and common experience of the people in the agricultural culture and setting that was common in Israel during that time.

He commenced His story by saying, "A farmer was sowing grain in his fields." As the man scattered seeds across the ground, the seeds he scattered fell into four different areas. Some fell beside a path, some fell on rocky soil, others fell among thorns, and some fell on good soil. The seed that fell beside a path was eaten by the birds. The seed that fell on the rocky soil withered and died because it was scorched by the hot sun because it had little root in the shallow soil. The seed that fell among thorns had its tender blades choked out. Only the seed that fell on good soil brought forth fruit, and some of it bore a hundredfold, some sixty, and some thirty.

Later, Jesus explained the meaning of the Parable of the Sower to His disciples. He said that the seed is the Word or message of the Kingdom. The different kinds of soil were the hearts of men. The birds were the evil or the wicked one. When someone hears the message of the Kingdom and does not understand it, then Satan comes and snatches away that seed from his heart. This was some of the seed that fell on the hard path.

As for what was sown on the rocky soil, this is someone who hears the Word and immediately receives it with joy, yet he has no root in himself. He endures for a while, but when tribulation or persecution arises on account of the Word, he immediately falls away.

As for what was sown among thorns, this is someone who hears the Word, but the cares of the world and the delight in riches choke the Word, and it proves unfruitful.

As for what was sown on good soil, this is someone who hears the Word and understands it, and he goes on to bear fruit. Jesus said this person can yield a hundredfold, sixty-fold or thirty-fold. Experts tell us that for farmers to exist, they need a 3 to 1 yield on their seed. 100 to 1, 60 to 1 and 30 to 1 are very successful averages. It may have been difficult in the rocky of terrain of Israel (before modern machinery, modern seeds, modern fertilizer and modern weed control to have nearly that much yield. Then, there were the birds that would catch away the seed sown. These were the main reasons that of the four kinds of soil, only one was fruitful.

Is it possible to improve and increase the crop yield even in these kinds of terrain? I believe so. But a farmer would have to put extra effort into ploughing hardened paths, removing offending stones, uprooting weeds and thorns and utilizing scarecrows to drive away the birds. This would take diligence and patience. This illustrates the fact that farming is a difficult job, and not many people like to farm these days. Most of the children of farmers do not want to continue their father's work. They would rather go to the city and look for other types of jobs. But farming can be very rewarding, especially when a farmer gets a bumper crop for harvesting. Besides feeding his family, he can also feed many other people through his harvests.

What does this parable speak to us today as contemporary Christians?

1. This parable challenges Christians around the world today to be fruitful!

2. It teaches us not to be satisfied with small harvests, but to believe for a hundredfold return.

3. It teaches us about obstacles that can hinder us in our Christian life and make us unfruitful.

What are these obstacles? Well, first of all, we have the devil. He is definitely our enemy, and we must not allow him to snatch away the Word of God from our hearts. The Word teaches:

And do not give the devil a foothold.   Ephesians 4:27, NIV

Remember what Jesus said:

The thief does not come except to steal, and to kill, and to destroy.   John 10:10

We must not harden our hearts to the Word of God:

Do not harden your hearts.   Hebrews 3:8

We must not allow persecutions, trials and difficulties to defeat us. We must not allow the lure of worldliness and the deceitfulness of riches to entangle and choke the Word of God in our lives. We must be strong in the Lord and be determined, be of strong resolve in our Christian moral conviction and integrity. Let us not compromise our Christian faith. Let this be our goal and mission!

How can we achieve this goal of being fruitful? This is what Jesus said:

I am the true vine, and My Father is the vinedresser. Every branch in Me that does not bear fruit He takes away; and every branch that bears fruit He prunes, that it may bear more fruit. You are already clean because of the word which I have spoken to you. Abide in Me, and I in you. As the branch cannot bear fruit of itself, unless it abides in the vine, neither can you, unless you abide in Me.

"I am the vine, you are the branches. He who abides in Me, and I in him, bears much fruit; for without Me you can do nothing. If anyone does not abide in Me, he is cast out as a branch and is withered; and they gather them and throw them into the fire, and they are burned. If you abide in Me, and My words abide in you, you will ask what you desire, and it shall be done for you. By this My Father is glorified, that you bear much fruit; so you will be My disciples."   John 15:1-8

How can we abide in Christ? How can this become practicable? The only way it can be practical is when we are *in* the Church because the Church is the Body of Christ here on earth. It is in the Church that the seed, the Word of God is constantly and regularly broadcast. It is in our connection with the Church that we grow by feeding on the Word of God. Jesus said:

Man shall not live by bread alone, but by every word of God.

Luke 4:4

God speaks through His servants the pastors, to sow the seed of the message of the Kingdom, to protect the members from the evil one through prayer, to warn and rebuke members so that they can be prevented from involvement and entanglement with worldliness and the deceitfulness of riches. Then, the members of the church grow spiritually and bear fruit.

There are spiritual fruits, and there are natural fruits:

But the fruit of the Spirit is love, joy, peace, longsuffering, kindness, goodness, faithfulness, gentleness, self-control.   Galatians 5:22-23

As the members continue to grow spiritually, they will be moved by the Spirit of God to persuade and convince others with boldness through the message of salvation in Christ Jesus, starting with their own family members. And, as the members in the church persevere in their goal and mission, the Lord will add souls to the church. Our God said, *"Be fruitful and multiply"* (Genesis 1:28)!

ᘓ **8** ᘔ

FROM HERE TO ETERNITY
(MAN'S JOURNEY AND DESTINY)

Text: 1 Corinthians 15:47-53

What is life? *Life* can be defined as "the quality that distinguishes a vital and functional being from a dead body." It is "a principle or force held to underlie the distinctive quality of animate beings." It is "an organic state characterized by a capacity for metabolism, growth, reaction to stimuli and reproduction." It is "the sequence of physical and mental experiences that make up the existence of an individual," and it is "the duration of an earthly existence."

There are categories of life on earth. These are plant life, animal life and human life.

What is eternity? It is "the state after death; immortality."

Let us confine here our focus on the human Life. Where did human life come from? The Bible has the answer to this question. In the opening pages of the book of Genesis, we read that after God created the earth with its plant and animal life, then:

57

Then god said, "let us make man in our image and in our likeness." Genesis 1:26

How did God make man?

And the Lord God formed man of the dust of the ground, and breathed into his nostrils the breath of life; and man became a living being. Genesis 2:7

So God created man in His own image; in the image of God He created him; male and female He created them. Genesis 1:27

Whereas the first man was created by God, the subsequent men were conceived by their mother.

Now Adam knew Eve his wife, and she conceived and bore Cain Genesis 4:1

And Cain knew his wife, and she conceived and bore Enoch.

Genesis 4:17

So, God intrinsically placed a reproductive capacity in every woman. But birth can only transpire with the contribution of a man through sexual intercourse. The only exception was the case of the Virgin Mary. The male's sperm cell meets the female's egg cell, which initiates fertilization, and conception, and the result is an embryo that grows into a fetus ... until the baby is born. This is the biological explanation, but it is God who gives life to the organs and engineers the entire process of reproduction.

After birth, man will experience three aspects of life. These are the physical life, the psychological life and the spiritual life. With the physical life, he will experience levels of growth and development. From infancy, he will grow into childhood and from childhood into adolescence. Along the way, he will also get involved in family, social and political life.

But not all men and women will experience spiritual life. Only those who have received Jesus Christ as their personal Savior and Lord of their lives after repentance will experience spiritual life. Why? Because man is born spiritually dead. That's why man needs to be born again.

While living, man has a lot of dreams, aspirations and expected achievements. All too often, these dreams and aspiration go unfulfilled and his achievements are cut short because he dies. Some die young and some die old. Some die of sickness, and some die violent deaths. But, everybody dies, and there is nothing he can do about it. Death has become a fact of life. This is quite ironic, but it is a reality. Every man is born to die. It is just a matter of time. Yes, there is *"a time to be born"* and *"a time to die"* (Ecclesiastes 3:2). Death is an inescapable reality in life.

The next question that is commonly asked is: Why does man die? Was sin the cause of his death, physical death, that is? If Adam and Eve had not sinned, would man have died? To answer these questions, let us go back to the time and examine the circumstances prior to and after the sin of Adam.

The Bible says that the Lord God took the man that He had created and put him in a garden, called the Garden of Eden, to work it and care for it. He said to man:

Of every tree of the garden you may freely eat; but of the tree of the knowledge of good and evil you shall not eat, for in the day that you eat of it you shall surely die. Genesis 2:16-17

When Adam violated God's command not to eat of the fruit of the forbidden tree that day, did he die physically? The answer is no, he did not die physically. Surely God would not lie, so Adam and Eve must have died that day. But they didn't.

What kind of death, then, was God contemplating as a consequence of their violation? It was clearly a spiritual death. Just as there is a spiritual life, so also there is a spiritual death. Then, why do people die a physical death if sin was not the cause of it?

Let us closely examine the pronouncement of God relative to the violation of His command. I believe that besides the punitive effect of sin, which is expressed in the pronouncement, *"You will surely die,"* it also implies the suggestion by God of the nature of man. And what is this nature? God was saying to Adam that he was mortal, and therefore he was going to die. This leads me to conclude that on this basis, sin or no sin, man was going to die anyway eventually.

Many people say that death is a mystery. What is a mystery? A *mystery* is "something which is beyond understanding." It is "an enigma." As earlier mentioned, death is a fact of life, and we witness that people die anytime and everywhere in our lifetime. The mystery that they perhaps refer to is what happens beyond death or, to simplify it in a question, "Is there life after death?" This is a mystery to many because they don't know the answer. Thank God that we have the Bible, which reveals to us what is mysterious to others.

My answer to the question, Is there life after death?, is yes and no. Let me explain. After a man dies, he is truly dead. (RIP) indeed. The notion that the human soul survives death and goes to Heaven or Hell immediately is false and those who believe and teach this doctrine misconstrue the interpretation of passages in the Bible such as 2 Corinthians 5:8, Matthew 10:28, and the story of Lazarus and the rich man, as well as Luke 23:43. It is very clear from the words of Jesus:

> *No one has ascended to heaven but He who came down from heaven, that is, the Son of Man who is in heaven.* John 3:13

So, where are the dead right now, and what will happen to them? All of the Old Testament saints, including Enoch and Elijah, the New Testament saints and all the Christians who already died are still here on earth. Their bodies have long ago turned to dust. They will remain dead, and they will not be conscious until the time and the day of resurrection (see 1 Thessalonians 4:13-18).

But, yes, there is life after death! Man lives again when he is resurrected. This is the *"blessed hope"* of the Christian.

What is resurrection? It is the raising up of those who died in Christ, including the Old Testament saints, never to die again! Jesus Christ is our pattern and example. He has been resurrected from the dead and is now in Heaven with God the Father and the angels. Look at what He said:

> *I am the resurrection and the life. He who believes in Me, though he may die, he shall live. And whoever lives and believes in Me shall never die. Do you believe this?* John 11:25-26

The Bible mentions two general resurrections besides that of Jesus. These are the first and the second resurrections.

The prophet Daniel prophesied:

And many of those who sleep in the dust of the earth shall awake, Some to everlasting life, Some to shame and everlasting contempt. Daniel 12:2

This truth was complemented, concurred and confirmed when Jesus said:

Do not marvel at this; for the hour is coming in which all who are in the graves will hear His voice and come forth—those who have done good, to the resurrection of life, and those who have done evil, to the resurrection of condemnation. John 5:28-29

Blessed and holy is he who has part in the first resurrection. Over such the second death has no power. Revelation 20:6

A More Abundant Life

Text: John 10:10

Jesus said, *"I came that they may have life, and that they may have it more abundantly."* Prior to this statement however, He also said, *"The thief comes only to steal, to kill and destroy."* The context of this statement is His discourse on the "The Shepherd and the Sheep." There He used a figure of speech illustrating His relationship with His flock. He is the Shepherd, and we are His sheep.

Jesus said hat He is the Good Shepherd who lays down His life for the sheep. He also knows His sheep, and His sheep know Him. His sheep know His voice, and they listen to Him and follow Him.

Then, Jesus also said that He is the Gate, or Door, of the sheep. *"If anyone enters by Me, he will be saved,"* He concluded (John 10:9). It is in this immediate context that He mentioned about the danger to the sheepfold. The Shepherd and the sheep have enemies. These are the thief and the wolves. Their intention is to steal, kill and destroy the flock.

Who is the thief? And who are the wolves? Was Jesus alluding to real persons? I believe so. The thief is the devil, who is also called Satan, and the wolves are people who are under the influence of demons. Both people and demons are cohorts of the devil. Their interests and intention concerning people, especially the people of God and the followers of Christ, is to steal and wreck havoc with death and destruction in their lives.

A classic example of this devilish, demonic and destructive activity is the case of Job in the Old Testament. Job was a righteous man who feared God and shunned evil. God blessed Job so that he was a wealthy man and the greatest among all the people of the east. However, his children and wife were not as godly as he.

Without his knowledge, Job was the subject of contention between God and Satan in Heaven. The Lord was proud of Job's godly integrity, and Satan was jealous of him. Satan said to the Lord that Job feared God only because God protected and blessed him and he challenged God, that if He removed His protection and blessing, Job would curse Him.

The Lord said to Satan, "Very well then, everything he has is in your hands, but on the man himself do not lay a finger." The result was that in one day all the wealth of Job, which was composed of livestock, was stolen or destroyed by what seemed like natural disasters. Then all of Job's children were killed while partying, when an extremely strong wind struck the house where they were, and it collapsed on them. All of this devastation and destruction was orchestrated by Satan and his cohorts.

Not satisfied, Satan also inflicted Job with an agonizing disease. Yet, in all these adversities, Job remained steadfastly faithful to God. He declared:

Though He slay me, yet will I trust Him.   Job 13:15

Another case of destructive demonic activity is found in the New Testament. In the Gospel of Mark, chapter 5, a demon possessed man, who lived in and came from the tombs, met Jesus. He was extremely violent, no one was strong enough to subdue him, and he could not be kept bound, even with a chain.

Night and day among the tombs and in the hills, this man would cry out and cut himself with stones. Now He ran to Jesus and fell on his knees in front of Him. Jesus rebuked the evil spirit and said, *"Come out of the man, unclean spirit!"* (Mark 5:8). The man was delivered from demon possession, and was later seen sitting in front of Jesus, dressed and in his right mind. Hallelujah! Praise the Lord!

So, if you are devastated by sickness and catastrophe, don't blame it on God. Blame the devil and his cohorts. They just attacked Stockholm, Sweden a few days ago, leaving at least five innocent people dead.

What did Jesus mean when He said, *"I came that they may have life and that they have it more abundantly?"* Why did He say this? Surely he was not referring to dead people that need life. He was referring to the spiritually dead people. Now let us clarify this matter of the life of man by looking into the aspects of his life. It is best to do this by going back to the dawn of the Creation of man.

Then God said, "Let Us make man in Our image, according to Our likeness."   Genesis 1:26

And the Lord God formed man of the dust of the ground, and breathed into his nostrils the breath of life; and man became a living being. Genesis 2:7

So God created man in His own image; in the image of God He created him; male and female He created them. Genesis 1:27

The image and likeness of God in man at the dawn of Creation resemble the physical life and the spiritual life of man. The image is the physical life, and the likeness is the spiritual life. After God created man, He put him in the Garden of Eden and commanded him not to eat from the tree of the knowledge of good and evil and warned that if he did, he would die. But Adam and Eve ate from the forbidden tree anyway and, thus, sinned against God. They did not die physically on the day they sinned against God, but they did die spiritually. And, since then, every man and woman (except Jesus Christ) who is born into this world is spiritually dead.

When Jesus said, *"I came that you may have life,"* He was referring to the need everyone has of spiritual life. Why do we all need it? Because every one of us is spiritually dead.

Jesus said to Nicodemus, *"You must be born again"* (John 3:7). Flesh gives birth to flesh, but the Spirit gives birth to spirit. Every person who receives Jesus Christ as his Lord and Savior has become spiritually alive.

The other divine imprint in man, which was the likeness of God, is now restored when Christ dwells in our hearts. This, too, was lost when man sinned against God. In Christ, man is complete again. He is now body, soul and spirit. The Bible says:

A More Abundant Life

For the wages of sin is death, but the gift of God is eternal life in
Christ Jesus our Lord. Romans 6:23

Without Christ in his life, man is a paradox. He is physically alive but spiritually dead!

Again Jesus said, *"That they may have it more abundantly."* As Christians grow and develop in their spiritual life, everything about their lives becomes more abundant ... until it becomes eternal life, which is a God-kind of life. This God-related abundant life is best described in Psalm 23, when David said:

The Lord is my shepherd;
I shall not want.
He makes me to lie down in green pastures;
He leads me beside the still waters.
He restores my soul;
He leads me in the paths of righteousness
For His name's sake.
Yea, though I walk through the valley of the shadow of death,
I will fear no evil;
For You are with me;
Your rod and Your staff, they comfort me.
You prepare a table before me in the presence of my enemies;
You anoint my head with oil;
My cup runs over.
Surely goodness and mercy shall follow me
All the days of my life;
And I will dwell in the house of the Lord
Forever. Psalm 23:1-6

God commanded the Israelites:

I set before you today life and prosperity, death and destruction. For I command you today to love the Lord your God, to walk in His ways, and to keep His commands, decrees and laws; then you will live and increase, and the Lord your God will bless you.

I have set you life and death, blessings and curses. Now choose life, so that you and your children may live and that you may love the lord god, listen to his voice, and hold fast to him. For the lord is your life and he will give you many years in the land.

Deuteronomy 30:15-16 and 19, NIV

Don't die without receiving Jesus into your heart as your personal Lord and Savior. Without Jesus in your life, there is no hope of salvation. He said:

I am the way, the truth, and the life. No one comes to the Father except through Me.   John 14:6

✄

ENJOYING THE CHRISTIAN LIFE GUILT-FREE

Text: 1 Timothy 6:17-19

There is a general notion among many people, even some Christians, that Christian life is the most miserable and unhappy life there is. Why is that? Because all you hear from these Christians, especially the faithful ones, is about trials, tribulations, persecutions, hardships, poverty and sacrifice. The devil is always giving them a hard time, and they never seem to overcome their adversities and have victory in their daily lives. Their testimonies, whether in church or elsewhere, are not good because they are so negative and do not glorify God or bless others.

Although it is undeniable that we will have unpleasant experiences in our Christian life (*"all who desire to live godly in Christ Jesus will suffer persecution"* [2 Timothy 3:12]), but to dwell only on that negates the work of Christ in our lives. (*"But thanks be to God, who gives us the victory through our Lord Jesus Christ"* [1 Corinthians 15:57]*). Trials and adversities must not dominate our Christian life.

Paul, the great apostle, suffered many things, but he wrote:

I can do all things through Christ who strengthens me.

Philippians 4:13

After the battle comes the victory, and after the victory comes the celebration. If there are people in the world who are most joyful despite the adversities they must face, it is the Christians. And I am proud to declare to the world that I am a one of them.

The fundamental reason that Christians are the most joyful and happy people in the world is because they have been forgiven of their sins. Their sins are washed away by the blood of Jesus Christ, the Lamb of God. They repented of their sins, and they received Jesus Christ as their personal Lord and Savior. That is why they are guilt free! Besides this, they now have faith, hope and love — faith in God through our Lord Jesus Christ, hope of eternal life in Heaven, and the love of God toward all people. This constitutes their new life.

Now, there is a serious misconception among some Christians with regards to the possession of wealth, money and things. They often quote: *"the love of money is the root of all evil"* (1 Timothy 6:10, KJV). They also quote: *"Love not the world, neither the things that are in the world"* (1 John 2:15, KJV). Of course, that is what the Bible says, so it is true. But does that mean that it is wrong for Christians to have money, especially lots of money? Is it wrong for Christians to be wealthy and have lots of things? The answer is a big NO! But that NO comes with a condition, and the condition is that the Christians did not steal, cheat, lie and defraud other people in order to acquire this money, wealth and things. If Christians are diligent,

70

hardworking, industrious and smart, and God blesses their efforts with wealth, money and things, then, it is all right. Those are blessings from God. Their wealth and possessions are beneficial to them, to support their family, support the church, to support missions and to bless others who are in need through their charitable and benevolent giving. Wealthy Christians are, however, warned not to trust in or be proud of their riches.

I believe that God desires and delights to bless His people with all spiritual blessings, and that includes wealth and riches. Jesus said, *"I have come that they may have life, and that they may have it more abundantly"* (John 10:10). He also said, *"But seek first the kingdom of God and His righteousness, and all these things shall be added to you."* (Matthew 6:33).

God blessed Abram so that he became very wealthy in livestock, in silver and in gold. God gave favor, power and abundance to Joseph, so that he saved Egypt from famine and his family was a part of that salvation. Besides wisdom, God gave Solomon wealth, riches and honor. This truth is clear: *"The blessing of the Lord makes one rich, and He adds no sorrow with it"* (Proverbs 10:22).

So, what should be the attitude of Christians toward money, wealth and the possession of things? It's a good question! Whereas Christians are precluded by God from loving money and the things in this world, they are allowed and given the privilege to enjoy all these things. Moreover, when God gives any man wealth and possessions and enables him to enjoy them, to accept his lot and be happy in his work, this is a gift of God.

What does it mean to enjoy these things? It means to have pleasure, satisfaction and be happy with the benefits of these things —for himself, his family and to help other people in need. It is a gift of God to enjoy these things. Sadly, there are people who have all the money and things in this world they need, but they don't enjoy them. When God blesses you with wealth, money and the possession of things, enjoy these blessings while you are still alive. Don't wait until you die, when somebody else will enjoy what you have worked hard for. It is not a sin to enjoy God's blessings.

Not long ago, a missionary approached me and asked me this question: "Why are you driving a Mercedes Benz?"

I answered, "Is it wrong?"

He answered, "Yes, because you're a pastor."

Another asked the question, "Why do you own your own home?" Another asked, "Why do you wear a Rolex watch? "How did you get these things?" The worst was a pastor who suggested that I was driving a Mercedes to "attract girls." I answered them all, "These are God's blessings to me, and I just enjoy these things, okay?"

It disappoints me when people insinuate that pastors must perpetually remain poor, remain beggars and have no right to enjoy the blessings of God. When you consider that these people are Christians, that's disgusting. People need to cleanse their minds of evil thoughts.

God wants us to enjoy, not only money, wealth and material possessions, but all things. Here it is:

Trust in ... the living God, who gives us richly all things to enjoy. 1 Timothy 6:17

What did God give me so that I might enjoy it? He gave me life, salvation, my wife, our children, our families, friends and brothers and sisters in the Lord. He gave me a job as a pastor and a school administrator. He gave us money, houses and cars. And I enjoy them all.

I enjoy my life, my salvation, my wife, my children, my family, my work and all the other things that God gives us every single day. My wife and I will celebrate our 47th year of marriage on October 10, and I have enjoyed her every day since the first day we were married until now. Praise god! Hallelujah! God is good indeed! ✳

OUR LORD'S PRAYER

Text: John 17:1-26

Solemn, somber and with sorrow, our Lord Jesus Christ prayed this prayer in the Garden of Gethsemane before His arrest and trial. Why was this moment filled with grief and sorrow? The reason for it was that our Lord Jesus Christ was about to leave His disciples and even this world. Soon He would return to the Father in Heaven. He also knew that the pain and the suffering of His crucifixion would come in the following days. That was why He prayed, *"O My Father, if this cup cannot pass away from Me unless I drink it, Your will be done"* (Matthew 26:42)." His prayer contains a profound petition regarding His divine glory and His intercession for His disciples then and now.

After Jesus said this, He looked toward heaven and prayed: *"Father, the time has come. Glorify your Son, that your Son may glorify you. For you granted him authority over all people that he might give eternal life to all those you have given him. Now this is eternal life: that they may know you, the only true God, and Jesus Christ, whom you have sent. I have brought you glory on earth by completing the work you gave*

74

me to do. And now Father, glorify me in your presence with the glory I had with you before the world began.

"I have revealed you to those whom you gave me out of the world. They were yours; you gave them to me and they have obeyed your word. Now they know that everything you have given me comes from you. For I gave them the words you gave me and they accepted them. They knew with certainty that I came from you, and they believe that you sent me. I pray for them. I am not praying for the world, but for those you have given me, for they are yours. All I have is yours, and all you have is mine. And glory has come to them. I will remain in the world no longer, but they are still in the world, and I am coming to you. Holy Father, protect them by the power of your name-the name you gave me."

"My prayer is not for them alone. I pray also for those who will believe in me through their message, that all of them may be one, Father, just as you are in me and I am in you. Father, I want those you have given me to be with me where I am, and see my glory, the glory you have given me before the creation of the world. Righteous Father, though the world does not know you, I know you, and they that know you have sent me. I have made you known to them, and will continue to make you known in order that the love you have for me may be in them and that I myself may be in them."

Our Lord Jesus Christ was consistent in His teachings regarding the correct pattern for prayer. He taught His disciples that when praying they must address God as their Father (as He does here in this prayer). But His first petition was rather mystifying. He was asking God the Father to *"glorify"* Him. What did He mean by that? Most Christians believe that Jesus is God incarnate, and therefore it would seem incumbent upon Him to already have the glory as God.

What is the meaning of *glory*? Concerning God, it is "the exhibition of His divine attributes and perfection or the radiance of

His presence." Glory is sometimes "the manifestation of God's personal revelation in order to get the attention of His people." For instance, He revealed Himself to Moses in a burning bush.

When Aaron made his first sacrifice as priest in the wilderness, God's glory appeared to all the people. The cloud of His glory also covered the Tabernacle in the wilderness. When King Solomon dedicated the Temple in Jerusalem, it was filled with a cloud, for the glory of the Lord filled the temple. In these manifestations, God revealed His righteousness, holiness, wisdom and love. His glory has been fully expressed through His Son, Jesus Christ.

And the Word became flesh and dwelt among us, and we beheld His glory, the glory as of the only begotten of the Father, full of grace and truth. John 1:14

This is the glory in which all believers in Christ share at the end of the age. Christians will be glorified in the heavenly presence of God, whose glory will be seen everywhere.

Now, if Jesus Christ is the glory of God, why was He asking God the Father to glorify Him? Are there other kinds of glory besides the glory that He has now? The answer is in the last line of the first paragraph of His prayer. He said, *"And now, Father, glorify me in your presence with the glory I had with you before the world began"* (John 17:5, NIV). So, there is an earthly glory, and there is a heavenly glory. It is apparent that when Jesus was incarnate, He relinquished the heavenly glory in order to fulfill His redemptive mission. And now, He was praying for that glory to be restored. [1]

1. Someone has made the suggestion that the star that guided the wise men to the birthplace of Jesus was actually the heavenly glory that Jesus had relinquished.

The second subject of Jesus' prayer was an intercessory one, cn behalf of His disciples and all the followers who had believed and would yet believe their message. What is an intercessory prayer? It is a prayer asking God for favor, in behalf and for the benefit of others. Jesus was endorsing to God His disciples and the Christian believers for unity, protection and keeping them from the evil one. Through the words that He spoke, they knew that He was not praying for the world.

Finally, Jesus asked the Father that those whom God had given Him would be with Him in Heaven to witness His heavenly glory. Jesus Christ has the power and authority to grant eternal life to those who believe in Him. Do you want to live forever in Heaven? Then repent of your sins today and receive Jesus Christ into your life, and you will become a child of God:

For the wages of sin is death, but the gift of God is eternal life in Christ Jesus our Lord. Romans 6:23

DELIVER ME!
(A PENITENT'S PRAYER)

Text: Psalm 51:1-5

These remorseful words are excerpts from the repentant prayer of King David in Psalm 51. This particular psalm of King David is rather unusual and unique compared with the rest of his psalms. Whereas, in the many of his other psalms, he praised and blessed God, here he pleaded with God for mercy and compassion.

To this first part he added:

Create in me a clean heart, O God,
And renew a steadfast spirit within me.
Do not cast me away from Your presence,
And do not take Your Holy Spirit from me.
Restore to me the joy of Your salvation,
And uphold me by Your generous Spirit.
Then I will teach transgressors Your ways,
And sinners shall be converted to You.
Deliver me from the guilt of bloodshed, O God,

DELIVER ME!

The God of my salvation,
And my tongue shall sing aloud of Your righteousness.

Psalm 51:10-124

Why was King David praying for God's mercy? What had happened to him? What did he do? First, let us look at the meaning of the word *mercy* because this was what he was asking from God.

Mercy means "compassion or forbearance shown to an offender or subject." It is "the withholding of a punishment, penalty or misery from a guilty party or sinner." This is one side of the coin of God's love. And what's on the other side of the coin of God's love? It is *grace*, and it means "the granting of forgiveness to the guilty party or sinner, although he doesn't deserve it." Grace has also been called an "unmerited favor." These are all God's divine and sovereign prerogatives.

This prayer of King David was the direct result of him being convicted by God through the parable of the prophet Nathan. The Lord sent Nathan to David, and when he came to king, he said:

There were two men in one city, one rich and the other poor. The rich man had exceedingly many flocks and herds. But the poor man had nothing, except one little ewe lamb which he had bought and nourished; and it grew up together with him and with his children. It ate of his own food and drank from his own cup and lay in his bosom; and it was like a daughter to him. And a traveler came to the rich man, who refused to take from his own flock and from his own herd to prepare one for the wayfaring man who had come to him; but he took the poor man's lamb and prepared it for the man who had come to him. 2 Samuel 12:1-4

When David heard this, he was very angry and said to Nathan:

As the Lord lives, the man who has done this shall surely die! And he shall restore fourfold for the lamb, because he did this thing and because he had no pity.   2 Samuel 12:5-6

David must have been very surprised when Nathan answered:

"You are the man! Thus says the Lord God of Israel: 'I anointed you king over Israel, and I delivered you from the hand of Saul. I gave you your master's house and your master's wives into your keeping, and gave you the house of Israel and Judah. And if that had been too little, I also would have given you much more! Why have you despised the commandment of the Lord, to do evil in His sight? You have killed Uriah the Hittite with the sword; you have taken his wife to be your wife, and have killed him with the sword of the people of Ammon. Now therefore, the sword shall never depart from your house, because you have despised Me, and have taken the wife of Uriah the Hittite to be your wife.' Thus says the Lord: 'Behold, I will raise up adversity against you from your own house; and I will take your wives before your eyes and give them to your neighbor, and he shall lie with your wives in the sight of this sun. For you did it secretly, but I will do this thing before all Israel, before the sun.'   2 Samuel 12:7-12

This brought David to his senses, and he said to Nathan:

I have sinned against the Lord.   2 Samuel 12:13

Nathan replied:

The Lord also has put away your sin; you shall not die.

2 Samuel 12:13

Although David was saved, the sword, the shame, the scandal and calamity in his family remained until the day he died. And no amount of prayer and fasting could save his son by Bathsheba. The child died.

David's son Amnon was killed by his half-brother Absalom because Amnon raped the sister of Absalom, whose name was Tamar. Absalom, the most beloved by David among his children was also killed when he grabbed power and the kingdom from his father. Adonijah, another son of David, was also killed when he prematurely declared himself king of Israel instead of Solomon. Tamar became a desolate woman after she was raped.

Do you remember David's pronouncement of judgment on the man who had done this thing? He said he deserved to die and must pay four times over. Well, four of his children died. What a painfully sad and tragic story!

What's the moral of the story of King David in this particular episode of his life? As God's servants and children, we cannot and must not abuse or misuse the authority and power that God has given us. Such misuse and abuse of power is contrary to morals, especially when it is used for personal gain and to the prejudice of others. They say that "power corrupts and absolute power corrupts absolutely." Bathsheba consented to King David's sexual advances because he was king, although such a relationship was adulterous. Joab obeyed King David in putting Uriah, Bathsheba's husband, in the heat of the battle so that he would be killed, although it was wrong. It was murder, and David was the mastermind of it!

As followers of Jesus Christ, we cannot be over-presumptuous of the Word of God or just take it for granted. Yes, David was king, and before that; he was *"a man after His [God's] own heart"* (1 Samuel 13:14), but no one is above the law. David tried to cover up his sin, but nothing is hidden in the sight of God.

Did David know that what he did was against the Law of God? I believe so! The judgments that came from his own mouth were based on legal and judicial principles, which he was aware of. Most of the times we are quick to judge others but adamant to justify ourselves. But sin is deadly! It will make you feel vile and disgusting! It will make you distant and detached from God. It will deny you the joy and gladness of salvation and make you feel condemned and guilty!

The Bible says clearly:

> *For the wages of sin is death, but the gift of God is eternal life in Christ Jesus our Lord.* Romans 6:23

> *Be sure your sin will find you out.* Deuteronomy 23:21

> *If we confess our sins, He is faithful and just to forgive us our sins and to cleanse us from all unrighteousness.* 1 John 1:9

ↈ **13** ↂ

Our Blessed Hope

Text: Titus 2:11-13

One of the essential and vital doctrines, or virtues, of our Christian faith is hope. The others are faith and love. Hope is something that is expected to happen in the future. As Christians, we are always looking forward to something good and positive. Our hope is based on the promises of God in the Bible.

There is a temporal hope, and there is an ultimate (or blessed) hope. Despite the many and multiple trials and hardship in our lives, Christians are the most hopeful people in the world. With perseverance in education, hard work, diligence, honesty, savings and blessings, and with divine providence, Christians are always hopeful of a better life. They live in sufficiency and contentment, with peace and joy in the Lord.

Contrary to the general perception of many Christians, however, not all hope in this world is pleasant, peaceful and positive. It could also be miserable. For instance, here's what the apostle Paul said regarding this miserable hope:

83

If in this life only we have hope in Christ, we are of all men most miserable.   1 Corinthians 15:19, KJV

This is an interesting, intriguing and ironic statement Paul made regarding this subject. Why did he say this? What did he mean by it? When I asked several of our brothers and sisters in the church what Paul meant when he said this, none of them could give a satisfactory answer. In order to understand what the apostle meant when he said this, we must go back in time.

Paul wrote this letter to the Corinthian Church during the first century A.D., and the Christians throughout the Roman world were suffering from severe persecution by the Romans at the time. Paul identified with these suffering Christians, when he said, *"We are of all men most miserable."* He was testifying of his own *"miserable"* circumstances as a minister of Christ, for he was frequently being imprisoned and threatened with death because of Christ.

He wrote:

From the Jews five times I received forty stripes minus one. 25 Three times I was beaten with rods; once I was stoned; three times I was shipwrecked; a night and a day I have been in the deep; 26 in journeys often, in perils of waters, in perils of robbers, in perils of my own countrymen, in perils of the Gentiles, in perils in the city, in perils in the wilderness, in perils in the sea, in perils among false brethren; 27 in weariness and toil, in sleeplessness often, in hunger and thirst, in fastings often, in cold and nakedness.   2 Corinthians 11:24-27

How about the rest of the Christians during that time? What were their circumstances? We know from the writer to the Hebrews and from history that they were tortured, suffered trials of cruel mockings and scourgings, were bound and imprisoned, were sawn asunder, were tempted, were slain with the sword, wandered about in sheep-skins and goatskins, being destitute, afflicted and tormented. They were hunted like criminals and were crucified and burned at a stake. They were made to fight and kill each other as gladiators in the arena, and some of them were even fed to hungry wild animals, to the delight and amusement of their Roman persecutors and spectators. It is believed that Peter was crucified upside down and that John was thrown into a boiling cauldron of oil. Yes, those early believers suffered because of their faith in Jesus Christ, and this is what the apostle meant when he said, *"If in this life only we have hope in Christ, we are of all men most miserable."*

Is this verse applicable or relevant to Christians today? Are there still Christians who are miserable in this life despite their hope in Christ? Well, for most Christians living in countries where there is religious freedom, this not applicable, and there is no relevance. Most don't even want to hear about suffering or misery. To them, it is as if God has abandoned you if you are suffering and in misery. This is true especially of those who are advocates of the so-called Prosperity Gospel. Many of these affluent and comfortable Christians in the West will certainly ignore the truth and reality of this message.

But there are many Christians today who are actually experiencing this type of suffering and misery. Christians, fore instance, in the ISIS-controlled parts of Iraq and Syria are suffering terribly. Their properties are being confiscated, and their women are being repeatedly raped by the ISIS militants. If they resist and refuse, they are beheaded—just because of their Christian faith. If Christians who are living in the free world try to go to countries like North Korea, Iran, Nigeria, Somalia, China and many of the Arab countries and preach the Gospel of Jesus Christ, you can almost be certain that they will suffer and be miserable, due to strong oppositions by the controlling regimes and the people of these countries who are against the Christian religion.

Even among those of us who live in free countries, there are still Christians who experience domestic suffering. No matter how they strive to improve their economic condition, they are still struggling with finances and in poverty. Despite God's promise of divine healing, there are those who are languishing in lingering sickness and disease. There are continuing bitter religious conflicts between husbands and wives because of different religious beliefs. Oftentimes this will eventually result in separation, leaving the poor wife with the enormous responsibility of raising and supporting the children. Many Christian parents are deeply frustrated and disappointed with their children's rebellious attitudes and behavior. And, what must be the worst nightmare for parents, when children are involved with and addicted to illegal and prohibited drugs, everyone suffers.

So, brothers and sisters in Christ, even though our expectations, dreams, aspirations and goals in this life, which are a part of our temporal hope in Christ, are not realized, we are exhorted to *"be steadfast, immovable, always abounding in the work of the Lord, knowing that in the Lord our labour is not in vain."* If our burdens are too much to bear, let us cast them upon Jesus, for He is always thinking about us and watching everything that concerns us. He said:

Come to Me, all you who labor and are heavy laden, and I will give you rest. Take My yoke upon you and learn from Me, for I am gentle and lowly in heart, and you will find rest for your souls. For My yoke is easy and My burden is light. Matthew 11:28-30

Of course, the ultimate of Christian hope, otherwise known as *our blessed hope*, is the return of Jesus Christ. This will be one of the greatest events in our future, when those who have died in Christ will be resurrected, and those who are alive will be changed into a glorified body, and together we will meet the Lord in the air, to be with the Lord and go to Heaven. This will be the moment in time when the following passage of Scripture will come true:

And God will wipe away every tear from their eyes; there shall be no more death, nor sorrow, nor crying. There shall be no more pain, for the former things have passed away.　　　　　Revelation 21:4

Jesus is coming again and soon! The signs of His soon coming, as predicted in the Bible, are unfolding and are evident in our generation. Are you ready to meet Him? Don't be left behind! If you are not ready, now is your day of salvation! Don't wait for tomorrow, when it may well be too late!

Call upon Him now, ask His forgiveness of your sins, repent and receive Him as your Lord and Savior, and you will be saved! He said:

"Come now, and let us reason together," says the Lord, "Though your sins are like scarlet, They shall be as white as snow.

Isaiah 1:18

Live for God the rest of your life, for the best is yet to come! Praise god! Hallelujah!

LAYING UP TREASURES IN HEAVEN

Text: Matthew 6:19-21

One among the messages of our Lord Jesus Christ to His followers in what has come to be called His Sermon on the Mount was about "Laying Up Treasures." There are two ways to lay up treasures that Jesus mentioned. The first was laying up treasures on earth, and the second was laying up treasures in Heaven. He precluded His followers from doing the first, by saying, *"Do not lay up for yourselves treasures on earth."* Why? Because, He said, moths and rust would destroy them, and thieves would break in and steal them. Instead, He challenged His followers to lay up for themselves *"treasures in Heaven, where moth and rust do not destroy, and where thieves do not break in and steal."*

What kind of treasures was our Lord Jesus Christ talking about? What are treasures, by the way? *Treasures* can be defined as "something of value which is laid aside, possessed or hidden by the owner or possessor and is, thus, valuable." *Treasure* is synonymous with *wealth* and *riches*.

In the old days, especially during the times of the patriarchs, treasures (wealth and riches) were measured mostly in livestock-sheep—goats, cattle, donkeys and camels. Other things, like land, houses, servants, slaves and precious metals like gold and silver, were also considered part of one's wealth and riches.

In the New Testament, gold, frankincense and myrrh were treasures that the wise men gifted the child Jesus during their visit to Bethlehem. Pearls were also of a great price during those days. In modern times, our treasures include expensive jewelry of gold and silver and precious stones like diamonds, rubies and emeralds, heirlooms, real estate, stocks and exotic and expensive cars.

In this text, known as the Olivet Discourse, Jesus confined the subject of treasures to two categories. The first was treasures which could be destroyed by moths or rust, and the second was treasures which could be broken into and stolen by thieves.

What were the treasures in those days which could be destroyed by moths? Precious garments were considered to be treasures back then. Unlike today, when we have industrial and hi-tech machines that produce textiles for our clothing, it was difficult to make garments in those days. The threads and yarn had to be manually prepared from flax or animal wool. Then, they had to be manually knitted or woven into material for garments.

Because garments were so difficult to produce, they were valuable commodities. Garments were objects of desire and temptation. For example, together with silver and gold, Achan hid the treasures of Babylonish garments. Samson bet thirty pieces of garments on his riddle, and Gehazi, Elisha's servant, coveted two garments from Naaman.

Garments, however, could be easily destroyed by moths. Today, we avoid this destruction by putting mothballs in our closets, and they protect our garments.

What were the treasures in those days that could be broken into and stolen by thieves? These were movable valuables, like precious metals (gold and silver), precious stones (like emeralds and rubies). This also included pearls. These were very vulnerable to thievery because the people had no banks, safes or safety deposit boxes in those days, and they had to find places to hide their treasures. They even hid them underground in the fields surrounding their dwellings.

This was illustrated by our Jesus Christ in His Parable of the Hidden Treasure and Parable of the Pearl of Great Price. He said:

The kingdom of heaven is like a merchant seeking beautiful pearls, who, when he had found one pearl of great price, went and sold all that he had and bought it.   Matthew 13:45-46

Unless they were well protected, livestock were also easily stolen by thieves. Job's numerous herds of cows and donkeys were all stolen by Sabean brigands.

Now, how do we lay up treasures in Heaven? The answer is that we can convert our earthly treasures into heavenly treasures. How is that done? A rich young ruler one day asked our Lord Jesus Christ this question, *"What must I do to inherit eternal life?"* (Luke 18:18). After Jesus challenged him regarding the mandates of the Law, his reply was, *"All these things I have kept from my youth"* (Luke 18:21). But that was only half of the commandment involving human relationship.

When Jesus heard this, He said to him, *"You still lack one thing. Sell all that you have and distribute to the poor, and you will have treasure in heaven; and come, follow Me"* (Luke 18:22). But when the young man heard this, he became very sad because he was a man of great wealth.

Yes, we can lay up for ourselves treasures in Heaven by first giving to God of our earthly treasures through the Church (which is God's agency here on earth). Every gift that we give to God in church, in the form of tithes and offerings, will be credited to our account in Heaven. Secondly, every gift or assistance that we give to the poor and the needy, whether in money or in kind, will also be credited to our account in Heaven.

The Scriptures declare:

Honor the Lord with your possessions,
And with the firstfruits of all your increase;
So your barns will be filled with plenty,
And your vats will overflow with new wine. Proverbs 3:9-10

Don't be greedy, like the rich man who ignored the poor Lazarus, when, in reality, he had plenty to share and could have helped. In the afterlife, their situations were reversed.

Why did the rich young ruler decline to obey Jesus? He was laying up for himself *treasures on earth.*

In the Gospel of our Lord Jesus Christ, there is more than just receiving salvation and going to Heaven! Jesus said, *"I came that they might have life [salvation and going to Heaven], and that they might have it more abundantly [treasures in Heaven]"* (John 10:10).

The heart of the matter, according to Jesus, is his: *"For where your treasure is, there will your heart be also"* (Matthew 6:21). According to the Jewish concept, the human heart is both the seat of the mind and the emotions. *"As he [a man] thinks in his heart, so is he"* (Proverbs

91

23:7). Compared with the modern computer, the heart is the central processing unit of the human personality. So, relative to the foregoing subject, the question is: "Have you been thinking of giving back to God through the Church? Have you been emotional about giving to the poor and needy? Do you pity the poor, so that you are moved with compassion and share your resources with them?" Check it out! Maybe your account in Heaven is totally empty! It is not too late to start being generous! Start giving now!   ✄

ෆ **15** ෨

ABSENT FROM THE BODY AND
PRESENT WITH THE LORD

Text: 2 Corinthians 5:8

Proponents of the mainstream Christian belief that, at death, the soul immediately goes to Heaven use this verse, among others, to support their allegation and argument. A closer look at the text and even the context, however, reveals that they don't even mention the word *death.*

"But doesn't *'absent from the body'* mean death?" some argue. "And no one goes to be with Lord (in Heaven) without undergoing death." That's true, as a general rule. But with every rule, there is an exception. And this is what Paul was contemplating here—the exception to the general rule.

How will that happen? He explained it in 1 Corinthians 15 and 1 Thessalonians 4: the sudden and abrupt change for those who are still alive at the coming again of our Lord Jesus Christ in the clouds to meet the saints in the air.

93

Assuming, however, for the sake of argument, that no one can 'be present with the Lord, meaning that no one can go to Heaven without undergoing death, this still cannot be immediately after death. As a rule, no one goes to Heaven without undergoing resurrection. The exception, of course, is the aforementioned. Jesus Christ is our pattern, our model. If He underwent resurrection before He ascended to Heaven, then so must every Christian who dies.

The main thrust of Paul's message here is found in the context. He was talking about two bodies, the earthly and the heavenly bodies. These two bodies are different, and he described the difference between the two by way of allegory. The first one was like a tent (the Tabernacle), and the other was like a building (the Temple). The former was temporary and the latter permanent. Both structures were indwelt by the presence of God, and there the Israelites met, served and worshipped Him.

Paul groaned, and he mentioned this groaning twice. It was an indication that he was in pain. And he was also burdened. It was apparent that the multiple trials he had previously mentioned (2 Corinthians 4:8, *troubled on every side, perplexed, persecuted, cast down and bearing about in the body the dying of our Lord Jesus*" had taken a toll on his body. At one time, he had a *"thorn in the flesh"* that he sought the Lord to remove. Was that some kind of health or physical issue as a consequence of his ministry?

Perhaps you and I can identify and relate with Paul in the many bodily infirmities that we suffer, especially as we become older. Our body is slowly deteriorating, and we have many aches: headaches, toothaches, backaches and even knee aches. Sometimes (or most of the time), we have no one to blame but ourselves. We have failed to take care of our body through indiscriminate, reckless, careless and callous living. We have abused and misused our body with uncontrollable vices. The excessive drinking of alcoholi beverages or addiction to tobacco smoking and prohibited and illegal drugs have weakened and destroyed our body's immure system so that we become weak and sick with diabetes, cancer, aids, and other maladies. Don't you know that your body is the temple of God? Therefore, we must keep it clean and holy. Do not defile the temple of God. Don't you know that God prohibits you from having tattoos on your body? Oh, the reality and the curse of being human.

There is some good news! God has prepared for us a new body which is heavenly. It is immortal, that is it will not die, but will live forever. It is incorruptible (not subject to decay and deterioration). It is powerful (not limited by time, space or the law of gravity). And is spiritual!

That sounds like Superman! Yes, God is preparing a new breed of people! Paul said, *"We know ... ."* How did they know? He fully explained that in 1 Corinthians 15, where he dealt with the subject of resurrection.

ᙿ **16** ᙒ

Prepare to Meet Your God

Text: Amos 4:12

There are two things which are certain in life. And what are those two things? They are taxation and death. Are they absolute? No, they are rules, and with every rule there is an exception.

Does this mean that there is an escape from any of these rules? With regards to taxation, at least in the Philippines, there are two escapes, and they are tax evasion and tax avoidance. The first one is illegal and has a criminal consequence. The second one is a legal remedy. Not everyone knows this, but lawyers know.

If one is found guilty of tax evasion, can he be imprisoned? Yes, because tax evasion takes on the nature of a crime. If one is guilty of tax evasion, can he compromise with the tax authorities in order to avoid being imprisoned? The answer is yes. Why? Because the goal of the tax authorities is to collect taxes, not to imprison taxpayers. But the tax evader will have to pay a hefty and heavy price in the form of penalties, surcharges and interest, besides his tax that is due. A piece of advice to taxpayers: pay your taxes, and pay your taxes on time.

Death is the least expected, if not the most unexpected, occurrence in most peoples' lives. If we are expecting something, we think about it and make preparation for it beforehand. Practical people prepare for the stark reality of death in their lives, especially when they get older or sick and sense that they may be dying.

Then people go into estate planning and prepare a will in order to apportion their estate properly to their surviving heirs, so that those heirs will not fight over the estate after owner's demise. They also prepare what is called a "life plan," which is actually a death plan. It includes arrangements for a funeral and burial once they have died.

It is interesting to observe that the elderly who make such preparations for death tend to be quite religious in the process. They go to church often and ask for prayers. Others, however, prepare only for the temporal things and but not for the everlasting.

Most young people are oblivious to death because they are still full of life and energy and have many dreams and aspirations. They fail to realize that death can strike them at any moment. Not long ago, fifteen college students suddenly died in a bus accident in Tanay, Rizal during a field trip. Those young people were filled with dreams and aspirations, and probably were not contemplating death, but very suddenly and unexpectedly it came to them.

In another sad case, a young man who was about to get married to his fiancée was riding a motorcycle when he was fatally shot in the head by an irate and trigger-happy gunman from a Land Cruiser SUV. The Bible says, *"Remember your Creator in the days of your youth, before the days of trouble come"* (Ecclesiastes 12:1, NIV).

What is the exception to the rule of death? Can death somehow be averted? The Scriptures say:

To everything there is a season,
A time for every purpose under heaven:
A time to be born,
And a time to die.   Ecclesiastes 3:1-2

And as it is appointed for men to die once, but after this the judg-
ment.   Hebrews 9:27

This is an appointment that no one can escape.

But there is an exception to this rule of death. There will be some people who will not experience death. How will this happen? And when will this happen? According to the apostle Paul, in his first letters to the Corinthians and to the Thessalonians, Christians who are still alive when Christ returns:

In a moment, in the twinkling of an eye, at the last trumpet. For
the trumpet will sound, and the dead will be raised incorruptible,
and we shall be changed.   1 Corinthians 15:52

Then we who are alive and remain shall be caught up together
with them in the clouds to meet the Lord in the air. And thus we
shall always be with the Lord.   1 Thessalonians 4:17

This extraordinary and remarkable event will transpire at the Second Coming of Jesus Christ, when He will descend from Heaven with a cry of command, with the archangel's call, and with the sound of the trumpet of God. Christians call this the Rapture.

Can death be suspended? The answer is yes! One good example from the Bible is the case of King Hezekiah, as recorded in 2 Kings 20:

In those days Hezekiah was sick and near death. And Isaiah the prophet, the son of Amoz, went to him and said to him, "Thus says the Lord: "Set your house in order, for you shall die, and not live."   2 Kings 20:1

In this way, King Hezekiah was issued a death warrant from God through the prophet Isaiah. But he did not die:

Then he [Hezekiah] turned his face toward the wall, and prayed to the Lord, saying, "Remember now, O Lord, I pray, how I have walked before You in truth and with a loyal heart, and have done what was good in Your sight." And Hezekiah wept bitterly.

And it happened, before Isaiah had gone out into the middle court, that the word of the Lord came to him, saying, "Return and tell Hezekiah the leader of My people, 'Thus says the Lord, the God of David your father: "I have heard your prayer, I have seen your tears; surely I will heal you. On the third day you shall go up to the house of the Lord. And I will add to your days fifteen years."   2 Kings 20:2-6

What is the implication of God's pronouncement to His people: *"prepare to meet your God"* (Amos 4:12)? Is it something optimistic or something pessimistic? Well, gleaning from the context of this verse, the sound of it is rather pessimistic. God gives a stern warning to pigheaded people that when they meet Him, it is something awful and dreadful! It is appointed to men once to die and after that comes the judgment. Just as no one escapes death (as a rule), no one will escape judgment either. At the Great White Throne Judgment, the sinful and wicked dead will be judged:

And I saw the dead, great and small, standing before the throne, and books were opened. Another book was opened, which is the book of life. The dead were judged according to what they had done as recorded in the books. Revelation 20:12, NIV

Then death and Hades were thrown into the lake of fire. The lake of fire is the second death. Anyone whose name was not found written in the book of life was thrown into the lake of fire.

Revelation 20:14-15, NIV

Today I have some very good news! Anyone who wants to can escape the dreadful judgment of God and not be thrown into the Lake of Fire. How and what must they do to be saved?

Believe on the Lord Jesus Christ, and you will be saved, you and your household. Acts 16:31

Nor is there salvation in any other, for there is no other name under heaven given among men by which we must be saved.

Acts 4:12

But now is the day of salvation. Don't wait until it's too late. Repent and confess your sins to God. Open your heart and receive Jesus Christ as your personal Lord and Savior.

For God so loved the world that He gave His only begotten Son, that whoever believes in Him should not perish but have everlasting life. John 3:16

For the wages of sin is death, but the gift of God is eternal life in Christ Jesus our Lord. Romans 6:23

THE UNKNOWN GOD REVEALED

Text: Acts 17:22-31

Of all of God's creation, man was His crown jewel. He was special and unique. And why is that so? The rest of God's creation, animate or inanimate, had only one connection—with earth—whereas man had two connections—with God and with earth. It was this connection with God that made man religious even after he fell into sin.

Only man was created in the image and likeness of God, only man was inbreathed by God, and only man had a direct and close contact with God. God was talking and walking with man. He gave man dominion over all His creation. Man was God's vicar on earth.

In olden times, rulers put their images on statues in their domain and also on their money (coins). This was to remind their subjects who ruled. God placed His image on man.

But when man fell into sin, his connection with God was cut off, and his fellowship with the Creator was severed. Man died spiritually and, slowly but surely, physical death crept in ... until

THE UNKNOWN GOD REVEALED

death had conquered man, and all men died. This was not only a sad and sorry episode in the history of mankind, but also a tragic one. Adam lost nearly everything, especially that which was of eternal value, which include his potential to become immortal. He relinquished to the devil his dominion over God's creation, and this was an act of treason and a betrayal of God. In the process, Adam gained Eve and the pleasure of being with her, but only for a season. In the end, they both died anyway, leaving behind a legacy of spiritual death, misery and a curse.

Since that time, man has wandered in darkness. Not only did the cataract of sin blur his spiritual vision, but his decision to be independent of God totally blinded him. However, despite the fallen nature of man, there is still a longing in him for God because of his created connection. This is a vacuum in his being that nothing and no one can fill and satisfy but God alone. So, man invented religions to try to fill this vacuum.

The problem was that these invented religions were based on an ignorance of the true God. Man chose to worship the creature instead of the Creator. He even worshipped idols, which God had prohibited him from doing. God said:

> *You shall not make for yourself a carved image — any likeness of anything that is in heaven above, or that is in the earth beneath, or that is in the water under the earth; you shall not bow down to them nor serve them. For I, the Lord your God, am a jealous God.* Exodus 20:4-5

> *Their idols are silver and gold,*
> *The work of men's hands.*

They have mouths, but they do not speak;
Eyes they have, but they do not see;
They have ears, but they do not hear;
Noses they have, but they do not smell;
They have hands, but they do not handle;
Feet they have, but they do not walk;
Nor do they mutter through their throat.
Those who make them are like them;
So is everyone who trusts in them.   Psalm 115:4-8

Although the evidence of God was overwhelming and undeniable visually through nature, still people did not know God, or maybe, they just ignored God. This is the reason there are so many religions in the world today.

Even the Greeks, who were advanced in and advocates of knowledge during the time of Paul, were ignorant of the true God. When Paul was in Athens, during one of his missionary journeys, he said to the Athenians:

I perceive that in all things you are very religious; for as I was passing through and considering the objects of your worship, I even found an altar with this inscription:

TO THE UNKNOWN GOD.

Therefore, the One whom you worship without knowing, Him I proclaim to you.   Acts 17:22-23

Through the preaching of Paul, God revealed to the Athenians the unknown God whom they worshiped as none other than our Lord Jesus Christ.

Paul concluded his preaching that day with these words:

Truly, these times of ignorance God overlooked, but now commands all men everywhere to repent, 31 because He has appointed a day on which He will judge the world in righteousness by the Man whom He has ordained. He has given assurance of this to all by raising Him from the dead.   Acts 17:30-31

I believe that there were two primary reasons why Jesus Christ came into this world. The first was that He wanted to reveal who God was to all the people of the world. In Christ, we see that God is omnipresent, omnipotent, omniscient and eternal and that God is love. Christ demonstrated all these divine attributes during His earthly ministry. He had power over sickness, sin, nature, demons and death.

The second reason Jesus came, of course, was to redeem mankind from sin through His sacrificial death on the cross of Calvary. He was resurrected from the dead in order to complete His redemptive mission for mankind.

Thank God that in His grace and mercy He did not want this ignorance of Him to continue. God revealed Himself first to individuals, like Abraham and Moses, and then to an entire nation (Israel). Prior to the advent of the New Testament, the Hebrew people were the only ones who had the knowledge of the true and the right concept of God. When Jesus came, the knowledge of God suddenly became available to all nations.

Whereas in nature, the evidence of God was visualized, in Jesus, it was verbalized (as the Word of God). Jesus Christ then became is *"the express image"* of the invisible God (Hebrews 1:3). This word *express* means "to make known." It also means "to speak." So, if we want to know God, all we have to do is look at Jesus. He is God!

So, look unto Jesus. Believe His words. Believe His works. Acquaint yourself with Him now and be at peace, so that good will come upon you. Repent of your sins, receive Jesus Christ as your personal Lord and Savior, and you will be saved!   ✄

$\mathcal{G}$ **18** $\mathcal{SO}$

GOD'S GIFT OF POWER, LOVE
AND A SOUND MIND

Text: 2 Timothy 1:7

The apostle Paul wrote his second letter to Timothy, his son in the faith, while he was imprisoned in Rome nearly two thousand years ago. The Bible, as the Word of God, is truly wonderful because, although this is an ancient text, its message has universal relevance and application.

It is believed that the apostle Paul was near to his martyrdom at the time of this writing. He longed to see his son in the faith, for that would bring him joy at this sad and lonely moment of his life. Many of Paul's co-workers in Asia had deserted him, maybe because he was imprisoned. Timothy was the pastor of the Church in Ephesus, when Paul wrote this letter, and the apostle informed him that he was constantly praying for him—night and day.

The initial subject of this letter was to encourage Timothy in his faith and in the gift of God relative to his service for God. This legacy of faith had been handed down to him by his mother and grandmother. Then the gift of God had been given to him through the laying on of Paul's hands. Paul was now reminding Timothy that he had these ministry gifts and was encouraging him to stir them up or fan them into flame.

Why was Timothy not using these ministry gifts? Apparently he was a rather reluctant servant of God and had some personal issues that hindered the use of these ministry gifts, leaving them rather dormant.

Had Timothy known that he had these ministry gifts? Well, whether or not he had previously know that he had them or not, Paul was telling him that he had.

What were Timothy's personal issues that hindered him from exercising these ministry gifts? One of these personal issues was fear or timidity. That's why Paul wrote to him:

For God has not given us a spirit of fear, but of power and of love and of a sound mind.   2 Timothy 1:7

What is fear or timidity in this context? It means that Timothy lacked the courage or self-confidence to exercise his God-given gifts of ministry. Paul added:

Therefore do not be ashamed of the testimony of our Lord, nor of me His prisoner.   2 Timothy 1:8

I believe that we are all servants of God. We, who are members of the clergy, are serving God under the category of sacred service, whereas those who are with the government and the private sector are also serving God, but under the category of secular service. We all have a mandate to serve God and our people, whether we are in the sacred or the secular service.

What we commonly call The Ten Commandments is actually a set of two duties. The first set is made up of our duties to God, which also is our sacred duty. The second set consists of our duties to our fellow beings, which also is our secular duty.

What is this *"power"* that God has given us, according to Paul? Jesus said:

> But you shall receive power when the Holy Spirit has come upon you; and you shall be witnesses to Me in Jerusalem, and in all Judea and Samaria, and to the end of the earth.   Acts 1:8

I believe that this is the power to witness, or testify, about our Lord Jesus Christ. It is the power to herald the Gospel of our Lord , and that Gospel brings life and hope of immortality. It is the Gospel of salvation. Like Paul, we may suffer because of the Gospel, but if we believe in Christ, He is able to guard what we entrust to Him for that day.

This promise of power is also related to our position in life, in government, in our society, in our work or even in our family and/ or church family. Power is also an authority. It has been said that "Power corrupts, and absolute power corrupts absolutely." What does it mean when power is corrupted? It means that someone who possesses power misuses or abuses it. He goes beyond the limits, or boundaries, of such power, as defined. This happens especially when power is being used for personal gain and to the prejudice of others. An abuse of power is also the exercise of such power beyond its jurisdiction, which is also called abuse of discretion. Some people, in order to perpetuate themselves in power, steal, kill and destroy. For example, the police have the power to apprehend suspected criminals, but when a policeman abuses his power instead of enforcing the law, he becomes a lawbreaker himself.

The first Christmas was not all that merry. When King Herod heard from the wise men that a new *"King of the Jews"* had been born, he massacred all the young children and infants in Bethlehem from the age of two years old and under. As a result, there was tremendous wailing in almost every house.

Today, even people in position of power in churches abuse or misuse such power. I am an apologist for the Christian faith and ministry, but I will not hesitate to rebuke corrupt and abusive ministers of the Gospel. I usually do not accept hearsay, but wait to come to an conclusion based on personal knowledge. Suffice it to say that there are pastors and others ministers today who use their position of power for personal gain, in order to enrich themselves.

Far too many have only one message, and that is: "Give, give, give! Money, money and more money!" They are not content with one offering. They scam the members of the church of more money with second offering or even a third. Oh, how they love money! I heard one man say, "My morality is money."

Some ministers also use their power, influence and words to sexually harass, seduce or abuse young women in the church. So, how can we prevent or avoid this type of corruption, abuse or misuse of power? The Bible shows that we must temper power with graces such as love and self–control.

What is love? Love is an emotion, usually a good and positive one. But there is also a bad kind of love. Why is it a bad love?

Because it is a forbidden love. For example, a married man is not to become romantically involved with a woman other than his wife. Those who are single are not to fall in love with a married man or a married woman.

Love is expressed in many and several ways. It is characterized by patience, kindness, humility, respect and gentleness. And, the Bible shows us, love does not delight in evil, but rejoices in the truth.

Another example of a bad kind of love is the love of money. Why is that? Because the Bible says that *"the love of money is a root of all kinds of evil"* (1 Timothy 6:10). When people love money, they are forced to lie, cheat, steal and defraud other people to get more of it

It is very embarrassing to read in the foreign and social media that our beloved Philippines is "the most, if not one of the most, corrupt countries in Asia." The challenge of this message to all of who live here is to reverse this bad reputation by serving God with fervor and integrity.

Love and self-control are like brakes on a motor vehicle. There is power in every car. But what would happen if there were no brakes? There would be many more collisions and total chaos on our roads and in our streets. In a spiritual sense, this is what is happening with many in the world today. There is chaos and confusion everywhere.

As believers in Christ, let us not be fearful in facing our future, knowing that God will always be with us. Let us face our life with all of its challenges and opportunities, with courage and self-confidence because God has promised to never leave us or forsake us.

෴ **19** ෴

GOD HAD SOMETHING BETTER FOR US

Text: Hebrews 11:40

Joseph in the Bible is one of the most sensational and inspiring of biblical characters. But just who was this Joseph? There are many Josephs in the Bible, so let us identify the one of whom we speak here. This Joseph was the eleventh son of Jacob and the first child of Rachel, Jacob's second wife.

Joseph was his father's favorite son. This was evident by the special coat that Jacob gave him. Unfortunately, this favoritism brought serious trouble for the whole family. The older ten brothers hated Joseph because he was their father's favorite. This hatred was aggravated when Joseph interpreted one of his dreams in what seemed like a rather conceited way, so that the brothers even plotted to kill him.

One day Joseph was told by his father to go look for his brothers (because they were all shepherds). When he found them, they seized him and set about to carry out their plan to kill him. This was foiled only because they were opposed by their elder brother, Reuben. Instead of being killed, Joseph was sold as a slave to some

112

Ishmaelite merchants who happened to pass by at that moment. Joseph was taken by this group of men to Egypt, where he was again sold, this time to a man named Potiphar.

Potiphar was an Egyptian official, Captain of the Guard for Pharaoh, the King of Egypt. The Lord was with Joseph in the house of Potiphar, and he found favor with him because the Lord caused all that he did to prosper in his hands (see Genesis 39:21). Unfortunately Potiphar's wife was jealous of Joseph, so she seduced him and then falsely accused him of attempting to rape her. The result was that his master put him in a prison where the Pharaoh's prisoners were confined. But, even while Joseph was there in the prison, God gave him favor in the sight of the prison warden, so that he was eventually in charge of the whole prison (see Genesis 39:21-23).

Then one day Joseph was summoned by Pharaoh, the King himself, to his palace:

> *Then Pharaoh sent and called Joseph, and they brought him quickly out of the dungeon; and he shaved, changed his clothing, and came to Pharaoh.*   Genesis 41:14

This was a momentous and crucial occasion because it could change the situation of Joseph and his family for the better, and this change would also affect the survival of the Jewish nation.

Why did Pharaoh summon Joseph? He wanted him to help interpret his dream. Pharaoh had a dream, it troubled him, and he sought wise men who might interpret it, but there were none. Then someone told him that Joseph could interpret dreams.

When he arrived at the palace, Joseph seemed very confident:

Joseph answered Pharaoh, saying, "... God will give Pharaoh an answer of peace."   Genesis 41:16

This was amazing because Joseph had just come from the prison. But it was what had happened there that gave him courage. There he had met two of Pharaoh's servants who had done something to displease him and therefore he had imprisoned them. One was said to be the king's butler and the other his baker.

What is a butler? A butler is "a chief male servant, having charge of the wines and liquors for the king."

While in the prison, both of these men had dreams which they could not interpret, and Joseph helped them interpret their dreams. As Joseph had foretold in his interpretation, after three days the baker was executed, and the butler was restored to his position. Before he left the prison, Joseph asked the butler to remember him when to the palace, but, as men often do, he forgot.

It was two years later that Pharaoh had his strange dream, and he had it twice. Something about the dream was so strange that he couldn't get it out of his mind, even though he had forgotten the details of it. He had man on staff who were considered to be wise, but none of them were able to help interpret the dream.

There was much noise in the palace over this dream and, hearing about it, the butler who had been with Joseph in prison finally remembered him and told Pharaoh about his ability to interpret dreams. And that was why he had been summoned to the palace.

Joseph did not accept any credit for his gift. He told Pharaoh:

GOD HAD SOMETHING BETTER FOR US

"I cannot do it, but God will give Pharaoh the answer he desires."   Genesis 41:16

Then, very quickly and seemingly very easily, he gave his answer. The two dreams, although slightly different, had the same meaning. There would be seven years of plenty, followed by seven years of famine. The famine would be so severe that the years of plenty would not be remembered. The fact that Pharaoh had dreamed the same dream twice meant that these events were fixed by God, and that He would shortly bring them to pass.

Joseph's suggestion to the Pharaoh was that he look for a man who was discreet and wise who could oversee the gathering and storage of twenty percent of all the harvests during the seven good years in preparation for the coming famine. Joseph must have been surprised when he was chosen by Pharaoh to be that man, and he was appointed ruler of all in Egypt, except in matters of the throne.

Pharaoh then took the signet ring from his finger and put it on Joseph's finger. He dressed Joseph in robes of fine linen and put a gold chain around his neck. He had Joseph ride in a chariot as his second-in-command, and men shouted before him, "Make way!" Wow! What a sensational and fantastic promotion and transition for Joseph! In one day, he had gone from prison to the palace! How amazing!

Eventually Joseph's brothers came to Egypt to buy grain because the famine that Joseph had predicted also affected Canaan. In a dramatic reunion with his brothers—the same brothers who had sold him into slavery in Egypt—Joseph revealed himself to them as their brother. They were, of course, shocked, but they were also terrified. The brother whom they had so wronged was now powerful. Joseph calmed their fears when he said:

115

But now, do not therefore be grieved or angry with yourselves because you sold me here; for God sent me before you to preserve life. Genesis 45:5

In this way, the one they had persecuted became the preserver of their lives. So, here are two perspectives of man's destiny—one human and the other divine. Sometimes people are hostile to us because of our faith in Jesus Christ (or for some other reason) but without any real meaning behind it at all, just because we are Christians. But let us be faithful and be patient and hope for divine providence!

Although the circumstances and situations in the life of Joseph changed, one thing was constant. Whether he was in Potiphar's house or in the prison, the Lord was with him and the Lord made him to prosper.

As followers of Christ, we can emulate Joseph, by trusting God in our adverse circumstances and situations in life, knowing full well that He has promised:

I will never leave you nor forsake you. Hebrews 13:5

Lo, I am with you always, even to the end of the age.

Matthew 28:20

And we know that all things work together for good to those who love God, to those who are the called according to His purpose.

Romans 8:28

Praise the Lord! Hallelujah!

He raises the poor from the dust and lifts the needy from the ash heap; he seats them with princes and has them inherit a throne of honor.   1 Samuel 2:8, NIV

But as it is written:

"Eye has not seen, nor ear heard,
Nor have entered into the heart of man
The things which God has prepared for those who love Him."

But God has revealed them to us through His Spirit.
                    1 Corinthians 2:9-10

Let not your heart be troubled; you believe in God, believe also in Me. In My Father's house are many mansions;[a] if it were not so, I would have told you. I go to prepare a place for you. And if I go and prepare a place for you, I will come again and receive you to Myself; that where I am, there you may be also.

                    John 14:1-3

The best is yet to come! Praise God! Hallelujah!

cs **20** so

THE GOSPEL ACCORDING TO THE APOSTLE PAUL

Text: 1 Corinthians 15:1-11

What is the Gospel? It is the Good News concerning Christ, the Kingdom of God and salvation. It is the message of Christianity, telling about the life, death and resurrection of Jesus Christ. The title *gospel* is also applied to the four inspired histories of the life and teachings of Christ. These four gospels were written by Matthew, Mark, Luke and John during the first century A.D.

Why four gospels? Each gospel writer wrote about Jesus to a different audience, for a different purpose, to give a unique perspective on His life. Together, the four gospels give us a complete picture of who Jesus was and what He accomplished during His earthly ministry.

The first three gospels are sometimes called synoptic because they see the whole together and present similar views of the life and teachings of Christ. Matthew presents Christ as the Messiah, Mark emphasizes His activities, Luke stresses His humanitarian interests, and John's gospel shows us His deity.

Different symbols for the gospels are also used to communicate the distinctiveness of each account. A lion, symbolizing Matthew, represents strength and royal authority; a bull, representing Mark, portrays service and power; the figure of a man, for Luke, stands for wisdom and character; and an eagle, John's symbol, represents Christ's deity.

The version of the Gospel I am calling the Gospel according to the apostle Paul is found in 1 Corinthians 15, and it is generally believed and accepted that the apostle Paul was the author of the letters to the Corinthians.

Is this a different Gospel, compared with that of the four previous ones? The answer is no! Let's see what Paul said about the Gospel:

> *Now, brothers and sisters, I want to remind you of the gospel I preached to you, which you received and on which you have taken your stand. By this gospel you are saved, if you hold firmly to the word I preached to you. Otherwise, you have believed in vain.*
>
> *For what I received I passed on to you as of first importance: that Christ died for our sins according to the Scriptures, that he was buried, that he was raised on the third day according to the Scriptures.* 1 Corinthians 15:1-4, NIV
> *"*

Whereas the books we call the four gospels narrate the birth, life and ministry of Jesus Christ, Paul's version focused on His death and resurrection. Prior to this statement, Paul had addressed a variety of problems in the lifestyle of the Corinthian believers. The Corinthians believers were engrossed in factions, lawsuits, immorality, other questionable practices, abuse of the Lord's Supper and spiritual gifts. Besides offering discipline and rebuke, Paul also gave answers and counsel to the questions and issues raised by the Corinthians.

Paul's Gospel was given to him; he did not write it himself. Somebody told him about the Gospel, and he had passed that knowledge on to the Corinthian believers when he had preached to them.

So, who gave Paul this Gospel? Was it Mark? Or Luke? We have no clue. Probably it was the Lord Jesus Himself who gave Paul the Gospel message after he met the Lord on the road to Damascus, where and when he was converted to Christianity. What was the essence of Paul's Gospel? It was the death, burial and resurrection of Jesus Christ.

Why did Paul stress the death and resurrection of Jesus in his Gospel? It was because the Greeks did not believe in the doctrine of resurrection from the dead. When Paul preached the Gospel of Jesus Christ on Mars Hill in Athens, he was mocked and laughed at by the Greeks. The Greeks believed that the body was a prison of the soul and that when a man died, he was finally free from that bodily prison. Paul, however, argued and established the fact and the truth of the doctrine of resurrection and, specifically, the death, burial and resurrection of Jesus Christ.

What is the significance of the word *death* in his argument regarding the resurrection? This word *death* is connected to resurrection. In order for a person to be resurrected, he must first die. There is no resurrection to talk about if there is not first a death. Resurrection is the raising from the dead of a person through the power of God, never to die again.

Furthermore, the death of Jesus Christ had redemptive implications. *Redemption, or deliverance from the enslavement of sin and release to a new freedom, is accomplished only through the sacrifice of the Redeemer, Jesus Christ Himself. The death of Christ was the redemptive price.*

The word *redemption* contains both the ideas of deliverance and the price of that deliverance or ransom. It was also a propitiation, in order to appease the wrath of God, so that His justice and holiness would be satisfied and He could forgive sin. Propitiation does not make God merciful; it makes divine forgiveness possible. For this, atonement must be provided, which is the death of Christ for man's sin. Through Christ's death, propitiation is made for man's sin.

In order to establish the fact and the truth of the resurrection of Jesus Christ, Paul presented several evidences. His first evidence was the sacred Scriptures. The scriptures referred to here were the books of the Old Testament, which is believed to be the Word of God. The death of Jesus Christ was *"according to the scriptures,"* and the resurrection of Jesus Christ was also *"according to the scriptures "*

Why did Jesus die? The Bible says, *"for our sins,"* as I have explained.

How did Jesus die? Did he commit suicide? Or was He murdered? No, Jesus did not commit suicide and neither was He murdered. He died of His own volition. He said:

> *No one takes it from Me, but I lay it down of Myself. I have power to lay it down, and I have power to take it again. This command I have received from My Father.* John 10:18

121

The next evidence that Paul presented was the testimony of the witnesses. The resurrected Christ was seen by these witnesses:

And that He was seen by Cephas, then by the twelve. After that He was seen by over five hundred brethren at once, of whom the greater part remain to the present, but some have fallen asleep. after that He was seen by James, then by all the apostles. Then last of all He was seen by me also, as by one born out of due time.

1 Corinthians 15:5-8

The last evidence Paul presented was *"res ipsa loquitor,"* meaning "the thing speaks for itself." Jesus Christ died and was buried, but now He is alive as seen by many witnesses:

To whom He also presented Himself alive after His suffering by many infallible proofs, being seen by them during forty days and speaking of the things pertaining to the kingdom of God

.   Acts 1:3

Now when He had spoken these things, while they watched, He was taken up, and a cloud received Him out of their sight.

Acts 1:9

What are the significance and the challenges of Paul's Gospel message? He was saying, "Instead of squabbling about divisions in the church, filing lawsuits against your fellow brethren, tolerating immorality in the lives of believers, and continuing other questionable practices ... instead of abusing the Lord's Supper and accepting confusion about spiritual gifts, you should concentrate on declaring and preaching the Gospel. When the Gospel is genuinely received, it can make us stand and will save us, if we believe in it. Believing the Gospel means committing our lives to receive Jesus Christ as our Lord and Savior with repentance and then following Him the rest of our lives. The Gospel according to the apostle Paul gives us hope of everlasting life! ✄

cs **21** so

Ninety Percent Ingrates

Text: Luke 17:11-19

Now it happened as He [Jesus] went to Jerusalem that He passed through the midst of Samaria and Galilee. Then as He entered a certain village, there met Him ten men who were lepers, who stood afar off. And they lifted up their voices and said, "Jesus, Master, have mercy on us!"

So when He saw them, He said to them, "Go, show yourselves to the priests." And so it was that as they went, they were cleansed.

And one of them, when he saw that he was healed, returned, and with a loud voice glorified God, and fell down on his face at His feet, giving Him thanks. And he was a Samaritan.

So Jesus answered and said, "Were there not ten cleansed? But where are the nine? Were there not any found who returned to give glory to God except this foreigner?" And He said to him, "Arise, go your way. Your faith has made you well."

Luke 17:11-19

Why did these ten men lift up their voices at a distance when they met Jesus? And why did they distance themselves from the crowd? The answer is because they were lepers. Leprosy was a rampant and serious disease in Israel before and during the time of Jesus. This disease was considered a plague and contagious. That's why the Mosaic Law required that lepers be isolated from the rest of society because of the need to control the spread of the disease, for which there was no cure. They had to cry out, "Unclean! Unclean!" so that everyone could avoid them. Any contact with a leper defiled the person who touched him.

There were prominent persons in the Old Testament who were victims of leprosy. For instance, there was Miriam, the sister of Moses. When she spoke against him, the Lord punished her with leprosy. There was Naaman, the Syrian. He was Captain of the Host of the King of Syria and was a great and honorable man and a mighty man of valor, but he had leprosy. He was miraculously healed when he dipped into the river Jordan seven times, as the prophet Elisha had told him to do. There was also King Uzziah, who was afflicted with leprosy until his death because he usurped the office of the priest. As with Naaman, sometimes the victims of leprosy were miraculously cured. Cleansing the lepers was part of the healing ministry of Jesus.

Why did the ten lepers say to Jesus, *"Have mercy on us!"* The other meaning of the word *mercy*, besides "forbearance of inflicting punishment upon an adversary or law-breaker" is "to ask for compassion, which causes one to help the weak, the sick, or the poor."

How did the lepers know that Jesus was in their village? And how did they know that He could help them or heal them? There is no doubt that they had heard about the fame of Jesus:

And Jesus went about all Galilee, teaching in their synagogues, preaching the gospel of the kingdom, and healing all kinds of sickness and all kinds of disease among the people. Then His fame went throughout all Syria; and they brought to Him all sick people who were afflicted with various diseases and torments, and those who were demon-possessed, epileptics, and paralytics; and He healed them.   Matthew 24:23-24

Why did Jesus tell the ten lepers to go to the priests? In the book of Leviticus, under the Mosaic Law, it was the priests who were given the task of examining the skin abnormalities of the people of Israel. The priests were to determine if a particular skin infection was the plague of leprosy. If so, they pronounced the person unclean, and the victim or victims were often quarantined. If the priests saw obvious symptoms of leprosy, the victims would be isolated for at least seven days. If there was improvement after the seven days of isolation, then the priests would pronounce the victim clean, and he or she could rejoin the camp. Otherwise, the victims might be isolated for life and pronounced unclean.

As these ten lepers obeyed Jesus, on their way to visit the priests, they were cleansed of their sickness. How did they know that they were cleansed of leprosy? There were obvious symptoms to look for, and in the case of these ten lepers, those obvious symptoms were gone. In the case of Naaman, the Syrian captain, his leprous skin was changed to look like the skin of a baby.

What was surprising is that after Jesus had healed the ten lepers, only one of them returned to Him and expressed his gratitude by glorifying God with a loud voice and falling down on his face at Jesus' feet, giving Him thanks. Interestingly enough, that man was a Samaritan.

Jesus then asked two questions regarding the ten lepers whom He had healed of leprosy. *"Were not ten cleansed? Where are the nine?"* Was Jesus expecting that all of the ten lepers who were healed by Him would return to Him and express their gratitude? I believe so. Was He disappointed with the nine who were healed but did not give Him thanks. Again, I believe so. This is implied in His two questions. And how would you feel if you were in Jesus' sandals? Would you expect that those for whom you had done good deeds or given good things would express thanks to you? Would you be disappointed if they forgot to give thanks, just as these nine lepers who were healed by Jesus? I would feel the same way!

And I know the feeling, believe me. It is not only disappointing, but it also huts. We have helped several pastors in rural areas outside Metro Manila with regular monthly financial support in the past, and we still are helping some. I require that every month they submit a church work or evangelism activity report, but some have failed to do so. One of them spread gossip around that I was somehow enriching myself from those church activity reports.

Based on a complaint from the elders of one of our churches, I advised another assigned pastor, whom we have helped in Pila, Laguna, to change his Sunday message delivery style. His message was always his testimony about himself, his wife, their sons and their family. I advised him, instead, to focus on the Word of God in the Bible. Instead of responding well, he chose to criticize me and my preaching. He didn't bother to say thank you for all the help we had extended to him and his family. Then he spread bad words about me.

So the nine unthankful healed lepers were typical of ungodly people who are ungrateful to God for all the blessings of life that they have received from Him. They are also unthankful to their parents and other people who have done them good. This is one of the characteristics of the ungodly and of people alive then and also of people in the last days. The apostle Paul said, in the book of Romans:

Although they knew God, they did not glorify Him as God, nor were thankful, but became futile in their thoughts, and their foolish hearts were darkened. Romans 1:21

In his letter to Timothy, he said:

For men will be lovers of themselves, lovers of money, boasters, proud, blasphemers, disobedient to parents, unthankful, unholy. 2 Timothy 3:2

Thank God that one of the ten lepers who were healed came back to thank Jesus. With a loud voice, he glorified God, falling down on his face at His feet giving Him thanks. Jesus said to this man, *"Get up and go your way. Your faith has saved you."* Whereas the nine ungrateful lepers received a temporary healing, the one who returned to Jesus received an everlasting healing besides. That was the healing of his soul from the sickness of sin. He received salvation for his soul in addition to the healing of his physical body.

Many brothers and sisters from our church have gone abroad, and most of them have been blessed by God and are now living a prosperous life. But there is one woman I really admire and appreciate in particular. She is an exemplary woman of God.

Like the rest, this woman has been blessed by God abroad. She now lives in the U.S. and has a good husband and a lovely daughter. She has a noble and respectable profession as a teacher. But she has not forgotten where she came from. She not only remembers her church and her family. She also expresses her gratitude and not only in words, but also with her offerings. She always and regularly sends money to help the church and her church family. I will not mention her name, so that her reward in Heaven will be kept intact. But, from the bottom of our hearts, we say thank you to our beloved sister. May God bless you even more.

Let us, as Christians, always give thanks to God for His abounding and numerous blessings in our lives! ✄

BEING HUMAN

Text: Genesis 1:26-28

Contrary to the allegations of the Theory of Evolution (that man originated and evolved from an ape-like ancestor that existed a few million years ago), the Bible clearly reveals that man was created by God:

Then God said, "Let Us make man in Our image, according to Our likeness."   Genesis 1:26

How did God do that? Again the Bible says:

And the Lord God formed man of the dust of the ground, and breathed into his nostrils the breath of life; and man became a living being.   Genesis 2:7

So God created man in His own image; in the image of God He created him; male and female He created them. Then God blessed

them, and God said to them, "Be fruitful and multiply; fill the
earth and subdue it. Genesis 1:27-28

Why did God create man? And what was His purpose for man from the beginning? God created man for the purpose of making man His vicar and co-regent over all of His creation, inanimate or animate, and over all the earth:

Then the LORD God took the man and put him in the garden of
Eden to tend and keep it. And the Lord God commanded the man,
saying, "Of every tree of the garden you may freely eat; but of
the tree of the knowledge of good and evil you shall not eat, for in
the day that you eat of it you shall surely die."
Genesis 2:15-17

Unfortunately, Adam disobeyed God and ate of the fruit of the forbidden tree. As a consequence, God said to Adam:

Cursed is the ground for your sake;
In toil you shall eat of it
All the days of your life.
Both thorns and thistles it shall bring forth for you,
And you shall eat the herb of the field.
In the sweat of your face you shall eat bread
Till you return to the ground,
For out of it you were taken;
For dust you are,
And to dust you shall return." Genesis 3:17-19

Man had a profound and an ideal beginning. He was created unique, compared with the other creations of God. He had a special connection with God through his nature and relationship. Man was a fusion and a hybrid of the earthly and the divine. He was a responsible being. He had a responsibility to God, to his environment and to himself. These responsibilities were his cultural mandate.

Man had a free will, but he was mortal. It was God Himself who pronounced man's mortality when He warned Adam of the consequence of eating the fruit of the forbidden tree: *"You will surely die!"* This divine pronouncement had two meanings. The first one was expressed. The violation of God's command has a punitive effect. The second one was implied. God was telling man that his nature was mortal, and that was why he would die. Therefore, whether man sinned or did not sin, he was to die anyway because that was his nature.

The first evidence of human mortality was recorded in Genesis 4, when Cain killed his brother Abel. It is sad to imagine that this killing was not done by an animal, but by another human being, and by Abel's own brother. This was, as a matter fact, a murder, the first murder.

Chapter 5 of Genesis contains the first recorded early human obituary:

So all the days that Adam lived were nine hundred and thirty years; and he died.   Genesis 5:5

Methuselah lived longer than any other man on record, but he also died:

BEING HUMAN

So all the days of Methuselah were nine hundred and sixty-nine years; and he died.   Genesis 5:27

The words *"and then he died"* were repeated for each of the patriarchs. Since then, death has reigned on humanity, and the Old Testament ended with the word *curse.* The advent of Jesus Christ, however, marked the beginning of the reversal of the cursed fate and destiny of mankind, especially for those who believe and follow Him. He is the Perfect Human, yet He suffered pain, misery and death for the sake of the redemption of humanity. But He rose again from the dead, to give us hope of resurrection and eternal life.

The Parable of the Good Samaritan (which has allusions to Christ), gives us a classic example of how humans must respond to the victims of cruelty by another human being. It is ironic that this is still a stark reality today:

A certain man went down from Jerusalem to Jericho, and fell among thieves, who stripped him of his clothing, wounded him, and departed, leaving him half dead. ...

But a certain Samaritan, as he journeyed, came where he was. And when he saw him, he had compassion. So he went to him and bandaged his wounds, pouring on oil and wine; and he set him on his own animal, brought him to an inn, and took care of him. On the next day, when he departed, he took out two denarii, gave them to the innkeeper, and said to him, "Take care of him; and whatever more you spend, when I come again, I will repay you."

Luke 10:30 and 33-35

Today, Europe is faced with an avalanche of complicated, complex crises and problems of migrants and refugees. These refugees and migrants, tens of thousands of young men, women and children, most of them coming from Syria, Iraq and Libya, flee the ravages and violence of war in their countries inflicted on them by their own cruel and despotic governments. They face the imminent mortal danger of crossing the Mediterranean Sa on overcrowded boats to reach Europe and find safe haven there.

We are witnesses (since we see these events on TV), to the deplorable, inhuman and brutal acts of the Asad regime and ISIS in Syria against these people. On the other hand, we salute, admire, honor and respect the European countries like Sweden, Norway, Iceland, France and Germany that have accommodated and welcomed these pitiful migrants and refugees. Their gesture and noble task in welcoming these people is one which is humanitarian. One of the European leaders put this into words: "There are no migrants and refugees but rather humanity, and our challenge in Europe is to help provide human dignity to these people. Yes, there are risks, but there are also opportunities, and the opportunities far outweigh the risks in this humanitarian endeavor."

On a personal perspective, why is it important for us, especially among Christians, to know and understand our nature and our humanity? The answer is: so that we should and must behave humanely and not act like brute beasts against our fellow human beings, knowing full well that they, too, are human beings created in the image of God (regardless of their culture or religion). We have to understand that we are responsible beings. Besides, as humans, we have to realize that we are subject to limitations and weaknesses. We get sick, we get old, we have failures, we get depressed, we get lonely, we get frustrated and disappointed. Sometimes, we lack resources and are in need ourselves.

Finally, because we are mortal, we die. All people eventually die. Understanding our humanity will soften the trauma of our human adversities and depravity. There's nothing we can do about it because that's who and what we are.

But wait a minute! There is some Good News! Through faith and trust in the Lord Jesus Christ, we can overcome all these human adversities and be victorious! Jesus said:

Come to Me, all you who labor and are heavy laden, and I will give you rest.   Matthew 11:28

He who believes in Me, though he may die, he shall live. 26 And whoever lives and believes in Me shall never die.

John 11:25-26

SMALL BUT TERRIBLE

Text: James 3:1-10

One of the poignant illustrations and reminders of James to the Christians of his day was about their indiscriminate judging of other people. He warned them in chapter 3 of his letter, not to be too eager to tell others their faults. His reason was, *"For we all make mistakes."* Only those who are perfect make none. And, for those who claim to be teachers of religion, who should know better but also do wrong, their punishment will be greater than it will be for others.

Who was this James? The author identifies himself as, *"James, a servant of God and the Lord Jesus Christ."* But there were at least five personalities in the New Testament named James. Bible scholars believe and concur that the author of this epistle was the James who was the brother of our Lord Jesus Christ. Although neither a disciple nor an apostle during the lifetime ministry of Jesus, James became a believer after the crucifixion and resurrection of Jesus. He emerged as the leader of the church in Jerusalem in the book of Acts. He called himself a *"servant"* rather than an apostle.

This letter was probably written in 60 A.D. In it, the focus of James' message is about the control and the misuse of the tongue. The tongue is a small part of the human body, but it can do an enormous amount of damage if it is out of control. James used three illustrations here to emphasize and underscore this point. The first was the control of a horse, the second was the control of a ship, and the third likens the tongue to a fire. The first two are positive, but the third is negative.

A horse is a strong and fast riding animal. What controls the horse when we want it to turn, to go faster or to slow down? It is a small bit that we place in its mouth. A ship is a large seaworthy vessel that carries passengers and cargoes across the world's seas. What turns the ship wherever the pilot wants it to go despite the strong wind and the rough seas? It is a small rudder.

The tongue is a flame of fire. It is a small thing, but it can set on fire a great forest by igniting just one tiny spark. Later, it can become a great wildfire, destroying properties and people. It is a blazing flame of destruction and disaster.

Every kind of beast, bird, reptile and sea creature can be tamed (and has been tamed) by mankind, but no human being can tame the tongue. It is a restless evil, full of deadly poison. With it we bless the Lord and the Father, and with it we curse men, who are made in the likeness of God. From the same mouth come blessing and cursing. *"This ought not to be,"* said James.

James' sermon on the indiscriminate judging of other people involving the tongue is consistent with the warning of our Lord Jesus Christ on this subject. He said:

"Judge not, that you be not judged. For with what judgment you judge, you will be judged; and with the measure you use, it will be measured back to you. And why do you look at the speck in your brother's eye, but do not consider the plank in your own eye? Or how can you say to your brother, 'Let me remove the speck from your eye'; and look, a plank is in your own eye? Hypocrite! First remove the plank from your own eye, and then you will see clearly to remove the speck from your brother's eye. Matthew 7:1-5

"But I say to you that for every idle word men may speak, they will give account of it in the day of judgment. For by your words you will be justified, and by your words you will be condemned."

Matthew 12:36-37

Some people today, including many Christians, are unaware of the fact that the misuse of their tongue and their careless utterances can cause them criminal liability, putting them in serious trouble. Crimes such as slander and libel or oral defamation may be committed, and these are punishable with imprisonment.

When I was in the seminary, one day one of my professors said, "Those pastors who drive Mercedes Benz cars and wear Rolex watches are crooks and thieves." I was the only one driving a Mercedes Benz and wearing a Rolex watch in the entire class during that time. I don't know why he said that. What he said was irrelevant to the subject we were discussing in the class. So I stood and said, "With all due respect, sir, are you accusing me of these crimes? Are you a judge? Do you have evidence to this accusation?" The man was dumbfounded and could not answer. He was fortunate that we were both Christians. Otherwise, I could have sued him in a court of law.

What is slander? Slander is "the false imputation of a crime subject to prosecution." Some of the elements of this crime are as follows:

- There must be an imputation of a crime, or of a vice or defect, real or imaginary.
- The imputation must be made publicly.
- The imputation must be malicious.
- The imputation must be directed at a natural or juridical person
- The imputation must cause dishonor, discredit or contempt of the person being defamed.

What is libel? Libel is "a malicious defamation, expressed in print or writing, or by sign or pictures, with the intent to injure the reputation, and thereby expose the person involved to public hatred, contempt or ridicule."

James was a staunch advocate of practical religion. The acid test of true religion, according to him, was in the doing and not just in the hearing or speaking. He said:

But be doers of the word, and not hearers only, deceiving your-selves.   James 1:22

Anyone who says he is a Christian but doesn't control his sharp tongue is just fooling himself, and his religion is not worth much.

Do not speak evil of one another, brethren. He who speaks evil of a brother and judges his brother, speaks evil of the law and judges the law. But if you judge the law, you are not a doer of the law but a judge. ... Who are you to judge another? James 4:11-12

Remember:

Evil communications corrupt good manners.

1 Corinthians 15:23

Not everyone who says to Me, "Lord, Lord," shall enter the kingdom of heaven, but he who does the will of My Father in heaven. Many will say to Me in that day, "Lord, Lord, have we not prophesied in Your name, cast out demons in Your name, and done many wonders in Your name?" And then I will declare to them, "I never knew you; depart from Me, you who practice lawlessness!" Matthew 7:21-23

❧ **24** ❧

POOR NO MORE

Text: Matthew 6:25-34

In this passage, the majority of Jesus' audience were poor people. Large crowds of such people were coming from the Galilee, Decapolis, Jerusalem, Judea and the regions across the Jordan, and they were following Him. Many of these poor people were sick with various diseases and suffering severe pain, and others were paralyzed and demon possessed, and He healed them.

Jesus said to these men and women:

> *"Therefore I say to you, do not worry about your life, what you will eat or what you will drink; nor about your body, what you will put on. Is not life more than food and the body more than clothing? Look at the birds of the air, for they neither sow nor reap nor gather into barns; yet your heavenly Father feeds them. Are you not of more value than they? Which of you by worrying can add one cubit to his stature?*

"So why do you worry about clothing? Consider the lilies of the field, how they grow: they neither toil nor spin; and yet I say to you that even Solomon in all his glory was not arrayed like one of these.   Matthew 6:25-29

What Jesus said was a comfort to these poor people. They no longer had to worry about their basic needs.

By the way, what exactly is worry? Worry is "a mental distress or agitation resulting from concerns, usually for something impending or anticipated; anxiety, trouble or difficulty." What specifically were these people worried about? Well, according to Jesus, they were worried about what were they going to eat and drink (about food), what were they going to wear (about clothes) and about their tomorrows (about the future). Jesus repeated the phrase *"Do not worry"* three times in these passages. When the Lord repeats something, it must be urgent or serious. And these things were, especially to the poor.

What were the reasons Jesus challenged His poor audience not to worry? First, He gave the illustration of the birds. Since the location of the occasion was on the open hillside, perhaps there were birds flying overhead or feeding nearby. He said, *"Look at the birds of the air; they do not sow or reap or store away in barns, and yet your heavenly Father feeds them. Are you not much more valuable than they?"*

With regards to the worry for clothing, Jesus said, *"See how the lilies of the field grow. They do not labor or spin. Yet I tell you that not even Solomon in his entire splendor was dressed like one of these. If that is how God clothes the grass of the field, which is here today and tomorrow is thrown into he fire, will he not much more cloth you? O you of little faith?"*

The third reason Jesus gave not to worry was: *"Your Heavenly Father knows that you need them."*

These pronouncements our Lord made that day, however, are never to serve as excuses for anyone to be indolent. Compared with other animate and inanimate creations of God, we humans are better, much better. In every way, we are superior to them. Whereas birds and other animals are guided by instinct, we have reason and are endowed by God with the ability and capability to be creative and productive in order to sustain our lives. We sow; we reap and gather into barns our food. We labor and spin to make our clothes. So, even if we were born poor, God gave us life and it is inherent in that life (because of our God-given gifts and talents) that we can rise above our situations, not only to survive, but also to live normally and comfortably. Even in extreme or extraordinary situations, God will providentially provide and sustain the life of His people.

The case of the Israelites during their wilderness journey to the Promised Land (Canaan) is a good example. They had no natural means to get food because they were in the wilderness. But for forty years, God gave them food to eat, their clothes and their shoes did not wear out. And they did not get sick. Now that is really amazing! Another example was when Jesus fed more than four thousand of His followers in a remote place with just seven loaves of bread and a few small fish.

A material quest and its accompanying apprehensions about tomorrow (the future) are the preoccupations of those who don't know God as their heavenly Father. But, as servants and followers of Jesus Christ, our first priority is to seek God's Kingdom and His righteousness, and then all these things will be given to us as well.

The Kingdom of God is not food and drink, but righteousness, peace and joy in the Holy Spirit (see Romans14:17) . Let us serve God faithfully. Let us trust and have faith in God for all our needs and let us learn to live day by day with God our heavenly Father. He is our great provider, and He answers our prayers. He said:

Ask, and it will be given to you; seek, and you will find; knock, and it will be opened to you. For everyone who asks receives, and he who seeks finds, and to him who knocks it will be opened.

Matthew 7:7-8

I was born poor, very poor, the eldest of nine siblings. My father was a barber, and my mother was a *lavandera* (she washed clothes for other people). We lived in a rickety shanty in a squatter's colony. At night, the whole family slept together in one room, and we were packed in like sardines. There was no electricity and no running water.

I remember a time when there was no food in the house and we children were all hungry. My mother told me to go to my father at the barber shop and ask him for money to buy food to feed us all. I waited there at the barbershop for a long time, but there was no money. Not many people were going to barbershops in those days because it was a time when the Beatles were popular, and young people didn't want their hair cut. That was bad for barbers! I shivered with hunger while I waited for the money. Eventually Dad just borrowed some money from his fellow barber.

That experience compelled me to look for work at a young age to earn extra money to help my parents feed the whole family. I started working as a shoe-shine boy in my very early teens. I worked on construction sites. I worked as a laborer in the port area, carrying heavy sacks of rice and corn. I worked as a house painter's helper. I even worked at the fish port in General Santos City in Mindanao, all the while continuing my education, so that I could have a better future.

Despite my poverty, I had dreams, lots of dreams and aspirations. I dreamt of having owning my own home and a car, of having a good paying job and a beautiful wife. At various times, I wanted to be a lawyer or a politician. I also wanted to travel and see the world. And I knew that education was my bridge to a brighter and better future.

There was one very funny experience I had during my high school days. I worked early in the morning at the fish port, and then I rushed to get to school. One day, I forgot to take a bath to get off the pungent fish smell and just rushed to my class. Many of my classmates kept their distance from me that day because I smelled so fishy. Through a scholarship, I was able to finish my high school as the class valedictorian. Besides taking the top academic honors, I was blessed because the prettiest coed on the campus (Cecilia Cortes, whom everyone called Liling) became my girlfriend. She later became my wife.

Since Liling and I became followers and servants of Jesus Christ, we don't have to worry about our food, clothing and our future. And when we refuse to worry about all these things, we find that we are no longer poor. All my dreams have been fulfilled. God has blessed us with our own home (now fully paid), with cars, and I was able to travel around the world twice. Now, however, I have a nobler and higher calling as pastor of a church. Our air-conditioned church building is located on a 720-square-meter property in West Crame, San Juan City, and that property, too, is also fully paid.

Besides this, God has also given us a school ministry, with more than 2,000 enrollment in both elementary and high school levels. One school is in Taytay, Rizal, and another is in Infanta, Quezon. The school property of about 6,500 square meters with building improvements is wholly owned by our mission, Star of Hope with no indebtedness. We have all the food and clothing we could ever desire, so that we give them away to our poor people in the church. Truly, our God whom we serve, is a God of abundance. Praise the Lord! Glory to God, and Hallelujah!

ଓ **25** ଓ

THE WEDDING INVITATIONS

Text: Matthew 22:1-14

In response to a question from the chief priests and Pharisees who were among those who heard Jesus preach one day, He spoke to them again in parables, saying:

> *The kingdom of heaven is like a certain king who arranged a marriage for his son, and sent out his servants to call those who were invited to the wedding; and they were not willing to come. Again, he sent out other servants, saying, "Tell those who are invited, 'See, I have prepared my dinner; my oxen and fatted cattle are killed, and all things are ready. Come to the wedding.'" But they made light of it and went their ways, one to his own farm, another to his business. And the rest seized his servants, treated them spitefully, and killed them.* Matthew 22:2-6

The king was angry, and he sent his army and destroyed those murderers and burned up their city. Then he said to his servants:

147

"The wedding is ready, but those who were invited were not worthy. Therefore go into the highways, and as many as you find, invite to the wedding." So those servants went out into the highways and gathered together all whom they found, both bad and good. And the wedding hall was filled with guests.

But when the king came in to see the guests, he saw a man there who did not have on a wedding garment. So he said to him, "Friend, how did you come in here without a wedding garment?" And he was speechless. Then the king said to the servants, "Bind him hand and foot, take him away, and cast him into outer darkness; there will be weeping and gnashing of teeth. For many are called, but few are chosen." Matthew 22:8-14

There are several questions with regards to the terminologies used in this narrative. First, there is the question of why Jesus frequently spoke in parables in His teachings about the Kingdom of God? Second, what are parables? What is the Kingdom of Heaven? Is it different from the Kingdom of God? There are varied answers as to why Jesus used parables in most of His teachings about the Kingdom of God. Some say that Jesus' intension and purpose in doing this was to use the parables to obscure the truth of the message of the Kingdom to the undiscerning and unbelieving listeners, but the truth of the message is revealed to His discerning disciples.

Another reason Jesus taught in parables was to answer the questions or needs of His listeners in a given situation. For example, in the Parable of the Good Samaritan, Jesus was asked a question by a lawyer who said, *"Who is my neighbour?"* The answer, of course, to that question, as narrated by Jesus in the parable, was the despised Samaritan and not the religious leaders.

One among Jesus' listeners asked a question regarding the division of inheritance with his brother. Jesus answered by way of a parable, warning about covetousness. That is why, in the beginning of this parable, it says: *"And Jesus answered and spoke to them again by parables."*

What is a parable? A parable is "a comparison: usually a short fictitious story that illustrates a moral attitude or a religious principle." How about a figure of speech? Is it related to a parable? A figure of speech is "a form of expression used to convey meaning or heightened effect often by comparing or identifying one thing with another that has a meaning or connotation familiar to the reader or listener." This is also used in this parable, as indicated by the word *like*. This figure of speech is called simile. *"The Kingdom of Heaven is like …"*

What is the Kingdom of Heaven? Is it different from the Kingdom of God? The Kingdom of God and the Kingdom of Heaven are the same. They are synonymous and are interchangeably used in the Bible. Some say that Matthew used *"kingdom of heaven"* in his gospel because of his Jewish audience. The Jews were cautious in using or mentioning the name of God because it was considered to be too holy to be spoken. So, instead of using the phrase *kingdom of God*, Matthew used *kingdom of heaven*. The audiences of Mark and Luke were mostly Gentiles and therefore non-Jewish, so they used the phrase *kingdom of God*.

What did Jesus mean when He spoke about the Kingdom of God or the Kingdom of Heaven? The word *kingdom* is defined as "the state or territory ruled by a king." Was Jesus talking about a new political state or just a new society? Others, like St. Augustine, espoused the idea that the Kingdom of God was the organized society called the Church. There has been a continuing debate among Christian theologians regarding this complex issue of the Kingdom of God. Some say that the Kingdom of God is a *de facto* kingdom, but others say that it is a *de jure* kingdom. There are also those who say that it is "already, but not yet."

The Kingdom of God is God's sovereign rule manifested in Jesus Christ, creating a people over whom He reigns and in which realm the power of God is experienced. All the people in the God's Kingdom voluntarily submit to the rule of God in their lives. And entrance into God's Kingdom is by the new birth.

In addition to the rule of God in the lives of people who are committed to Him, God's rule is something that can be demonstrated and can influence the world at large. The Kingdom of God started like a seed and then grew into a tree and a yeast that leavens the whole bread. In the future, all the kingdoms of this world will become the Kingdom of God and of Jesus Christ.

What is the point of this parable? The point is that God is a good God. He is also generous and sovereign. He wants to share His joy with us by inviting us to His Kingdom. He is the ruler of the Kingdom, and will not allow the subjects of His Kingdom to disobey, disregard or disrespect him. He is a God of justice. This means that there will be consequences for those who disregard and disobey His sovereign rule. These consequences are in the form of punishments.

This parable also has eschatological implications. It is unfortunate that the man who was already in the wedding was found without the necessary wedding garment, and he was cast out because of it. Today, God's servants continue to invite to come into God's Kingdom people from all walks of life, despite the potential dangers of persecution, suffering and death. And those who come must discard their old garments and put on the new garment of the Kingdom. The man who was cast represents those who are in the church today but who take lightly this garment issue, starting with pastors and other ministers of the Gospel. Most pastors today have abandoned decent attire while preaching in the pulpit. They look like bums wearing T-shirts, blue jeans and sandals in the church. But, remember: Pastors and other ministers of the Gospel are officers of the Church, representing the Kingdom of God. You could be cited for indirect contempt by the Judge if you are a litigation lawyer in a court of law. Christian women also must dress modestly, especially when they are attending church.

The invitation to come to the Kingdom of God still stands today:

Come now, and let us reason together,"
Says the Lord,
"Though your sins are like scarlet,
They shall be as white as snow;
Though they are red like crimson,
They shall be as wool.   Isaiah 1:18

Come to Me, all you who labor and are heavy laden, and I will give you rest. Take My yoke upon you and learn from Me, for I am gentle and lowly in heart, and you will find rest for your souls.   Matthew 11:28-29

Get to know your King, and good things will come to you. Repent of your sins and commit your life to God by receiving Jesus Christ as your personal Lord and Savior. Be among the chosen few. The Kingdom of God is Jesus Christ Himself. That is why He said, *"The Kingdom of God is within you."*   ✵

THE LUCKIEST GUY IN THE WORLD

Text: 2 Chronicles 9:13-28

It is an undisputed fact that King Solomon of Israel was the luckiest guy in the world. At a young age, he became the most powerful person in Israel, when he was crowned King. He was also endowed with extraordinary wisdom, knowledge and an understanding heart. The Bible says:

> *God gave Solomon wisdom and very great insight, and a breadth of understanding as measureless as the sand on the seashore. Solomon's wisdom was greater than the wisdom of all the people of the East, and greater than all the wisdom of Egypt. He was wiser than anyone else.*   1 Kings 4:29-31, NIV

Solomon spoke three thousand proverbs, and his songs numbered a thousand and five. He described plant life, taught about animals and birds, reptiles and fish. Men of all nations came to listen to Solomon's wisdom, sent by all the kings of the world, who had heard of his

152

wisdom. So, King Solomon became famous around the world because of his gift of wisdom.

During the first twenty years of his reign as King of Israel, Solomon also built the Temple in Jerusalem and his palace. It took thirteen years to complete the construction of his palace, which was made of high-grade stones and timbers of cedar from Lebanon.

King Solomon also built ships for trade, commerce and to deliver gold to him. The weight of gold that Solomon received yearly was 666 talents, not including the revenues from merchants and traders and from all the Arabian kings and governors of the land. His shields were made of gold, his throne was made of ivory and inlaid with gold, and his goblets and household articles were all made of gold.

Solomon had also 1,400 chariots and 12,000 horses. He was greater in riches and wisdom than all the other kings of the earth. The whole world sought audience with Solomon, to hear the wisdom God had put in his heart. Year after year, everyone who came brought a gift— articles of silver and gold, robes, weapons, spices, horses and mules.

For all of the positive things we can say about him, however, King Solomon also took many foreign wives and concubines.

They were from the nations about which the Lord had told the Israelites, "You must not intermarry with them, because they will surely turn your hearts after their gods." Nevertheless, Solomon held fast to them in love. He had seven hundred wives of royal birth and three hundred concubines, and his wives led him astray. As Solomon grew old, his wives turned his heart after other gods, and his heart was not fully devoted to the Lord his God, as the heart of David his father had been. ... So Solomon did evil in the eyes of the Lord; he did not follow the Lord completely, as David his father had done.1 Kings 11:2-4 and 6

He built high place for the gods of Moab, and for Molech the detestable god of the Ammonites. He did the same for all his foreign wives, who burned incense and offered sacrifices to their gods. Because of this, the Lord became angry with Solomon, since his heart had turned away from the Lord, the God of Israel who had appeared to him twice.

How did King Solomon amass those enormous fortunes? It was through his extraordinary wisdom. His wisdom was sought after the world over. For example, the Queen of Sheba, hearing about the fame of Solomon, traveled to Jerusalem to test the king with hard questions. Solomon answered all her questions; nothing was too hard for him to explain to her. After she was satisfied, she gave him lots of gold, large quantities of spices and precious stones. Never again were so many spices brought in as those the Queen of Sheba gave to King Solomon. In those days, spices were very valuable commodities, like gold and precious stones.

How did Solomon get his wisdom? It was given to him by God as an answer to his prayer when he assumed the throne as king over Israel. Besides his power, fame and fortune, Solomon lived in palaces and had 1,400 chariots and 12,000 horses. Each of those chariots were equivalent to a Rolls Royce luxury car today. Can you imagine having more than a thousand Rolls Royces? Those horses he had were like exotic and imported sports cars today. Whoa! Hold your horses guys!

Solomon had an intimate relationship with a thousand women, seven hundred of them his wives and three hundred his concubines. Quite honestly, I have to ask this question: How could he do that? How did he do that? As for me (and most men), one is enough—more than enough. But Solomon had a thousand.

How and why were these women attracted to Solomon? Was it his power, position, prestige, money or manhood? Was he handsome? Surely, considering all of the aforementioned, King Solomon was the envy of many, if not of most, men. To many of these men, he must have seemed like the luckiest guy who had ever lived!

But let us ask this question regarding King Solomon, who was considered the luckiest of men, in terms of position, possessions and everyday life. Was he happy? Did he find the meaning of life in all that he had? We might be surprised to hear his answer. Despite his privileged life of extravagance, luxury, flamboyance, excess and sensuality, his life was filled with remorse and regrets, especially during his old age. From the beginning to the ending of the book of Ecclesiastes, evaluating his life and endeavor with multiple repetitions, Solomon said, *"Meaningless! Meaningless! Utterly meaningless! Everything is meaningless!"* (Ecclesiastes 1:2, NIV).

Solomon's answer was quite ironic, if you ask me. Did he suggest an alternative? Yes, as a matter of fact, he did. He said:

Remember your Creator
  in the days of your youth,
before the days of trouble come
  and the years approach when you will say,
  "I find no pleasure in them."   Ecclesiastes 12:1

In other words, "Don't forget the Lord while you are young!"

Fear God and keep his commandments,
  for this is the duty of all mankind.
For God will bring every deed into judgment,
  including every hidden thing,
  whether it is good or evil.   Ecclesiastes 12:13-14, NIV

155

Centuries after King Solomon, another King appeared in Jerusalem. He was no ordinary king. He was and is the King of Kings and Lord of Lords. He was greater than Solomon. He was, in fact, the greatest Man who ever lived. He changed people and changed the world.

This man was Jesus Christ, the Son of God, who was incarnate in the flesh. Ironically, He was born in a manger and lived a simple and humble life. He had no palace to live in and neither chariots nor horses to ride like King Solomon. Instead, He rode on a borrowed donkey.

He spoke the most profound of words, the wisdom of God, the Word of God and the word of life. He demonstrated the power of God by healing the sick, delivering people from demon possession, calming the raging storm, and bringing back to life some who had died. Finally, He Himself rose from the dead. It was He who said:

For what will it profit a man if he gains the whole world, and loses his own soul? Or what will a man give in exchange for his soul?

Mark 8:36-37

"What must I do to be saved?" Believe on the Lord Jesus and you will be saved, you and your household.   Acts 16:30-31

✄

cs **27** so

THE GOOD AND GENEROUS FATHER

Text: Luke 15:11-32

Much has been spoken and written about the prodigal son
of Luke 15, but if we can turn our focus on the father, we will
find an equally, if not more, profound message. Just as the son
was a prodigal son, this father was a prodigal father. Why do
I say that the father was also a prodigal? It is because he was
so lavishly extravagant toward his sons.

This whole parable (like the two that precede it) was an
answer from Jesus directed to the scribes and Pharisees who
murmured and said, *"This man receives sinners and eats with
them"* (Luke 15:2). In reply, Jesus told them this story:

*A certain man had two sons. And the younger of them said
to his father, "Father, give me the portion of goods that
falls to me." So he divided to them his livelihood.*

Luke 15:11-12

157

Before we continue, let us ask the question: What is a parable? A parable is "a story in which things in the spiritual realm are compared with the events that could happen in the temporal realm; or an earthly story with a heavenly meaning." This was a characteristic teaching method used by our Lord Jesus Christ. In short, a parable is "a comparison; a short fictitious story that illustrates a moral attitude or a religious principle." So, did this story really happen? The answer is no. A parable has no factual reality; it is imaginary. It is neither a simile nor a metaphor in this case. Could it happen? Yes, it might happen or it could happen.

When the younger son asked his father for his portion of the father's estate, his father gave it to him—no questions asked. He went even further, dividing his entire estate between the two sons. But there were legal implications in the act of the younger son and in the act of the father. Under the law (The Law on Succession), the general rule is that the heirs (children in this case) may not inherit from their parents until their parents have died. When the younger son demanded his share of his father's estate while his father was still living, in effect he was stating that he wanted his father dead.

Is there an exception to this rule? Yes, there is. While the parents are still alive, they may give their estate to their children under the law of donation, but this is discretionary on the part of the parents and must not be demanded. Yet the son demanded, and the father acquiesced to those demands.

After squandering his wealth in wild living in a distant country, the younger son came back to his father, destitute but repentant:

When he came to his senses, he said, "How many of my father's hired servants have food to spare, and here I am starving to death!

I will set out and go back to my father and say to him: Father, I have sinned against heaven and against you. I am no longer worthy to be called your son; make me like one of your hired servants." Luke 15:17-19

So he got up and went to his father. But while he was still a long way off, his father saw him and was filled with compassion for him; he ran to his son, threw his arms around him and kissed him.

The son said to him, "Father, I have sinned against heaven and against you. I am no longer worthy to be called your son."

But the father said to his servants, "Quick! Bring the best robe and put it on him. Put a ring on his finger and sandals on his feet. Bring the fattened calf and kill it. Let's have a feast and celebrate. For this son of mine was dead and is alive again; he was lost and is found." So they began to celebrate. Luke 15:20-24

The celebration caused some hard feelings with the son who had remained faithfully at home:

Meanwhile, the older son was in the field. When he came near the house, he heard music and dancing. So he called one of the servants and asked him what was going on. "Your brother has come," he replied, "and your father has killed the fattened calf because he has him back safe and sound."

The older brother became angry and refused to go in. So his father went out and pleaded with him. But he answered his father, "Look! All these years I've been slaving for you and never disobeyed your orders. Yet you never gave me even a young goat so I could

159

celebrate with my friends. But when this son of yours who has squandered your property with prostitutes comes home, you kill the fattened calf for him!"

"My son," the father said, "you are always with me, and every-thing I have is yours. But we had to celebrate and be glad, because this brother of yours was dead and is alive again; he was lost and is found."   Luke 15:25-32

What a generous and exemplary father! This father was an ideal father, worthy of emulation by all fathers everywhere. He was an unselfish father and one who was willing to give all his wealth and earthly possessions for the welfare and benefit of his sons. He was an understanding, forgiving, accepting, accommodating, caring, loving and restoring father, even to his wayward younger son. Whereas the two sons revealed their true character by their words and attitudes, the father was steadfast and constant with his character and kept his integrity intact. He was not intimidated by his sons' wicked behaviors, and he did not come down to their level when confronted with such behaviors. He did not react or retaliate against his sons. I wish that all fathers today could be like him.

This story is a reflective picture of the character of our heavenly Father. Our God is a good and generous God, equally so to the good and also to the bad. He is no respecter of persons. He delights in giving good things to His children, and His entire Kingdom is reserved for them as an inheritance.

In this story, we see genuine repentance, as demonstrated by the younger son. True repentance has several elements besides the needed change of mind. When one is truly repentant, he must admit his sins, confess his sins, act to discard and leave his sinful life and then return to the Father as evidence of that action. When this is one, God will receive, accept and embrace every repentant sinner with open arms:

Your Father in heaven is not willing that any of these little ones should perish. Matthew 18:14

The Lord is not slow in keeping his promise, as some understand slowness. Instead he is patient with you, not wanting anyone to perish, but everyone to come to repentance. 2 Peter 3:9

Happy Father's Day, everyone! ✄

CႽŠ **28** ᖬ

THE PARADOX OF PATERNITY
(THE END JUSTIFIES THE MEANS)

Today we celebrate Fathers' Day. We honor, salute and pay tribute to all our fathers around the world. We acknowledge and appreciate the roles and responsibilities of our fathers, who greatly help us grow and develop as children. Our father is our provider, protector and guide. Many fathers sacrifice their lives, working very hard, in order to provide food, clothing, shelter and education for their children. Besides this, they raise their children with tender loving care, bringing them up in the discipline and instruction of the Lord. These are what we call ideal and exemplary fathers.

If there are good fathers, there are also bad fathers. These bad fathers mistreat their children with physical and verbal abuse and always provoke their children to anger for no valid reason. They are just mean, always shouting at their children, and sometimes cursing them. Many fathers also neglect to provide for the basic needs and necessities of their children, and sometime they just totally abandoned them, leaving them no means of support. There are fathers today who, instead of protecting their young daughters, become monsters by committing incestuous rape with them. This happens in most cases when the mothers are not around, perhaps because they are working abroad.

We now face an alarming situation here in the Philippines, especially in many poor areas called squatters colonies where families all sleep together in the same room. When the father arrives home drunk, and the mother is absent due to work abroad as a domestic helper, this pitiful and unfortunate incident happens all too often. With threats and intimidation, the drunken father sexually assaults his young daughters. Star of Hope helps these poor young girls with free basic education. Sometimes they don't attend classes, and we wonder why. One of the young girls confided to my wife that her problem was just what I have described here. To help these young girls, victims of circumstances, Star of Hope in Taytay, Rizal is building a Girls' Sanctuary where girls can sleep at night in order to avoid and prevent such untoward incidents.

There were fathers in the Bible whose behavior relative to a son or daughter was puzzling and even mind-boggling. First, let us consider Abraham.

Abraham took his young son Isaac to the land of Moriah to sacrifice him there as a burnt offering. This was his response to the command of God, and he obeyed, no questions asked. As they neared the place, Isaac asked him, *"Look, the fire and the wood, but where is the lamb for a burnt offering?"* (Genesis 22:7). Abraham answered, *"My son, God will provide for Himself the lamb for a burnt offering"* (Genesis 22:8). Abraham proceeded to build an altar and then bind Isaac and was about to plunge the knife into him when the angel of the Lord called from Heaven, restraining him from harming the boy. When Abraham looked, he saw a ram nearby, its horns caught in a thicket, and that ram was used as a sacrifice in lieu of Isaac.

This episode in Abraham's life was, of course, another test of his faith in God, and he passed it. Today we are privileged to be spectators in this divine/human drama, but if we had been in Abraham's shoes, what would have been our response to God's command? What was Abraham thinking? And what would you be thinking? We can only speculate what was going on in Abraham's mind. If this happened to us today, maybe we would question the voice. "Is that really You, God?" The Bible, however, is silent about what was going on in Abraham's mind. From the human standpoint, what kind of a father was Abraham? And how could he do that to his son?

Another father whose behavior toward his daughter was rather bizarre was considered a mighty man of valor. His story is found in the book of Judges. He made a vow to God that if he would be victorious against his enemies in battle that he would make a sacrifice unto the Lord of whatever or whoever first met him coming from his house. Then, tragically, after his conquest of the enemies he was met by his only daughter, coming out with timbrel and dance to help him celebrate his victory. He was, of course, extremely sad that he now had to sacrifice his only daughter in order to fulfil his vow to the Lord. But did he really kill his daughter? Is human sacrifice sanctioned by God? Could we say that these two fathers were religious fanatics?

The most bizarre case, of course, was what happened to our Lord Jesus Christ. From the human standpoint, we can ask so many questions: Why did God allow the suffering, torment, torture and agony that Jesus experienced before and during His crucifixion? How was God able to stand the suffering and death of His Son? Was it necessary for Jesus to suffer and die? Could He not have just directly forgiven penitent sinners? Was God a cruel Father for allowing those sinful people to beat and torture Jesus? The all-powerful God did not intervene to save His Son from human cruelty and wickedness! Why? Ah, this was divine justice! And justice had to be satisfied through the sacrificial death of God's Son, so that man could be saved through Jesus Christ!

Every time I think about what Jesus Christ did for me on the cross, I can't help but weep. I weep because I realized how much God loves me and how much He loves all of us. The Bible says:

You see, at just the right time, when we were still powerless, Christ died for the ungodly. Romans 5:6, NIV

Since we have now been justified by his blood, how much more shall we be saved from God's wrath through him! For if, while we were God's enemies, we were reconciled to him through the death of his Son, how much more, having been reconciled, shall we be saved through his life! Romans 5:9-10, NIV

Therefore, there is now no condemnation for those who are in Christ Jesus. Romans 8:1

Happy Father's Day, everyone! ✄

THE GOOD FIGHT OF FAITH

Text: 2 Timothy 4:7-8

I have fought the good fight, I have finished the race, I have kept the faith. Finally, there is laid up for me the crown of righteousness, which the Lord, the righteous Judge, will give to me on that Day, and not to me only but also to all who have loved His appearing.

These were the last words of encouragement that the great apostle Paul gave to his faithful attendant and son in the faith, Timothy. The apostle was nearing his martyrdom and, for that reason, he said in the previous verse, *"For I am already being poured out like a drink offering, and the time for my departure is near."*

This second letter of Paul to Timothy was written in Rome during his house arrest, due to his appeal to Caesar, arising from the case charged against him by the Jews in Judea. It was about 67 A.D., Nero was the Roman Emperor during this time, and he was waging severe and deadly persecutions against the Christians.

Prior to this solemn statement by Paul, he charged Timothy before the Lord regarding his sacred duty:

> Preach the word; be prepared in season and out of season; correct, rebuke and encourage — with great patience and careful instruction. For the time will come when people will not put up with sound doctrine. Instead, to suit their own desires, they will gather around them a great number of teachers to say what their itching ears want to hear. They will turn their ears away from the truth and turn aside to myths. But you, keep your head in all situations, endure hardship, do the work of an evangelist, discharge all the duties of your ministry. 2 Timothy 4:2-5

What was Paul implying in verse seven? What kind of fight was he in? How was it a "good" fight? Paul was giving a personal testimony of his life's career and purpose since he had become a Christian. His mission was a kind of fight, a fight of faith. He had gone through many obstacles and hindrances in order to accomplish his purpose and goal in Christ, and that was to proclaim the message of the Gospel of Jesus Christ, especially to the Gentiles. He testified:

> We are hard pressed on every side, but not crushed; perplexed, but not in despair; persecuted, but not abandoned; struck down, but not destroyed. 2 Corinthians 4:8-9, NIV

> But none of these things move me; nor do I count my life dear to myself, so that I may finish my race with joy, and the ministry which I received from the Lord Jesus, to testify to the gospel of the grace of God. Acts 20:24

It was a *"good"* fight of faith for Paul, as indicated in the latter part of verse seven. *"I have finished my course. I have kept the faith,"* he said.

In his first letter to Timothy, Paul challenged him about having godliness with contentment, fighting the good fight of faith and laying hold of eternal life. What is faith? In his letter to the Hebrews, Paul defined faith as: *"the substance of things hoped for, the evidence of things not seen"* (Hebrews 11:1).

And how do we obtain faith?

So then faith comes by hearing, and hearing by the word of God.   Romans 10:17

There are two kinds of faith. These are the right faith and the wrong faith. The right faith is based on the hearing of the Word of God, whereas the wrong faith is based on the word of men.

How did the apostle Paul finish his course? The answer is by keeping the faith. How did Paul keep the faith? By laying hold on eternal life.

How important and significant is faith in our Christian life? Faith is important and significant because:

Without faith it is impossible to please Him, for he who comes to God must believe that He is, and that He is a rewarder of those who diligently seek Him.   Hebrews 11:6

By faith we understand that the universe was formed at God's command, so that what is seen was not made out of what was visible.   Hebrews 11:3

THE GOOD FIGHT OF FAITH

*For it is by grace you have been saved, through faith—and this
is not from yourselves, it is the gift of God*   Ephesians 2:8

Today, two of our very own countrymen, Manny Paquiao and Nonito Donaire, are fighting inside the ring in Las Vegas, Nevada. They are both professional boxers although Manny Paquiao is now also a Philippine senator. Both boxers have been knocked out in the ring. Unlike other boxers who have been knocked out and then stayed down and quit in the bout, these two got up, fought again and won. I really admire these two boxers, and we are proud of them as Filipinos.

All Christians are in a fighting match, just like the apostle Paul and Timothy. Some Christians are unaware of the fact that our opponents are not flesh and blood, but principalities, powers and rulers of darkness of this world and spiritual wickedness in high places. That is why, in order to prevail in this faith fight and stand against our enemies, we all need to take on the whole armor of God:

Therefore put on the full armor of God, so that when the day of evil comes, you may be able to stand your ground, and after you have done everything, to stand. Stand firm then, with the belt of truth buckled around your waist, with the breastplate of righteousness in place, and with your feet fitted with the readiness that comes from the gospel of peace. In addition to all this, take up the shield of faith, with which you can extinguish all the flaming arrows of the evil one. Take the helmet of salvation and the sword of the Spirit, which is the word of God. And pray in the Spirit on all occasions with all kinds of prayers and requests.

Ephesians 6:13-18, NIV

Was there another reason the apostle Paul fought the good fight of faith besides keeping the faith? Yes, there was. What is it? He said:

Now there is in store for me the crown of righteousness, which the Lord, the righteous Judge, will award to me on that day—and not only to me, but also to all who have longed for his appearing.

2 Timothy 4:8, NIV

What is a crown? It is "a special headgear used to symbolize a person's high status, honor and authority, especially in the Greek and Roman worlds." Crowns are worn by kings and queens. In the Grecians games, the crown was "a wreath of leaves awarded the winner of an athletic competition."

In reality, and quite honestly, today there are many Christians who fall because of their adverse circumstances and unpleasant situations in life. I remember one of the songs of Bob Carlyle, which says:

And the saints are just sinners who fall down and get up!
We fall down, we get up, we fall down, we get up! [1]

It is such a comfort to know the Word of God in times like these:

The steps of a good man are ordered by the Lord,
And He delights in his way.

---

1. Copyright © 1998, worshiptogether.com songs (administered by Capitol CMG Publishing)

Though he fall, he shall not be utterly cast down;
For the Lord upholds him with His hand.   Psalm 37:23-24

It will be worth it all when we hear the word of the Lord in His presence in Heaven:

Well done, good and faithful servant; you have been faithful over
a few things, I will make you ruler over many things. Enter into
the joy of your Lord.   Matthew 25:23

✄

OUR CHRISTIAN DUTIES AND CONDUCTS

Text: Romans 12-13

Now that we are Christians, what are our responses to our relationships and connections? Surely, our responses now are completely different from those which we were used to before we were converted to Christ. That's why the Bible says: *"Therefore, if anyone is in Christ, he is a new creation; old things have passed away; behold, all things have become new"* (2 Corinthians 5:17). These responses are also understood as our personal conducts. Sometimes these new conducts are also synonymous with our Christian duties, obligations and services. In chapters 12 and 13 of the book of Romans, the apostle Paul enumerated several of our Christian duties and conducts.

What is a duty? A duty is "a moral or legal obligation, a service required." What is obligation? It is "an act of obligating oneself to a course of action." It is "a bond with a condition annexed and a penalty for non fulfilment." Simply put, an obligation is "something that one is bound to do." The apostle Paul placed our Christian duties and conducts into two categories. The first one is sacred, and the second is secular. What is sacred? Sacred means "a duty or service set apart and related to our worship of God." Secular is "our duty, conduct or service relating to the worldly or temporal; not specifically religious."

As we continue, let us used the terms *duty* and *duties*, first because this is similar to our conduct or service, but it has a more obligatory weight. It means that it is our moral and legal obligation, which is a required service. Under our sacred duty, our service or obligation is related to God and the Church. Under our secular duty or obligation, our service or conduct is related to other people (not necessarily Christians), our government (or the state) and even our enemies.

So, how do we respond to God under our sacred duty? After a lengthy discussion, eleven chapters in all, about the redemptive provisions of God through Christ, the apostle Paul now appealed to Christians by the mercies of God to serve Him through worship. One of the important and significant elements of worship is sacrifice. Whereas, in the Old Testament, the sacrifices offered in worship were dead animals, we are urged to offer ourselves (our bodies) as a holy and living sacrifice, which is acceptable and our reasonable service to God.

Besides this, Christians are precluded from conforming with the present worldly system but are urged to be transformed by the renewal of their minds in order to experience what is the good, acceptable and perfect will of God. It is unfortunate that many Christians today are physically present in the church, but they are mentally absent. No wonder there are so many Christians today who are spiritually malnourished, despite the fact that they have been in the church for so long a time!

Our duty to the church and the members of the church must be practiced with tempered and humble attitude relative to the gifts that we must exercise. There are different gifts that God gives to the members, to use for the edification and welfare of all the members of the Church and for the glory of God. These ministry gifts are: prophecy, preaching, practical service, teaching, counselling and financial contributions. All these ministry gifts must be used in proportion to our faith, serving others well with serious responsibility, generosity and Christian cheer.

As to our relationships with non-Christians, our attitude to them must be based on conduct rather than duty. What is conduct? Conduct is "a mode or standard of personal behavior especially as based on moral principles and Christian conviction":

Love must be sincere. Hate what is evil; cling to what is good. Be devoted to one another in love. Honor one another above yourselves. Never be lacking in zeal, but keep your spiritual fervor, serving the Lord. Be joyful in hope, patient in affliction, faithful in prayer. Share with the Lord's people who are in need. Practice hospitality.

Bless those who persecute you; bless and do not curse. Rejoice with those who rejoice; mourn with those who mourn. Live in harmony with one another. Do not be proud, but be willing to associate with people of low position. Do not be conceited.

Do not repay anyone evil for evil. Be careful to do what is right in the eyes of everyone. If it is possible, as far as it depends on you, live at peace with everyone. Do not take revenge, my dear friends, but leave room for God's wrath, for it is written: "It is mine to avenge; I will repay," says the Lord. Romans 12:9-17, NIV

And there was more:

Owe no one anything except to love one another, for he who loves another has fulfilled the law. For the commandments, "You shall not commit adultery." "You shall not murder," "You shall not steal," "You shall not bear false witness," "You shall not covet," and if there is any other commandment, are all summed up in this saying, namely, "You shall love your neighbor as yourself." Love does no harm to a neighbor; therefore love is the fulfillment of the law.

And do this, knowing the time, that now it is high time to awake out of sleep; for now our salvation is nearer than when we first believed. The night is far spent, the day is at hand. Therefore let us cast off the works of darkness, and let us put on the armor of light. Let us walk properly, as in the day, not in revelry and drunkenness, not in lewdness and lust, not in strife and envy. But put on the Lord Jesus Christ, and make no provision for the flesh, to fulfill its lusts.   Romans 13:8-14

With regards to the government or the state, our conduct is one which is governed by duty:

Let every soul be subject to the governing authorities. For there is no authority except from God, and the authorities that exist are appointed by God. Therefore whoever resists the authority resists the ordinance of God, and those who resist will bring judgment on themselves. For rulers are not a terror to good works, but to evil. Do you want to be unafraid of the authority? Do what is good, and you will have praise from the same. For he is God's minister to you for good. But if you do evil, be afraid; for he does not bear the sword in vain; for he is God's minister, an avenger to execute wrath on him who practices evil. Therefore you must be subject, not only because of wrath but also for conscience' sake. For because of this you also pay taxes, for they are God's ministers attending continually to this very thing. Render therefore to all their due: taxes to whom taxes are due, customs to whom customs, fear to whom fear, honor to whom honor.

Romans 13:1-7

Jesus summed this all up together when He said, *"Render therefore to Caesar the things that are Caesar's, and to God the things that are God's"* (Matthew 22:21).

Paul now says, *"Don't quarrel with anyone. If possible, so far as it depends upon you, live peaceably with all."* Christians have enemies despite our non-aggressive conduct toward other people. There are evil and wicked people in this world who are hostile and cruel to Christians. And what should be the Christian's conduct against these bad people, especially when the Christians are experiencing extreme prejudice? Must Christians take things to the law? The answer is no:

Beloved, do not avenge yourselves, but rather give place to wrath; for it is written, "Vengeance is Mine, I will repay," says the Lord. Romans 12:19

Paul concluded:

Therefore

"If your enemy is hungry, feed him;

If he is thirsty, give him a drink;

For in so doing you will heap coals of fire on his head."

Do not be overcome by evil, but overcome evil with good.

Romans 12:20-21

❧ **31** ☙

CALM AND CONSISTENT CHRISTIANS

Text: Acts 21:20-25

On the way to Rome, the apostle Paul, together with his other 275 companions in the ship, encountered a violent storm called a northeaster:

Now when neither sun nor stars appeared for many days, and no small tempest beat on us, all hope that we would be saved was finally given up. But after long abstinence from food, then Paul stood in the midst of them and said, "Men, you should have listened to me, and not have sailed from Crete and incurred this disaster and loss. And now I urge you to take heart, for there will be no loss of life among you, but only of the ship. For there stood by me this night an angel of the God to whom I belong and whom I serve, saying, 'Do not be afraid, Paul; you must be brought before Caesar; and indeed God has granted you all those who sail with you.' Therefore take heart, men, for I believe God that it will be just as it was told me." Acts 27:20-25

Why was Paul in this situation? Why was he going to stand trial before Caesar? The two questions are connected, and the answer to these questions are also connected. Prior to this trip to Rome, Paul was charged by the Jews in Jerusalem with unfounded accusations. These fanatical Jews seized him while he was in the Temple, and they dragged him away and tried to kill him. The uproar reached the Roman authorities, and when rioters saw the Roman commander and his soldiers, they stopped beating Paul.

Later on, Paul was taken to the barracks of the Roman regiment, and there they attempted to flog him, but Paul invoked his Roman citizenship in order to stop the flogging. After that, he gained favor with the Roman commander and was taken to Caesarea so that he was rescued from the sinister plot of the Jews in Jerusalem to kill him.

There in Caesarea, Paul stood before two governor's courts, that of Felix and Festus. The chief priests and Jewish leaders in Jerusalem had urged and appealed to Festus to bring Paul back to Jerusalem so that they might kill him, but Festus declined, and when he arrived in Caesarea, Festus convened the court, and Paul was brought before him.

In his defense, Paul refused to be brought back to Jerusalem and, instead, made an appeal to Caesar in Rome. This left Festus in a dilemma. It happened that King Agrippa (the grandson of Herod the Great, the King who had slaughtered many infants at the time of Jesus' birth) was visiting Caesarea right then, and Festus conferred to him Paul's case. Agrippa wanted to hear Paul, and it was an opportunity for Paul to testify to him and to those who were listening during the hearing. After Paul had spoken, King Agrippa said to him, *"You almost persuade me to become a Christian"* (Acts 26:28). To Festus, he said, *"This man might have been set free if he had not appealed to Caesar"* (Acts 26:32). And that is why Paul was sent to Rome.

As contemporary Christians, what do we learn from this episode and experiences of the apostle Paul's life? How do we live or respond in a given or similar situation? First of all, we learn that it is not easy to live a dedicated and devoted Christian life. We must expect and anticipate persecutions. In fact, Paul himself said:

> *All who desire to live godly in Christ Jesus will suffer persecution.* 2 Timothy 3:12

The irony of Paul's case is that the persecutions come from his own people. It was not the Gentiles or the Romans who persecuted Paul, but his own people, the Jews and their leaders in Jerusalem.

What was the cause or causes that Paul was persecuted? Paul was preaching, testifying and teaching about Jesus Christ and His resurrection from the dead. Can we avoid such persecution today? Yes, you can. But that means that you will have to avoid living a Christian life.

Secondly, we learn that Christians are not exempt from the devastation of natural calamities. Disasters like earthquakes, volcanic eruptions, hurricanes or super-typhoons, etc. are beyond our human control. Can they be avoided? To some extent, yes. How? By means of precautionary measures, vigilance and preparedness, damages, losses and casualties can be minimized or prevented.

As for Paul, there was nothing he could do about it because he was overruled by the Centurion and the owner of the ship. They chose to ignore his advice and sail anyway. Despite the impending

CALM AND CONSISTENT CHRISTIANS

danger, Paul was constrained to stay in the ship because he had to go to Rome to stand trial before Caesar.

How do we live our Christian life or respond in a similar situation? Just like the apostle Paul, let us not be intimidated by our persecutors, whether they be religious leaders or people belonging to the higher echelon of society. Oftentimes, our persecutors come from our own family. Even in times of natural calamities, let us not lose hope, as if God had abandoned us. Rather, let us be bold and be steadfast in our fortitude of faith and hope through our life and testimony about our Lord and Savior Jesus Christ.

Let no Christian capitulate or compromise his Christian faith under pressure from whoever or whatever persecution or trials, knowing, understanding and experiencing full well the reality and the providential power of the God whom we serve. As long as we have done no wrong, anything illegal or immoral, we have no reason to be afraid of the storms ahead of us because:

For God has not given us a spirit of fear, but of power and of love and of a sound mind.   2 Timothy 1:7

For He shall give His angels charge over you,
To keep you in all your ways.   Psalm 91:11

There are troubles in this world, but we have peace in Jesus Christ!   ✄

ℭℬ **32** ℬ

WHY CHRISTIANS DO NOT
WORSHIP IDOLS AND IMAGES

Text: Exodus 20:3-6

Idolatry is forbidden by God and is a dangerous and deceitful sin. God spoke and said to His people:

> *You shall have no other gods before Me. You shall not make for yourself a carved image—any likeness of anything that is in heaven above, or that is in the earth beneath, or that is in the water under the earth; you shall not bow down to them nor serve them. For I, the Lord your God, am a jealous God, visiting the iniquity of the fathers upon the children to the third and fourth generations of those who hate Me, but showing mercy to thousands, to those who love Me and keep My commandments.*

What is idolatry? Idolatry is "the worship of something created as opposed to the worship of the Creator Himself." There are many references to the practice of idolatry in the Old Testament. The ancient neighbors of Israel were idolatrous nations. They worshipped many different gods. Some people insist that idols and images are only an aid to worship and not the object of worship itself, but whether these idols or images are gods or representation of gods, the Bible strictly forbids the making of idols or images because these do receive worship, a worship which absolutely and exclusively is reserved for the true and living God.

A notable violation by God's people of this law occurred when Moses delayed coming down from Mount Sinai. Aaron and the people made a golden calf and worshipped it. The Lord was angry and, had it not been for the prayer and intervention of Moses, the entire people of Israel could have been wiped out.

Even after the conquest of Canaan, this sin of idolatry was a recurring refrain for the Israelites:

And the children of Israel did that which was evil in the sight of Jehovah, and forgat Jehovah their God, and served the Baalim and the Asheroth. Judges 3:7, ASV

During the period of the united kingdom under Kings David and Solomon, idolatry was nearly eradicated, but then it recurred after the division of the kingdom. That's why the prophets like Elijah preached against it strongly and vigorously during their time.

What are idols or images? These are "representations or symbols of an object of worship; false gods." Most of the time, however, images refer to "statues or something of human manufacture which people have substituted for the true living God."

Images is synonymous with *idols*. They are made in different ways and of various kinds of materials, like metal, stone or wood. Sometimes they can be described as "carved images or molded images." The image in Nebuchadnezzar's dream was made of gold, silver, bronze, iron and clay.

Perhaps the best definition of an idol is "something we make ourselves into a god." It does not have to be an idol or an image. It can be anything that stands between us and God or something we substitute for God.

The apostle Paul, in the New Testament, warned Christians against idolatry, and still today we live in a world filled with idols. When Paul was in Athens, Greece, he saw that the city was given over to idols. So, why did so many people then and why do so many people now continue to worship idols and images? That's because they are blinded by their sin. They have no knowledge and understanding about the one true God.

There are those even today who claim to be Christians but they have idols and images in their churches, in their homes and in their altars. I say that these are counterfeit Christians, but this is just my personal opinion.

Since Emperor Constantine declared Christianity as the official religion of the Roman Empire, Christianity has been split into two churches. The first and the original church was founded by Jesus Christ in Jerusalem, and the other was founded by Emperor Constantine (which later became what is today the Roman Catholic religion). The problem with the declaration of Constantine was that most subjects of Rome during that time embraced and adopted the Christian religion without experiencing Christ as their Lord and Savior. Instead, they just carried over their previous cultural and religious practices.

The resulting theology is a confusing one. Instead of keeping their previous gods under the Greek and Roman belief, they replaced those with the statues and images of the saints. They even worship Mary, the mother of our Lord Jesus Christ, as God, by praying to her. That's why we need to reach out and preach the Gospel to them, and they need to be born again.

Today idolatry may not come in the form of bowing before a statue or image, but it can become rather subtle and sophisticated in the mind of some Christian believers. Obsession with the possession of material things like cars, houses, lands and money can be became objects of worship as they take God's rightful place in our lives. Other objects of worship can be pride, hobbies, fame and even deeds done in the name of the Lord. We must be constantly on guard that we let nothing come between us and God. When anything or anyone comes between us and God, that is an idol.

A classic example of this form of idolatry is the story of the rich young man in Matthew 19. He came to Jesus and asked what he must do in order to have eternal life. But when Jesus answered him:

If you want to be perfect, go, sell what you have and give to the poor, and you will have treasure in heaven; and come, follow Me. Matthew 19:21

When he had heard this answer, *"the young man ... went away sorrowful: for he had great possessions"* (Matthew 19:22)

SHOULD CHRISTIANS BE APOLITICAL?

Text: Romans 13:1-7

Obey the government, for God is the one who has put it there. There is no government anywhere that God has not placed in power. So those who refuse to obey the laws of the land are refusing to obey God, and punishment will follow. For the policeman does not frighten people who are doing right; but those doing evil will always fear him. So if you don't want to be afraid, keep the laws and you will get along well. The policeman is sent by God to help you. But if you are doing something wrong, of course you should be afraid, for he will have you punished. He is sent by God for that very purpose. Obey the laws, then, for two reasons: first, to keep from being punished, and second, just because you know you should.

Pay your taxes too, for these same two reasons. For government workers need to be paid so that they can keep on doing God's work, serving you. Pay everyone whatever he ought to have: pay your taxes and import duties gladly, obey those over you, and give honor and respect to all those to whom it is due. (TLB)

The Epistle to the Romans was written by the Apostle Paul probably in Corinth about 57 to 58 A.D. After expounding on the Christian doctrine of salvation in chapters 1 through 11, he began discussing the practical consequences of the Gospel, which are our duties and responsibilities starting with chapter 12.

What are these Christian duties and responsibilities? First, we have a duty to God, to serve Him, with our bodies as living sacrifices and with our renewed mind according to the will of God. Second, we have responsibilities and duties to our society. Third, we have duties and responsibilities to our government. And fourth, we have duties and responsibilities to our neighbors.

Let us now focus on this third category of duties and responsibilities according the first part of chapter 13. Can you imagine Paul saying, *"Obey the government"* during his time? Other translations say, *"Let every soul be subject unto the higher powers."* And who was the power during this time? It was the Roman Empire under Emperor Nero.

Nero was notorious for his suspected burning of Rome, but he blamed it on the Christians. A severe and deadly persecution followed after that, which led to the martyrdom of the apostle Paul and many other Christians. Despite the brutality and oppression of the Roman power, Paul said, *"Obey the government!"* What was his basis for that statement? He said, *"This power or authority is sanctioned by God!"* I find this very ironic indeed, but this is the Word of God, and we have to obey it.

There are several factors that we have to seriously consider regarding our responsibilities and duties with our government. If we resist the authorities, we are also resisting God. The reason, according to Paul, is that these authorities or powers are instituted and appointed by God Himself. If we are law-abiding, we have nothing to fear. But if we violate the law, then we will be punished. These powers and authorities are also God's servant to execute His wrath on every wrongdoer.

For the same reason, we also need to pay our taxes, because the government is made up of ministers of God, and they need to be paid to keep on doing God's work of serving us. Pay all of them their dues, taxes to whom taxes are due, revenue to whom revenue is due, respect to whom respect is due, honor to whom honor is due.

I believe that this message is relevant today, due to the recent and current political developments here and in America. The body of former President Marcos was immediately and clandestinely buried by his surviving family at the *Libingan ng mga Bayani* (Cemetery for Heroes). The anti-Marcos oppositionists were caught unaware. The burial of former President Marcos was quite an issue that divided the Filipino populace. For more than two decades, his body was lying at the mausoleum in Ilocos Norte province. Finally, with the advent of the new administration, President Duterte allowed the burial of the former President. This was, of course, met with opposition and protests until it reached the Supreme Court. The Court issued a TRO, but this month, the Supreme Court finally allowed the burial with a vote of 9 to 5, citing as their basis that President Duterte did not abuse his discretion when he decided to allow the burial. Besides, there is no law that precludes this burial.

Opposition lawmakers, anti-Marcos groups and even students from the academia took to the streets in protests, lambasting the former president, that he was a dictator, a criminal and a thief. They are also enraged, furious and in contempt of the decision of the Supreme Court and of President Duterte. They say that former

President Marcos is not fit to be buried at the Heroes Cemetery because he was no hero. They say that these decisions and actions on the issue of the matter is a disrespect of law. But the President has legal basis for his decisions and actions. First, there was the go signal from the Supreme Court. Former President Marcos was a President of the Philippines, and third, he was a soldier. All these qualify him to be buried at the *Libingan ng mga Bayani*.

What concerns me is that there are so many young people today joining these demonstrations and rallies chanting that Marcos was a dictator, a thief and he was not a hero. But what do they know about martial law? I assume they were not yet born during those days. It is apparent that their teachers and professors taught them about the atrocities of the martial in their schools. They should ask in the first place why the martial law that was declared by then President Marcos.

Martial law is one of the legal remedies of the state in order to quell rebellion or invasion. There were communist insurgents attacking everywhere, and Muslim separatist rebels in Mindanao, undermining the peace and stability of our country. I believe that President Marcos did what was necessary, although it was a necessary evil. It is unfortunate that those who fought against the government became collateral casualties. Such is the scenario and consequences in a political struggle.

These young people today must be re-educated because right now, they are acting violently and, I am afraid, are becoming potential rebels because of their attitude. Remember, evil communication corrupt good manners. To me, the late President Marcos was a good president. He was, in fact, the best of Philippine presidents so far, and I admire him. I was among the many witnesses of the progress and development of our country during his time. No other president can match his achievements. He built infrastructures such as roads and bridges to interconnect the islands with accessible land transport. He was a champion of social justice. He signed into law the 13th month pay, which was a bane to employers but a blessing to the workers.

We are now enjoying and benefiting from convenient and comfortable travel on the road to the north and to the south by means of expressways. Significant among these is the Candaba Viaduct in Pampanga.

President Marcos built dams in order to increase and improve agricultural and rice productivity by means of irrigation in the Masagana 99 program. So, our farmers can increase their harvests from one to three times a year because of irrigation. He developed alternative energy sources, like hydroelectric, geothermal and nuclear plants. We would be paying much more for electricity today if these projects had not been pushed through.

President Marcos devised a buffer fund called OPSF (Oil Price Stabilization fund) to help protect the motorists due to the sudden spike in oil prices when Saudi Arabia cut oil production because of war in the Middle East. He also built steel mills which are vital components of our industrialization.

In order to prevent the perennial problem of flooding in Manila during rainy season, President Marcos built the floodway. These are just several of his achievements that I can remember. I am sure there are many more. During the EDSA People Power Movement, Fabian Ver, one of Marcos' generals, was ready to fire on civilians, but President Marcos commanded him to stand down. Instead, he abdicated Malacañang Palace, in order to save thousands of lives. What a magnanimous President!

After Donald Trump was overwhelming elected as President of the United States, many of the Clinton supporters also demonstrated in the streets in several states for days denouncing Trump. They said, "Trump is not our President." These demonstrators have no legal basis for their rallies. Are they Americans or foreigners? Well, it doesn't matter. Whether they like it or not, Donald Trump is the President-elect of the United States of America.

As Christians, we must be good and obedient citizens of our country. So, in matters involving our responsibilities and duties to the state, we cannot be apolitical. We have to respect the duly elected President and leaders of our country. But, if a Christian wants to enter politics and run for public office, it is his choice and decision to undertake at his own risk.   ✄

ᘓ **34** ᘔ

CAVEAT, CHRISTIANS!

"Know and understand this ... ," said the Apostle Paul in his second letter to Timothy, *"in the last days perilous times will come."* In another translation, it says, *"It is going to be very difficult to be a Christian,"* and the Paul enumerated the reasons for this statement:

> *For people will love only themselves and their money. They will be boastful and proud, scoffing at God, disobedient to their parents, and ungrateful. They will consider nothing sacred. They will be unloving and unforgiving; they will slander others and have no self-control. They will be cruel and hate what is good. They will betray their friends, be reckless, be puffed up with pride, and love pleasure rather than God. They will act religious, but they will reject the power that could make them godly. Stay away from people like that!*
>
> 2 Timothy 3:2-5, NLT

It goes on:

192

CAVEAT, CHRISTIANS!

They are the kind who work their way into people's homes and win the confidence of vulnerable women who are burdened with the guilt of sin and controlled by various desires. (Such women are forever following new teachings, but they are never able to understand the truth.) These teachers oppose the truth just as Jannes and Jambres opposed Moses. They have depraved minds and a counterfeit faith. But they won't get away with this for long. Someday everyone will recognize what fools they are, just as with Jannes and Jambres. 2 Timothy 3:6-9, NLT

These are words of stern warning from the apostle Paul, especially to Christian believers in the last days. It will be dangerous, stressful and more difficult to live a Christian life.

Are we in the last days now? Do we see the fulfillment of the predictions of the apostle Paul with regards to the decline and the total collapse of morality in the lives of the people today? Is this the age of apostasy?

Many, if not most, Christians today believe that we are now in the last days. The many signs of the imminent return of Christ are evident in our generation. False Christs and false prophets abound nowadays, deceiving many. There never were more deadly and bloody wars being fought in the history of the mankind than in our generation (with combined casualties of more than 100 million people during World War I and II, not to mention scores of millions more who died in wars of atrocities between nations in our generation. Natural calamities, like earthquakes and other disasters, are very frequent today compared with those occurrences in the past. And, because wickedness has increased, the love of many will grow cold.

193

The apostle Paul's writings on the last days is focused on the moral decline and depravity of the people. Many people today are conceited and egocentric; they are materialistic and lovers of money. They don't care if they prejudice the interests and rights of others, as long as they get money and get it quickly. The apostle Paul also wrote: *"The love of money is the root of all evil"* (1 Timothy 6:19). That is why people become proud, constant liars, reckless, ingrates, lovers of pleasure rather than lovers of God. They have become religious hypocrites. They are sensual, carnal and sexually perverted.

The danger today is that these worldly people have crept into the church and contaminated the innocent and naive Christians. The church now is a mixed multitude. This term was given to the Israelite congregation when they left Egypt and non-Hebrews joined them and became problems for the Hebrews later on. The ulterior motive of such people is to take advantage and defraud Christians of their money through their fictitious business proposals. There are far too many Christians who would rather go to ball games, recreations and do shopping in malls rather than going to church and attending services on Sundays. There are those Christians who are so obsessed with and addicted to their smart phones that while the pastor is preaching or teaching, they keep browsing their phones rather than paying attention to the message. This is disrespectful, not only to the pastor, but also to God Himself.

No, we are not yet in the age of apostasy, but the proliferation of immoral and wicked phenomena that we are witnessing in our time are indeed a prelude to usher in that age. Today, LGBT lifestyles and same-sex marriage have been legalized in America, and this has become the trend and is now widely accepted around the world. I must say this, Not all things that are legal are moral!

There are two things that will need to transpire before the age of apostasy will come, according to 2 Thessalonians 2:2-4. First, there will be a time of great rebellion against God. Second, the man of rebellion will come—the son of perdition.

So, how should the true Christians respond to this present last-day situation, when evil men and impostors will go from bad to worse, deceiving and being deceived? The answer is: we must not compromise our faith, but we must continue in what we have learned about the Scriptures, which makes us wise for salvation through faith in Christ Jesus.

All Scripture is God-breathed and is useful for teaching, rebuking, correcting and training in righteousness, so that the servant of God may be thoroughly equipped for every good work.

2 Timothy 3:16-17, NIV

We must be resolute in our faith, patience, endurance, sufferings and even in persecutions. Everyone who lives a godly life in Christ Jesus will be persecuted. But the Lord will rescue the faithful Christians from all of it.   ✄

Ignorance of the Law

But I do not want you to be ignorant, brethren, concerning ...

1 Thessalonians 4:13

There is a legal maxim in our Civil Code (Philippine Law) which provides that: "Ignorance of the Law excuses no one from compliance therewith." The case of Mary Jane Veloso, who was convicted of drug trafficking in Indonesia, is a good example of this law. She is now incarcerated in one of the prisons in Indonesia, awaiting the undisclosed date of her execution. She previously got a reprieve from an earlier date of execution through the kind intervention of our President Aquino, but recently her family was notified that of her execution is impending.

Of course, the family of Mary Jane Veloso is saying that she is innocent and that she is only a victim, a victim of her illegal recruiter and the International Drug syndicate. Did she know the law in Indonesia when she smuggled in a large quantity of prohibited drugs? Did she know the consequences of the violation of that law? Apparently she did not know. Had she known the penalty for her violation of serving as a drug mule, she would not have

196

done it, realizing that she would lose her life. Many commented on social media that Mary Jane Veloso was convicted because she was poor. I don't think so. The law has no such distinction of for criminals, rich or poor.

If my personal opinion were to be asked regarding this issue, I would say, yes, let this Filipina be penalized. Let her suffer the consequence of her crime, remaining in prison for a lifetime without any remedy of an appeal whatsoever. But, I am against the penalty of death on drug cases. Why? Because human life is much too precious compared with those drugs that she smuggled in to Indonesia.

As a Christian pastor, I believe that capital punishment must only be used exclusively on the a-life-for-a-life basis espoused in the justice systems based on biblical principles. Some politicians are playing God, and others think themselves even wiser than God. If the same bill or a piece of legislation is proposed here in our country, I will vigorously object and oppose it. But that is the law in Indonesia. There is nothing we can do but respect their law: *Dura Lex Sed Lex!*

There is another crime which is worse than ignorance of the law, and this is ignoring the law. The recent incident of fire in a Valenzuela City, Bulacan plastics factory should serve as a stern and stark warning regarding ignoring the law. More than seventy factory workers were burned alive on the second floor of that factory because there was no fire escape. The factory building was a death trap. This tragic incident with the untimely loss of many lives could have been avoided if there had been compliance by the factory owner regarding the law on fire safety.

But some people never seem to learn their lesson. We had another tragic incident of Ozone and a hotel in Cubao, where one hundred people were burned to death because of non-compliance with the fire safety laws.

There are many Christians today in the church who seem to have hyper-faith. They issue checks to pay their obligations, even when there is not enough funds in their bank account. I have long warned people against this practice, but some of them insist, "I believe that God will put the money in my bank account, and that's why I issued the checks in advance."

I said, "That's not going to happen." You are the one who must put the money in your bank account. Sure enough, their checks bounced. There were two laws violated in this transaction. The Bouncing Check Law (BP 22) and *Estafa* (Fraud). These laws have Criminal implications. Offenders will be imprisoned pending investigation and conviction. The only good thing in that case I mentioned was that the wronged party was also a Christian, so no lawsuit was filed, but only because the offending party promised to pay the obligations in cash and in a timely manner.

Scammers abound these days, and I have also warned Christians about the lure of quick-profits or quick-money schemes such as the many pyramid and networking scams. Tragically, there are many Christians involved in these scams. I say to them, "Stop now, before you get yourself in trouble—big trouble!

Many years ago now I warned the members of our church against what was being called "Pre-Need Investments." "Can you not manage your own money?" I asked them. "Why do you trust other people to manage your money for you?" The result was that our members withdrew their investments in those companies. As the years passed, those Pre-Need Companies closed one by one and were unable to reimburse their investors. Many had invested, hoping to send their children to college through the Pre-Need

Companies, but, instead, they lost their money and were unab le to give their children a good education. I had been right!

Facebook account holders be warned also because there are lots of scammers at work in the social media. Often they post the face of celebrities or use well-known names, but most of them are scammers from Nigeria who want to swindle your money. Even when they urge you to contribute money for orphanages in Africa, many of them are a hoax.

So, Christians, caveat! We don't have to be victims and suffer the consequences of ignorance. Saint Paul repeated this warning to Christians: *"We don't want you to be ignorant ..."* Be very careful, then, how you live, not as unwise but as wise, making the most of every opportunity, because the days are evil. Therefore, do not be foolish, but understand what the Lord's will is.

This is the time that we, as Christians, must exercise the gift of discerning even outside the church. If any lacks wisdom, let him ask of God. Jesus said, *"Ask, and it will be given you."*

The book of Proverbs has a lot to say about wisdom, knowledge and an understanding heart. In dealing with people; Jesus said, *"Be wise ..."* ✳

cs **36** &

DISPUTES AND JUDICIAL ISSUES
BETWEEN AND AMONG CHRISTIANS
(TO SUE OR NOT TO SUE!)

Text: 1 Corinthians 6:1-7

The Corinthian Church, during the days of the apostle Paul was a complicated and problematic church. They had problems about immaturity, divisions in the church, questioning the credibility and the apostleship of Paul, immorality, issues regarding marriage, food, and the exercise of the gifts of the Spirit relative to worship and about Christian belief (for instance, the subject of resurrection). That was why the apostle Paul wrote two letters to the members of the Corinthian church, in order to rectify these errors, problems and confusions. These two letters of Paul contained the proper and correct theological perspectives, which brought resolve to the besetting problems in the church.

Among the concerns of the apostle Paul was the problem of lawsuits between and among the Corinthian Christian believers. He rebuked them and precluded them from doing this. He said that it was embarrassing and not a good testimony for them to file cases against another brother or sister in the church. Instead of filing cases in the courts of law, especially when the judge was an unbeliever, they should have just settled their disputes between themselves within the church. They should have looked for a brother wise enough to judge the disputes.

In the first place, there should not have been disputes among these believers. As believers in Christ, they were expected to not do wrong against any brother or sister in the Lord. And even if a wrong had been done, the offended party should have been able to "suffer" that wrong done to him. This is, of course, more easily said than done!

Today, as our economic life improves, there are arising similar cases of disputes in our Christian churches. These disputes, in most cases, arise from money matters involving the members of the church. This usually happens when one member of the church lends money to another member, and the transaction is not documented. Then, when the due date for repayment of the loan accrues, the borrower is not able to meet his obligation or, in the worst cases, may even deny that he owes money to the lender.

This is a reminder to all kind-hearted Christians who are willing to help fellow members of the church by lending them money. In order to protect your interests (money) in such a transaction, you must put into a document (a contract of sorts) the details of your transaction, especially when the amount involved is more than five thousand pesos. This is consistent with the legal provision under the "Statute of Fraud." In order for the contract to be enforceable, it "must" be documented. Besides that, the contract must be signed by the contracting parties.

When the loan money involves a large amount, let us say one hundred thousand pesos, it is best that there is a corresponding

201

security for it. This security may be an immovable or personal property. In the case of immovable property, the contract is called an Antichresis, and in the case of the personal property, the contract is called a Pledge.

What is an Antichresis? It is "a written pledge and transfer from a debtor to a creditor of possession of immovable property, like land or buildings, giving the creditor the right to the fruits (as rents) of the property."

What is a Pledge? It is "the delivery of especially personal property, such as a car or valuable jewelry, as a security for a debt or other obligation."

Then we have the question of criminal cases. Should a Christian pursue or file a criminal case against his fellow Christian in the church? First of all, it is unlikely that a criminal offense will happen between or among Christians in the church. But if it does happen, which perhaps is a remote case, the Christian brother has the liberty to file a case or not. So, what then is the judicial norm in the church involving disputes between and among Christians? Let us listen to the ruling of our Lord Jesus Christ regarding these issues:

> Moreover if your brother sins against you [civil or criminal offenses], go and tell him his fault between you and him alone. If he hears you, you have gained your brother. But if he will not hear, take with you one or two more, that "by the mouth of two or three witnesses every word may be established." And if he refuses to hear them, tell it to the church. But if he refuses even to hear the church, let him be to you like a heathen and a tax collector.

Matthew 18:15-17

Furthermore, the Bible shows that there are sanctions even for Christians in the Church who do wrong. These are possible punishments for the wrongdoer. These are sanctions from the church and from the government, which are both authorities established by God. But all of these sanctions can be avoided if we love our neighbor as ourselves because *"love does no harm to a neighbor"* (Romans 13:10).

✂

∞ **37** ∞

DENIED APPEALS

Text: Luke 16:19-31

The story of the Rich Man and Lazarus in the Gospel according to St. Luke is a controversial one. The controversy arises from some issues in the narrative. The first issue is whether or not this story is a parable. Some contend that this was a true story because of the word *certain* being used to describe the rich man and also the mention of particular real names like Abraham and Lazarus in some translations. But, according to biblical experts, there is no doubt that this is indeed a parable because the story is among and within a series of parables that Jesus taught. It is important to determine that it is a parable because of its significant reference to the Doctrine of Eschatology.

So what is a parable? A parable is "a story or fable for the illustration of moral or spiritual truth." It is also "an allegory." In other words, the story did not really happen. It had no factual reality.

This premise considered, therefore we cannot use this parable as a reference to the Christian Doctrine of Life After Death, especially in the immediacy of life after death. In other words, there is no intermediate life after death.

This is the second issue. There is a thin line between what is factual reality and truth. The determinative factors that this story is fiction and, therefore, there is no factual reality are, first of all, that it is a parable. Secondly, it did not happen. But there are spiritual and moral truths in this parable.

Truth is more comprehensive and transcendent than factual reality. The truth in this parable is that there is social inequality in this life between the rich and the poor. But both the rich man and the poor man died (sometime and somewhere) and their situation in the afterlife was suddenly reversed. The rich man was in torment, while Lazarus was comforted.

The scene of the story has now shifted to the afterlife, with the rich man in the active role, while Lazarus is passive. The rich man saw Abraham and Lazarus at his side, so he called to Abraham:

Father Abraham, have mercy on me, and send Lazarus that he may dip the tip of his finger in water and cool my tongue; for I am tormented in this flame.   Luke 16:24

But Abraham replied:

Son, remember that in your lifetime you received your good things, and likewise Lazarus evil things; but now he is comforted and you are tormented. And besides all this, between us and you there is a great gulf fixed, so that those who want to pass from here to you cannot, nor can those from there pass to us.

Luke 16:25-26

The rich man made another plea:

I beg you therefore, father, that you would send him to my father's house, for I have five brothers, that he may testify to them, lest they also come to this place of torment. Luke 16:27-28

But Abraham replied:

They have Moses and the prophets; let them hear them.

Luke 16:29

But the rich man was not finished his pleading:

No, father Abraham; but if one goes to them from the dead, they will repent. Luke 16:30

Abraham's answer was definitive:

But he said to him, "If they do not hear Moses and the prophets, neither will they be persuaded though one rise from the dead."

Luke 16:31

This dialogue was between the rich man and Abraham, who played active roles in this narrative and it confirms that indeed this story is a parable. According to the proponents of the view that the human soul survives death and immediately goes either to Heaven or Hell, the soul of the rich man was in Hell after he died. He could even talk, see and feel. The question is: how could a disembodied spirit (the human soul, as they say) talk, see and feel? The rich man in Hell needed a body in order for him to talk, see and feel. He needed a body to face judgment and punishment. Yes! There is truth in this parable, and that truth is that there is a Hell, a place of torment, and sinners will go there if they don't repent and receive Jesus Christ as their Lord and Savior!

How will the sinners and the unrepentant go to Hell after they have died? After sinners die, they cease to exist. It is the end of their life on Earth. That is the status of the Christians as well. There is no soul to talk about going to Heaven or going to Hell. *Soul* means "life," so what soul are they talking about when the person is dead? Both of them would have to wait for the resurrection before they could be conscious again.

Why is that? Because resurrection by divine power will provide a body and soul for those who have died, never to die again. It is only then that those who have been resurrected can be conscious and can talk, feel and see. There is a resurrection to life and there is a resurrection to damnation. The rich man is among those who are included in the resurrection to damnation.

So, what's the moral of this story? The moral of the story is this: man has time to repent and turn to God now while he is still alive! He has time to convince others and to pray for them, including his brothers, to do the same. This lifetime of opportunity to turn to God is called grace. You are now in a period of grace. There is one who came back from the dead, and His name is Jesus Christ. So, listen to the One who came back from the dead. He said:

He who believes in Him is not condemned; but he who does not believe is condemned already, because he has not believed in the name of the only begotten Son of God. John 3:18

Paul wrote:

For all have sinned and fall short of the glory of God. Romans 3:23

For the wages of sin is death, but the gift of God is eternal life in Christ Jesus our Lord. Romans 6:23

In our criminal justice system, after a conviction, the accused has a period of time to appeal the judgment of his conviction, with the hope of reversing it and thus exonerating himself from punishment. This time is called "The Period to Appeal the Conviction," and usually runs for fifteen days after the judge promulgates the verdict. If an appeal is made, the case is then elevated to a higher court or tribunal for retrial. But if the accused is negligent and does not act to file a notice of appeal as one of the remedies to stay execution, the judgment will become final and executory. Thereafter, the accused will stand convicted and will be incarcerated.

This is what happened to the rich man. His appeal came too late! First, he appealed for himself and then for his brothers. Although both appeals were heard, both were also denied. Don't go to sleep tonight without first repenting of your sins and accepting Jesus Christ as your personal Lord and Savior. He is our only remedy to avoid judgment. You might not wake up tomorrow, but the next time you wake up, you will already be in Hell! Now is the day of salvation!

ॐ **38** ॐ

EMANCIPATION CELEBRATION
JUNE 12: PHILIPPINE INDEPENDENCE DAY

Text: Exodus 12:3-13 and 51

Every year, when we celebrate our Independence Day, we remember and honor the struggles and sacrifices of our forefathers and heroes who fought to bring us freedom. Not only did these heroes fight and shed their blood, but they also gave their lives and thousands of them died so that we could be free as a nation from foreign occupation, domination and oppression. Freedom is not without a price, and the price is high. How nice and wonderful it is for us today to enjoy liberty and to be free indeed!

A very long time ago, God's people, the Israelites, were in bondage in a foreign land, Egypt. The Bible says that a new king in Egypt came to power who did not know Joseph. Joseph was one of Jacob's children, who was sold into slavery in Egypt by his brothers, but by divine Providence, he rose to prominence and power when he saved the nation of Egypt from perishing by reason of severe and extreme famine that hit the entire region for seven years.

Because he had gained favor with the Pharaoh, Joseph was able to bring his whole family to Egypt, including his father Jacob, and there they lived alongside the Egyptians. But, now, many years later, this new king in Egypt became suspicious of the Israelites because they were becoming so numerous, and he was afraid that they might connive with Egypt's enemies in the case that war broke out. So, this new Pharaoh (the Egyptian title for their king) began to cruelly oppress the Israelites by putting them into forced labor and setting slave masters over them.

Strangely, the more the Israelites were oppressed, the more they multiplied, so that the Egyptians dreaded them and made their lives bitter with hard labor in brick and mortar and with all kinds of work in the fields. The Egyptians used and abused these people ruthlessly.

Then, in desperation, the Pharaoh ordered the Hebrew midwives to kill the Israelites baby boys and spare the baby girls. They declined to obey him. Then Pharaoh ordered them to throw the baby boys into the river as soon as they were born.

It was during these difficult and trying times for the Israelites that Moses was born of Hebrew slave parents. One day Pharaoh's daughter found him in a papyrus basket floating in the River Nile, and she adopted him as her son. Once Moses was of age, he discovered his true identity as a Hebrew and attempted to deliver his nation by killing an Egyptian, but he failed miserably.

After the Pharaoh heard of this incident, he tried to kill Moses and Moses fled into Midian. After some time, Moses had an encounter with God in a burning bush and God spoke to him. The Lord said:

Now therefore, behold, the cry of the children of Israel has come to Me, and I have also seen the oppression with which the Egyptians oppress them. Come now, therefore, and I will send you to Pharaoh that you may bring My people, the children of Israel, out of Egypt.   Exodus 3:9-10

With reluctance and hesitance, Moses agreed to return to Egypt to deliver the Israelites out of Egyptian bondage. But how could he do that? Moses and the Israelites had a secret weapon to use against the Egyptians, so that they could finally be set free. Despite the enormous devastation done to Egypt due to the first plagues God sent, Pharaoh was still so pig-headed that he refused to let the Israelites go to serve the Lord. And what was their secret weapon? It was the blood of the Lamb!

The Lord instructed Moses and Aaron, his brother, to prepare special lambs, about a year old and without defect. Each Israelite household must take such a lamb and kill it at twilight. They were to take some of the lamb's blood and put it on the sides and the tops of the door frames of the houses where they then ate of the roasted lamb. The blood would be a sign, and when the Lord saw the blood, no destructive plague would touch that house or its inhabitants.

Because the Egyptian houses had no blood overing, the Lord struck down all the firstborn in Egypt that night at midnight, including the firstborn of Pharaoh, and there was death in every Egyptian house that night. This broke the impasse, and finally Pharaoh released the Israelites into freedom! It was a day for Israelites to celebrate for generations to come, a lasting ordinance, a festival to the Lord!

But what do have these Old Testament narratives have to do with us contemporary Christians? Is there any relevance or significance in them for our Christian Faith today? The answer is in the affirmative! As followers of Christ, we must understand that both the Old and the New Testament are intertwined. Whereas, to the early Christians, the Old Testament was the Scriptures, we contemporary Christians recognize both the Old and the New Testaments as Holy Scripture.

The Passover Lamb was a symbol of Jesus Christ, the Lamb of God who takes away the sins of the world. His suffering, death on the cross and the shedding of His blood were His acts of redemption. The apostle Peter said:

You were not redeemed with corruptible things, like silver or gold, from your aimless conduct received by tradition from your fathers, 19 but with the precious blood of Christ, as of a lamb without blemish and without spot. 1 Peter 1:18-19

Just as the firstborn of the Israelites were spared from death during that Passover night because they appropriated the blood of the lamb on their door frames, so also is everyone who believes in Jesus Christ. They will not perish but will have eternal life! *"If the Son makes you free, you shall be free indeed"* (John 8:36). We always remember and celebrate the redemptive sacrifice of our Lord Jesus Christ in the communion. This is one of our traditional Christian worship rituals. The bread, which is broken and partaken by church members, symbolizes the body of Christ, and the wine symbolizes His blood. Thus, every Christian partakes of Christ in the Communion. Hallelujah! Praise the Lord!

⚝ **39** ⚝

OUR PERILOUS TIMES

Text: 2 Timothy 3:1-5

But know this, that in the last days perilous times will come.

2 Timothy 3:1

Other Bible translation confirm that in the last days it will be difficult to be a Christian. This was part of the opening statement of the apostle Paul in his second letter to his son in the faith, Timothy. His words seem to connote a warning to Timothy that there was some danger ahead, as indicated by the words *perilous times*. The phrase *perilous times* is preceded by the words *last days*. Does this mean that the last days will be characterized by danger and difficulty? The answer is yes, as the statement implies.

Were they already in the last days when Paul told Timothy these things? Or was he talking about some coming, future days closer to the Second Coming of Jesus? What are the last days and when will they commence? According to many Bible scholars (and scholars seem to concur on this point), the last days started with the advent or beginning of the ministry of Jesus Christ on earth. This period of time in the redemptive plan of God for mankind will culminate in the Second Coming of Jesus Christ.

The phrase *last days* is synonymous with *last things* under the broad study of Eschatology, according to theologians. So now we understand why Paul started exhorting and encouraging Timothy to be bold and be strong in the grace that was in Christ Jesus. Besides the challenges and responsibilities of his task as a servant of God, he also had to resist and repel the pressures and the danger of the opposing forces of evil.

What Paul was saying to Timothy was based on his own ministry experiences. In 2 Corinthians 11, he spoke of the various perils he had encountered. He had been under constant death threats. He was beaten with rods, he was stoned three times and he suffered shipwreck and had to float on the sea until he was rescued. He was in perils on his journeys, in perils of water, in perils at the hands of his own countrymen, in perils at the hands of the heathen, in perils in the city, in perils in the wilderness and in perils among false brethren. He had been in weariness and painfulness, in watchings often, in hunger and thirst, in fastings often and in cold and nakedness.

Are we now living in the last days? Are we in perilous times? What are the indicators that we are now in the perilous times which are characteristic of the last days? In answer to these questions, Paul said, *"For men will be lovers of themselves"* (1 Timothy 3:2). How can we know that men (meaning people) are lovers of their own selves? When men are, as Paul described, *"lovers of money, boasters, proud, blasphemers, disobedient to parents, unthankful, unholy, unloving, unforgiving, slanderers, without self-control, brutal, despisers of good, traitors, headstrong, haughty, lovers of pleasure rather than lovers of God, having a form of godliness but denying its power"* (2 Timothy 3:2-5). Today we are witnesses to the moral degeneration, decline, deterioration and decay of our society. There are so many upsurges of criminality, violence, murder, robbery, the proliferation and addiction to illegal and prohibited drugs and fraud among our people. Some of us have even been victims of these crimes. We are living in dangerous times, and this is the outcome when *"Men are lovers of their own selves!"*

If we can examine closely the immoral and evil characteristics of these men who are lovers of their own selves, we see a reverse of what Jesus said, that we must love God first, then our neighbors and ourselves last. Here, only one love is present, and that is love of self, minus the two other loves—the love of God and the love of neighbors.

This is human pride, which is only focused on self, and it's dangerous because a proud person will do anything—even to the detriment and the prejudice of other people—in order to satisfy his pride. He has no regard and respect for the rights, property and even for the lives of others, including his parents and family. He even has a religion in order to cover up his evil deeds, but this is just a *"form"* without power (substance).

What is this *"power"* of God? The Bible says that Jesus Christ is the power of God. Any religion without focus on Jesus Christ is an empty religion without substance. We have so many religions today which focus only on man and not on Christ. This is danger-ous! Paul's warning was:

From such people turn away!   1 Timothy 3:5

As the return of our Lord Jesus Christ is nearing, evil men and impostors will go from bad to worse, deceiving and being deceived. What must be the Christian's response in this situation? Just like Timothy (because Christians are spiritual Timothys), we must continue to fully know our doctrine by studying the Word of God, the Holy Scriptures. They are given by inspiration of God and are useful to teach us what is true and to make us realize what is wrong in our lives. The Word of God straightens us out and helps us to do what is right. It is God's way of making us well prepared at every point, fully equipped to do good to everyone.

When prejudiced, or even extremely prejudiced, by these violent and ruthless people in these dangerous times, we must not take the law into our own hands, for God says:

Vengeance is Mine, I will repay. Romans 12:19

We must not fear either because Jesus said:

And do not fear those who kill the body but cannot kill the soul. But rather fear Him who is able to destroy both soul and body in hell. Matthew 10:28

Earlier, Paul said to Timothy:

For God has not given us a spirit of fear, but of power and of love and of a sound mind. 2 Timothy 1:7

OUR PERILOUS TIMES

The psalmist declared:

If you make the Lord your refuge,
*   if you make the Most High your shelter,*
no evil will conquer you;
*   no plague will come near your home.*
For he will order his angels
*   to protect you wherever you go.*   Psalm 91:9-11, NLT

Paul wrote to the Romans:

If God is for us, who can ever be against us?

Romans 8:31, NLT

✿

217

🕉 **40** 🕉

LET'S BRING A FRIEND TO JESUS!

Text: Mark 2:1-12

A paralytic man, carried on a stretcher by four friends, was brought to Jesus, and He instantly healed the man. Then Jesus said to him, *"Pick up your stretcher and go on home, for you are healed"* (verse 11). The man jumped up, took the stretcher, and pushed his way through the stunned onlookers. As a result of this miracle, the people praised God, saying, *"We've never seen anything like this before!"* (verse 12). This same miraculous account is recorded in chapter 9 of the book of Matthew.

The circumstances surrounding this event were rather extraordinary. When Jesus arrived in Capernaum, after His evangelistic campaign on the other side of the huge lake known as the Sea of Galilee, the news of His arrival spread quickly through the city. Capernaum was the new hometown of Jesus and was the hub of His evangelistic activity. Soon the house where He was staying was so packed with visitors that there wasn't room for a single person more, not even outside the door.

As Jesus preached the Word to those who had gathered, the four men arrived carrying the paralyzed man on a stretcher. They couldn't get to Jesus through the crowd, so they dug through the clay roof above his head and lowered the sick man on a stretcher, right down in front of Jesus. The Scriptures declare:

> *Seeing their faith, Jesus said to the paralyzed man, "My child, your sins are forgiven."*   Verse 5

Some of the Jewish religious leaders who were there questioned in their hearts. *"Why does this man speak thus? It is blasphemy! Who can forgive sins but God alone?"* (Verses 6 and 7).

Jesus, of course, knew what was in their hearts, so He said to them: *"Why do you question thus in your hearts?" Which is easier, to say to the paralytic, 'Your sins are forgiven,' or to say, 'Rise up, take up your stretcher and walk?' But that you may know that the Son of man has authority on earth to forgive sins ..."*

And that was when the told the paralytic man to get up and go home. He was healed.

Why was Jesus thronged by such multitude of people wherever He went? Who were these people and why were they following Jesus? The Bible has the answer to these questions:

> *Jesus went throughout Galilee, teaching in their synagogues, proclaiming the good news of the kingdom, and healing every disease and sickness among the people. News about him spread all over Syria, and people brought to him all who were ill with various diseases, those suffering severe pain, the demon-possessed, those*

219

having seizures, and the paralyzed; and he healed them. Large crowds from Galilee, the Decapolis, Jerusalem, Judea and the region across the Jordan followed him.   Matthew 4:23-25, NIV

The healing of this paralytic man was an interesting particular case. Paralysis, by the way, is a sickness which is "a partial or complete loss of function, especially when involving a motion or sensation in a part of a body." It is "the loss of the ability to move; a state of powerlessness or incapacity to act." A *paralytic*, therefore, is "one who suffers from a nerve dysfunction, disease, or injury which damages muscle function; particularly one who cannot walk." It was a common sickness during those days. What is interesting in this case is that this paralytic was brought on a stretcher by four men to Jesus. These were men of faith. They were also men of concern, love and compassion.

What was the relationship of the four men with the paralytic? Was he a relative or was he a friend? We don't know. What we do know is that these four men had a strong faith and a strong will. No obstacle could hinder them in their mission of bringing the paralytic to Jesus, not even the crowd. Where there is faith, there is a way. So, they climbed to the rooftop of the house, bringing with them the paralytic on a stretcher. Then, they removed the roof above Him, and when they had made an opening, they lowered the paralytic on the stretcher, right down in front of Jesus.

These men must have been looking down through that hole with great anticipation of what would happen next, for when Jesus saw their faith, He said unto the paralytic, *"Son, your sins are forgiven!"* And before long, the miracle happened, and the paralytic was healed!

Looking closely at the scene, starting with the words, *"When Jesus saw their faith,"* we can learn some profound lessons about our own faith. Although faith is abstract, it can be obvious through our actions. Our active faith in God will significantly contribute to the salvation and healing of other people. These four men of great faith and their friend on a stretcher received from Jesus more than they had expected, more than healing. They received the forgiveness of sins. Some people say, "It is better to be sick and go to Heaven than to be well and go to Hell," but in this case, God wants us to be well in body, as well as in our soul. And there can be no doubt about His desire for us all to go to Heaven. Praise the Lord!

Does Jesus heal today? The answer is yes! The Bible says, *"Jesus Christ is the same yesterday, today, and forever"* (Hebrews 13:8). We had a difficult time during our first year of serving God, and my wife and I were contemplating quitting the ministry. Our eldest son had an epileptic seizure during this time, and we could not bear the sight of his suffering. He was about a year old then. I took and raise him up to the Lord with my two hands, and I said, "Here, take our son, Lord; otherwise heal him, and we will serve You the rest of our lives." That was his last seizure, and he is now a grown man with his own family. Glory to God!

Not long ago, a man came to me after one of the services in our church and gave me US $50. I told him that he should have dropped the money into the offering basket during the service. But he told me that this was his personal love gift to me because he was grateful to me for my message. He said that several years back a friend of his had invited him to attend our church. Although hesitant, he did not want to disappoint his friend, so he came. During the service that he heard my message of salvation, gave his life to Jesus and was converted. He became a new man after

221

that and was able to get a job in the Middle East. He had just come home for a vacation when he gave me that money.

Recently, a lady doctor sent a friend request to my Facebook account. I checked her background first, and since I remembered her and recognized her face, I accepted her as a Facebook friend. She told me, through a private message, that she used to attend our church services as a visitor invited by a doctor friend who was a member of our church member. I remembered her hostile look at me during my preaching time. Either she didn't like my preaching or she didn't like me. Now, she told me that she was already a doctor and that she was also pastoring a church somewhere in Mindoro. I was so happy to know this.

Today I want to challenge you to bring a friend to Jesus. Let them hear the Word of God. He said of His Word:

So shall My word be that goes forth from My mouth;
It shall not return to Me void,
But it shall accomplish what I please,
And it shall prosper in the thing for which I sent it.

Isaiah 55:11

Hallelujah!

Cʒ **41** ꝏ

WEALTH OR WISDOM?
(A PRAYER'S PETITION)

Text: 2 Chronicles 1:7-12

If God appeared to you in a dream and asked you this question, *"Ask for whatever you want me to give you"* (Verse 7, NIV), what would be your answer? Perhaps the answer of most people, especially the poor, the destitute and the needy, would be, "Give me money, lots of it, tons of it. And please, God, make it in U.S. dollars!" But would that be the right answer to God?

Could we blame the people who might answer in this way? They would surely have their own reasons for their answer. In their minds, their personal circumstances would somehow justify their answers. And, maybe, if we were in the same situation, we would answer as they would.

But in an ordinary situation, when and where we are not in such dire need of the basic necessities of life, but we are faced with tremendous challenges consisting of responsibilities and opportunities, would our answer be the same?

223

What is *wealth* by the way? *Wealth* is "an abundance of valuable material possessions and resources, including money." Given the choice between wealth and wisdom, what would be our answer to the foregoing question by God? You might be surprised to know that many people still choose wealth over wisdom, especially when they don't know and understand the superiority of wisdom.

What is wisdom? *Wisdom* is "the ability to discern inner qualities and relationships; an insight, a wise judgment and attitude or course of action."

In the Parable of the Lost Son, it was a very big mistake when the younger son asked his father for his share of the father's estate. This shows that he was naive and reckless. Sure enough, after he received his share of his father's estate, he went to a distant country and there squandered his wealth in wild living.

After he had spent everything, there was a severe famine in that country, and he began to be in great need. In order to survive, he took the basest of jobs, feeding swine, for no one gave him anything. What a condescending and degrading life that must have been for him! Fortunately, his circumstances forced him to come to his senses, and he remembered the abundance of his father's house. Therefore he was repentant and went back to his father, and his father joyfully welcomed and received him.

Today, there are so many people like that prodigal son. They are not only naive and reckless, but also torpid and gullible to the lure of get-rich-quick schemes. They easily become the victims of scammers who offer them enormous returns for their money in a very short a time, under the pretext of these payments being "investments." These people are dubious swindlers who use a Ponzi scheme approach, in order to defraud people of their money. Such transactions are also known as a pyramid scheme.

What is a Ponzi scheme? It is "a fraudulent investment operation where the operator, an individual or organization, pays returns to its investors from new capital paid to the operators by new investors, rather than from profit earned by the operator." The biggest scammer in this regard was Bernard "Bernie" Madoff in the U.S. who conned $50 billion from his investors. [1] I feel the need to always remind and warn people: CAVEAT! BEWARE!

Actually, this phrase *"Ask for whatever you want me to give you,"* was a question asked by God to King Solomon in a dream. Solomon was the newly-installed King of Israel, but he was young and inexperienced in matters of ruling and governing a kingdom. His answer showed wisdom and should be emulated by everyone when confronted with the same question.

First, King Solomon acknowledged his father David. Then, he also acknowledged his great responsibility in governing his people and the affairs of the kingdom. His answer to God was:

Give me wisdom and knowledge, that I may lead this people, for who is able to govern this great people of yours? 2 Chronicles 1:10

In another version, Solomon is quoted as saying, *"Give your servant an understanding heart to govern your people and to distinguish between right and wrong."* Simply put, *wisdom* is "the ability to discern what is right and what is wrong." So, the Lord was pleased that Solomon had asked wisely and said to him:

Because this was in your heart, and you have not asked riches or wealth or honor or the life of your enemies, nor have you asked

1. https://en.wikipedia.org/wiki/Bernard_Madoff

long life—but have asked wisdom and knowledge for yourself, that you may judge My people over whom I have made you king—wisdom and knowledge are granted to you; and I will give you riches and wealth and honor, such as none of the kings have had who were before you, nor shall any after you have the like.

2 Chronicles 1:11-12

So, God gave Solomon what he had asked for and also what he had *not* asked for. The result was that Solomon's wisdom was greater than that of all the men of the east and greater than all the wisdom of Egypt. He spoke three thousand proverbs, and his songs numbered one thousand and five. Men of all nations, sent by the kings of the world who had heard of Solomon's wisdom, came to confer with him.

This great wisdom and judgment of Solomon was tested one day when two women came to him, each claiming a surviving infant as her own. One of the women had lain on her child during the night, and he had died. She then took the living child of the other woman and replaced him with her dead child.

When the other woman awoke in the morning, she saw that the child next to her was dead, but she quickly realized that it was not her child. She also realized what the other woman had done. As you can image, the disagreement between the two woman was so heated that the matter was brought directly to Solomon.

When King Solomon saw how resolutely each of the mothers stuck to her story, he called for a sword to be brought. Then, in the hearing of the two women, he ordered his servants to cut the living child in half and give half to each of the women. The reaction of the two women to this suggestion was very different:

WEALTH OR WISDOM?

Then the woman whose son was living spoke to the king, for she
yearned with compassion for her son; and she said, "O my lord,
give her the living child, and by no means kill him!" But the
other said, "Let him be neither mine nor yours, but divide him."

1 Kings 3:26

Watching this exchange very carefully, the king now knew what must be done:

So the king answered and said, "Give the first woman the living
child, and by no means kill him; she is his mother."   Verse 27

Such wisdom rightly impressed the people who heard about this matter:

And all Israel heard of the judgment which the king had rendered;
and they feared the king, for they saw that the wisdom of God was
in him to administer justice.   Verse 28

So, which will you ask God for—wealth or wisdom? If you only have wealth and not wisdom, your wealth can be easily lost. But wisdom is a wealth that can never be lost or stolen.

When our youngest son finished college and was working in a bank in Makati, earning a good income, my wife and I challenged him to choose between a trust account to be set up for him in the amount of half a million pesos or his expenses to take up the study of Law. He chose to take up Law, and is now a practicing lawyer. Praise God that he chose wisely, to further his studies in Law.

How do we get wisdom? The Bible says:

The fear of the Lord is the beginning of wisdom. Psalm 110:10

If any of you lacks wisdom, let him ask of God, who gives to all liberally and without reproach, and it will be given to him.

James 1:5

What are you waiting for? Get your share of this treasure.   �֍

CR **42** &

SERVING GOD AND OTHERS WITH INTEGRITY

Text: Romans 13:8-14

These verses are part of the letter of Saint Paul to the Romans. He wrote this letter while he was in Corinth between 57 and 58 A.D. In it, from chapters 1 through 11, he argued and explained the great need and necessity of salvation for all people. He summarized this message of salvation in three verses:

1. *"All have sinned and fall short of the glory of God."* (3:23)

2. *"For the wages of sin is death, but the gift of God is eternal life in Christ Jesus our Lord."* (6:23)

3. *"There is therefore now no condemnation to those who are in Christ Jesus, who do not walk according to the flesh, but according to the Spirit."* (8:1)

Starting in chapter 12, the apostle Paul enumerated several and different duties and responsibilities of a Christian after he has been saved. What is a duty? A *duty* is "a moral or legal obligation, a service required."

What is an obligation? An *obligation* is "an act of obligating one-self to a course of action." It is "a bond with a condition annexed and a penalty for non-fulfilment." Simply put, it is something that we are bound to do.

The apostle Paul categorized our Christian duties into two. The first one is sacred duty, and the second one is secular duty. Under our sacred duty, our service or obligation is related to God and His Church. Under our secular duty, our service is related to other people, our government (or the state) and even our enemies. We are all servants of God!

So, what is our first duty as a Christian according to the apostle Paul? Our first duty is serving God. How are we to fulfil that? Answer: By presenting our bodies and renewed mind as living sacrifices. In other words, we are to regularly worship God. We are precluded from conforming to this world but are rather encouraged to seek His good, acceptable and perfect will in our lives.

Our second duty is toward our fellow beings. Our relationship with them must be in the conduct of love and patience:

Repay no one evil for evil. Have regard for good things in the sight of all men. If it is possible, as much as depends on you, live peaceably with all men. Romans 12:17-18

Do not be overcome by evil, but overcome evil with good.

Romans 12:21

Our third duty is toward our government (the state). We are to obey our government, the Bible teaches. Why? Because it is God who put that government in power. The government is mandated and tasked to maintain peace and order, execute judgment and punishment on criminals and those who violate the law. It is for this reason that we are to pay our taxes, so that government workers can keep on doing God's work and service to the people. Besides this, we are to honor and pay respect to all those to whom it is due. Christians are law-abiding citizens.

In all these endeavors, whether sacred or secular, we must seriously consider our cooperation with others in order to achieve reasonable success. In other words, we need each other. Just as there are many parts to our bodies, so it is with Christ's Body. We are all parts of it, and it takes every one of us to make it complete, for we each have a different work to do. So, we belong to each other, and each needs all the others:

God has given each of us the ability to do certain things well. So if God has given you the ability to prophesy, then prophesy whenever you can—as often as your faith is strong enough to receive a message from God. If your gift is that of serving others, serve them well. If you are a teacher, do a good job of teaching. If you are a preacher, see to it that your sermons are strong and helpful. If God has given you money, be generous in helping others with it. If God has given you administrative ability and put you in charge of the work of others, take the responsibility seriously. Those who offer comfort to the sorrowing should do so with Christian cheer.

Romans 12:6-8, TLB

231

What did Paul mean when he said, *"Owe no one anything"* (Romans 13:8)? Was he referring to money or valuable material things that we need to repay to our creditors? Debt does not only refer to money, but it can also mean "sin or trespass." This, in fact, is the reiteration of chapter 8, which provides that those who are in Christ Jesus no longer walk in the flesh. What Paul is saying is this: "Do not sin or violate the rights of your fellow beings." This explains why, in the following statements, he said: " *'You shall not commit adultery,' 'You shall not murder,' 'You shall not steal,' 'You shall not bear false witness,' 'You shall not covet,' "* (Romans 13:9). Instead, he taught, " *'You shall love your neighbor as yourself.' Love does no harm to a neighbor; therefore love is the fulfillment of the law"* (Romans 13:9-10).

Sin is a violation of God's law. Sin, like a coin, has two faces. When God precludes us from doing something and we do it anyway, it is called a sin of commission. But when God tells us to do something and we don't do it, that is called a sin of omission. So, which is our debt?

Sin is likened to the darkness of night, while living for God is likened to daylight. Since we are now in Christ, let us cast away the darkness of sin in our lives. God is light, and those who are with God live in the light of God. Jesus said:

You are the light of the world. A city that is set on a hill cannot be hidden. Nor do they light a lamp and put it under a basket, but on a lampstand, and it gives light to all who are in the house. Let your light so shine before men, that they may see your good works and glorify your Father in heaven.

Matthew 5:14-16

Finally, we also have duties to ourselves. We are encouraged:

*Let us walk properly, as in the day, not in revelry and drunken-
ness, not in lewdness and lust, not in strife and envy.*

Romans 13:13

Let us ask the Lord Jesus Christ to help us live as Christians and
don't make plans to enjoy evil:

*But put on the Lord Jesus Christ, and make no provision for the
flesh, to fulfill its lusts.* Romans 13:14

❧

cs **43** so

WHAT BEING A CHRISTIAN MEANS

Text: Acts 11:26

Who were and who are the Christians? The word *Christian* signifies "followers of Christ." This word appears only three times in the New Testament.

In the book of Acts (11:26), we read that in Antioch, the disciples were, for the first time, called Christians.

When the apostle Paul witnessed to King Agrippa about the Gospel of Jesus Christ, the King's response to Paul was, *"You almost persuade me to become a Christian"* (Acts 26:28).

Suffering and Christianity were closely related in the early Church and still are in many countries today. So, the apostle Peter said that it was never a shame to suffer for being a Christian (see 1 Peter 4:16). Praise God for the privilege of being in Christ's family and being called by His wonderful name!

During and after the Day of Pentecost, multitudes of people both Jews and proselytes (persons of Gentile origin who had accepted the Jewish religion), came from Mesopotamia, Judea, Cappadocia, in Pontus and Asia, Phrygia, and Pamphylia, in Egypt, and in the parts of Libya, Cyrene, from Rome, Crete and Arabia and were saved. Three thousand souls were added to the Church in a single day. This was the result of an extraordinary phenomenon, the outpouring of the Holy Spirit upon the apostles, as they spoke the message of God in the native languages of the people who had come from those different places *"the wonderful works of God"* (Acts 2:11). With boldness, Peter stood up that day and preached the Gospel of Jesus Christ, challenging the people to repent and be baptized in the name of Jesus Christ for the remission of sins.

In the days to come, signs, wonders and miracles were performed by Peter and John in the name of Jesus, particularly the healing of a man who had been lame since birth and who sat at the gate of the Temple, asking for alms. This miracle was witnessed by many, and this gave the apostles another opportunity to preach the Gospel of Jesus Christ.

Despite opposition from the priests, the captain of the Temple and the Sadducees, Peter, being filled with the Holy Spirit, boldly proclaimed to the people: *"Nor is there salvation in any other, for there is no other name under heaven given among men by which we must be saved"* (Acts 4:12). The result was that multitudes believed, and the wave of glory continued:

> *And with great power the apostles gave witness to the resurrection of the Lord Jesus. And great grace was upon them all.*

Acts 4:33

The disciples, as those who followed Christ were then called, lived communally. Those who had lands or houses sold them, and

235

brought the proceeds thereof to the apostles, and distribution was made unto every man, according as he had need (see Acts 4:35).

As the number of disciples multiplied, a management oversight involving the daily distribution of food occurred. The apostles suggested that the church congregation pick out from among them men of good character to look into these matters. One among the chosen men was Stephen, who was mightily used by God with signs and wonders among the people. The religious leaders of that day vehemently opposed Stephen, but they could not withstand the wisdom and the Spirit with which he spoke (see Acts 6:10).

After Stephen's arrest, he faced the council, and those who saw him said that his face was like the face of an angel (see Acts 6:15). In response to a question from the current high priest, Stephen delivered one of the most profound Old Testament expositions. Unfortunately, this led to his martyrdom.

Then a great persecution of the disciples of Christ began that scattered them beyond the regions of Judea and Samaria, but wherever the disciples of Christ were scattered, they continued preaching the Word. A Pharisee named Saul spearheaded a very aggressive persecution of the followers of Christ. In fact, he had consented to the death of Stephen. Now breathing with threats and murder, he pursued the men and women who belonged to "the Way" (another name for the Church at the time).

However, while he was traveling on the Damascus road, Saul, whose name later on would be changed to Paul, was confronted by the Lord Jesus Christ with a blinding light and with a voice saying to him, *"Saul, Saul, why are you persecuting me?"* (Acts 9:4),

Saul answered, *"Who are You, Lord?"* (verse 5).

The Lord said, *"I am Jesus, whom you are persecuting. ... Arise and go into the city, and you will be told what you must do"* (Acts 9:5-6). The result was that Paul was converted to Christianity after he met Jesus Christ on that road to Damascus. After his conversion, he spent several years in his home city of Tarsus, until one day Barnabas went there and asked him to join him in a venture to teach the newly-formed church at Antioch. Paul became a faithful follower of Christ, a dedicated missionary and a respected leader in the early Church. He was the great apostle to the Gentiles.

Paul participated in three missionary journeys. Among his many travelling companions at various times were Barnabas, John Mark, Silas and Luke. One of his journeys took him back to Jerusalem, where he was taken prisoner and then sent to Rome to await trial. He suffered martyrdom in Rome under the reign of Nero. Paul was believed to be the author of thirteen of the letters found in the New Testament.

After the time of Paul and the early Church, Christians suffered severe persecutions of trial and torture under the Roman Empire. They were hunted down like criminals. They were imprisoned, stoned, sawn asunder, crucified upside down, thrown into boiling cauldrons of oil. They were slain with the sword and were fed to hungry wild animals in the arena. Being destitute, afflicted, tormented, they wandered in deserts, and in mountains, in dens and caves of the earth. None of these things, however, could separate these Christians from the love of Christ. Paul declared:

Who shall separate us from the love of Christ? Shall tribulation, or distress, or persecution, or famine, or nakedness, or peril, or sword? As it is written:

*"For Your sake we are killed all day long;
We are accounted as sheep for the slaughter."*

Yet in all these things we are more than conquerors through Him who loved us. For I am persuaded that neither death nor life, nor angels nor principalities nor powers, nor things present nor things to come, nor height nor depth, nor any other created thing, shall be able to separate us from the love of God which is in Christ Jesus our Lord. Romans 8:35-39

These things could not separate Christians from God then, and they cannot separate us from God now. No, in all things we Christians are more than conquerors through Him who loved us. Yes, Christians are people who are full of God, full of love, full of faith, full of hope and full of life. Praise God and Hallelujah!

THE ISSUE OF LYING
(A SITUATIONAL ETHIC)

Text: Exodus 20:16

The ninth commandment says: *"You must not lie"* (TLB). Other translations say *"You shall not bear false witness against your neighbor."* Is this an absolute rule or a general rule for all the people of God? Personally, I believe that this commandment is both an absolute and a general rule. (And there is always an exception to the rule.)

What is lying? The word *lying* is the present participle form of the verb *to lie.* So the root word of *lying* is *lie.* It means "an assertion of something known or believed by the speaker to be untrue and false with the intent to deceive or mislead."

The first recorded lie in the Bible was uttered by the devil appearing as a serpent in the Garden of Eden. God precluded Adam and Eve from eating of the fruit of the forbidden tree in the midst of the Garden and swore that they would *"surely die"* if they eat of it (Genesis 2:17). But the serpent said to Eve, *"You will not surely die"* (Genesis 3:4). Who was telling the truth? And who was telling a lie? Of course, God was telling the truth, and the devil was telling a lie. Still, Adam and Eve believed the lie of the devil instead of the truth of God. Why did they believe the lie of the devil? Eve was deceived, and Adam ate the fruit of the forbidden tree because of her.

The second incident of lying in the Bible was committed by Cain. After he killed his brother Abel, God asked him where his brother was, and he answered, "I don't know," although he knew very well that he had killed him.

Abram and Sarah his wife both lied to Pharaoh, King of Egypt regarding their status. Abram persuaded Sarah to tell Pharaoh that she was his sister instead of his wife.

We can say that Isaac, Abraham's son, was like his father. Like Abraham, he lied to King Abimelech regarding his wife Rebekah, for fear of his life. I guess lying ran in the family of Abraham because even Jacob, Abraham's grandson, also lied. He lied to Isaac, his father, involving Isaac's blessing. With the connivance of his mother, he pretended to be his brother Esau, in order to get his patriarchal blessing.

Before the Israelites entered Canaan, Joshua sent two spies to Jericho. They went to the house of a woman named Rahab, who was a prostitute, and were hoping to spend the night there. Before long, however, someone informed the King of Jericho that two Israelites who were suspected of being spies had arrived in the city that night. The king sent word to Rahab to surrender the men who had come to her house, but she hid them on the roof, and when the search party from the king arrived, she told them that the men were gone and that they should pursue after them. So, these men went out looking for the two spies all day. Rahab, of course, had lied to them because the Israelite spies were still hidden in her house.

In chapter 5 of the book of Acts, Ananias and his wife Sapphira sold a piece of property and brought only part of the money as an offering, but claimed that it was the full price, both having agreed beforehand to this deception. Peter was not pleased with this charade. He said to them:

"Ananias, why has Satan filled your heart to lie to the Holy Spirit and keep back part of the price of the land for yourself? 4 While it remained, was it not your own? And after it was sold, was it not in your own control? Why have you conceived this thing in your heart? You have not lied to men but to God." Acts 5:3-4

When they heard these words from Peter, both husband and wife dropped to the floor dead. The conclusion was:

So great fear came upon all the church and upon all who heard these things. Acts 5:11

Based on these examples on the issue of lying or telling a lie, I can safely conclude that the ninth commandment is both an absolute and a general rule. When it comes to our relationship with God, the command is absolute. We must never lie, or tell a lie, to God. When it comes to our relationship with our fellow beings, we are also precluded from lying or telling a lie as a general rule. With every rule however, there is an exception. So, what is the exception here? The exception is situational. This means that when a human life is in danger, lying is sanctioned. Abram, Isaac and Rahab were forced to lie in order to save their own lives and the lives of others, and they were not punished for their lies.

Another translations that says, *"You shall not witness falsely against your neighbour"* suggests a judicial proceeding. Under oath in a court of law, we are precluded from giving false testimony against the accused, especially when such testimony will extremely prejudice the life of the accused. What is the rationale behind this principle? It is that human life is sacred and precious, whether one is a sinner or a saint. The Bible says that man is made *"in the image of God"* (Genesis 1:27).

What are the consequences of lying or telling a lie? With regards to the absolute and the general rule that *"you must not lie,"* the consequences of disobeying are fatal and destructive. Lying is the root of the culture of corruption that complicates our relationships and lives and that will eventually ruin us. Lying is relative to cheating, falsehood, dishonesty and fraud. This is the moral turpitude that permeates the many sectors of our present society, including politics, government, business, education and, it is sad to say, even some churches.

One of our Christian challenges as the *"light"* and *"salt"* of this world is to live honest and truthful lives. They say that honesty is the best policy, and the opposite of a lie is the truth.

Jesus called the devil the *"father"* of all liars:

When he speaks a lie, he speaks from his own resources, for he is a liar and the father of it.   John 8:44

In contrast, Jesus said, *"I am ... the truth"*:

Jesus said to him, "I am the way, the truth, and the life. No one comes to the Father except through Me.   *john 14:6*

As Christians, we are to speak the truth in love:

But, speaking the truth in love, may grow up in all things into Him who is the head — Christ.   Ephesians 4:15

The Bible adds:

Then Jesus said to those Jews who believed Him, "If you abide in My word, you are My disciples indeed. And you shall know the truth, and the truth shall make you free."   John 8:31-3.2

Don't tell a lie, but, at the same time, you don't have to always tell the whole truth:

But outside are dogs and sorcerers and sexually immoral and murderers and idolaters, and whoever loves and practices a lie.

Revelation 22:15

But the cowardly, unbelieving, abominable, murderers, sexually immoral, sorcerers, idolaters, and all liars shall have their part in the lake which burns with fire and brimstone, which is the second death.   Revelation 21:8

�֎

cʒ **45** ꙍ

THE RENEWING OF OUR MINDS

Text: Romans 12:2

One of the important areas of a Christian's life which needs renewal, a radical renewal, is his mind. As a matter of fact, repentance must take place in the person's mind. He must acknowledge that he is a sinner and that he needs forgiveness from God. He must be convinced in his mind of the truth of the Gospel of Jesus Christ and that believing and receiving Jesus as his personal Lord and Savior is the only way of salvation.

How important is this mind renewal? It is important, very important, because this renewal of mind will affect and determine a person's spiritual and secular dimensions, as well as his eternal perspective on life. It is from the person's mind that the attitude is formed depending on the informational data received. Then, from the person's attitude, emanate his behaviors and conduct. Compared with the computer, the mind is the central processing unit of every person.

The mind is one element of the human soul, the others being the emotions and the will. The mind is the seat of our human intellect and reason. It is where our thinking processes come from. In the Bible, however, the person's mind is referred to as his heart. For example: the book of Proverbs says, *"For as he [a man] thinks in his heart, so is he"* (Proverbs 23:7). Jesus said, *"For from within, out of the heart of men, proceed evil thoughts, adulteries, fornications, murders, thefts, covetousness, wickedness, deceit, lewdness, an evil eye, blasphemy, pride, foolishness. All these evil things come from within and defile a man"* (Mark 7:21-23). To the Jewish understanding, these two terms — the mind and the heart — were and are interchangeably used. Both mind and heart form the very core of a person's human personality. Paul wrote, *"Therefore, if anyone is in Christ, he is a new creation; old things have passed away; behold, all things have become new"* (2 Corinthians 5:17). There is a transition here, a renewal, from the old to the new.

What are the things that have been renewed? Surely, this is the same person with the same face, the same stature and in a similar social or economic status, but what has been renewed is his mind. Whereas his mind before he received Jesus Christ into his life was reprobate, perverted, corrupt, carnal, blinded with spiritual things and without knowledge and understanding about spiritual things, now, in Christ Jesus, it is totally different. The Christian has a renewed mind.

The questions are: How does a Christian think? And what are the things that he should be thinking about? First of all, the Christian must always think about humility and obedience, following the example of Jesus Christ. Although Jesus was God, He humbled Himself and became a servant, and He was obedient to the will of the Father, even to death on the cross.

Secondly, the Christian should think about things which are true, things which are noble, things which are right, whatever is pure, whatever is lovely and whatever is admirable. If anything is excellent or praiseworthy (see Philippians 4:8). Add to these thoughts of compassion, kindness, gentleness, patience, forgiveness and love. The opposite of these were our former thoughts, which were filled with sexual immorality, impurity, lust, evil desires and greed, which are all another form of idolatry. A Christian must also discard all thoughts of anger, rage, malice, slander, filthy language and all lies! Finally, we must bring into captivity every thought or imagination to the obedience of Christ (see 2 Corinthians 10:5).

A Christian must also think about Heaven. Many Christians only think about Heaven when they are dying. Paul said that, as Christians, we must set our hearts and minds on things above where Christ is seated at the right hand of the Father (see Colossians 3:2). Jesus is preparing a place for us in Heaven, and He will come again and take us to be with Him (see John 14:3). Therefore, let us remember, as Christians, that our citizenship is from Heaven, and this world is not our home. We are just passing through. One day, someday, we are going Home.

This is why Jesus said that we should lay up for ourselves treasures in Heaven and not on earth (see Matthew 6:19-21). Why? Because the things of this world are temporal, while heavenly things are eternal. There will be no more curses or sickness there, God will wipe away the tears from His people's eyes, and there will be no more death. All will be eternal bliss in the beauty of Paradise and the splendor of the Holy City of New Jerusalem forever. Oh, how wonderful it is to think about Heaven!

Earlier I mentioned about the three elements of the human soul, namely the mind, the emotions and the will. In reality and oftentimes, there are contentions and tensions between the mind and the emotions. Whichever prevails becomes the will of that person, which boils down to his decision on whatever issue or issues he is confronted with at the moment. When we allow our emotions to overrule our reason (mind), there are always problems, big problems, as a consequence. However, if we allow our reason to dominate, we become callous and insensitive, especially when it involves the needs of other people. There must be a balance between these two, if we are to arrive at a favorable and reasonable decision. As a rule, the emotions must be subservient to our reason (the mind), if we are to avoid big problems.

There is another player in this decision dilemma of man, which is more confined to Christians. This is concerning and involving the will of God. After the struggle between the emotions and reason (mind), which result in the will of man, now comes the struggle between the will of man and the will of God. As Christians, we want to always do the will of God relative to whatever decision or actions we wish to take. How can we know and understand that what we decide to do is the will of God? It's a good question.

There is the general will of God, and there is the particular will of God. The general will of God is revealed in the Bible relative to our issues. The particular will of God is not written in the Bible, but there are similar or related principles that can be applied. One needs to be patient and wait, making consultations and seeking advice from parents, pastors or elders and saying lots of prayers, if he or she wants to know the particular will of God:

I beseech you therefore, brethren, by the mercies of God, that you present your bodies a living sacrifice, holy, acceptable to God, which is your reasonable service. And do not be conformed

247

*to this world, but be transformed by the renewing of your mind,
that you may prove what is that good and acceptable and perfect
will of God.*   Romans 12:1-2

How can we do this? The answer is by presenting ourselves to God. And where? There were always designated places in olden times where sacrifices were offered to God. Today, it is done in the church as Christian believers congregate and worship God.

Our worship is a sacrifice to God and, as we go out from the church, we must not live worldly lives. As we go back to church regularly and listen to the preaching and teaching of the Word of God, we are transformed, and our mind is renewed. Yes, Christians have a renewed mind because they are born again, and they have the mind of Christ!   ✄

YES, OBEDIENCE IS BETTER THAN SACRIFICE

Text: Philippians 4:19

When I went to the United States fairly early in my ministry, my intentions were good. I was not abandoning my faith or my ministry. I felt that I was doing the responsible thing by looking for other ways to provide for my family. Surely I could find the answer I needed in the land of opportunity. The United States proved to be all that I had dreamed of and more.

Then, however, after I was there for less than six months, the Lord spoke to me to come back home to the Philippines. I really struggled with that decision. In the end, I asked a pastor friend to help me pray about it, and he confirmed the Lord's will for me to return.

Reluctantly, having experienced the difficulty of meeting my family's needs, I obeyed the Lord. After all, He was Lord, and surely He knew what He was doing. True to His Word, within a few years, the Lord had given us, fully paid, our own church building in West Crame, San Juan (and the building is fully air-conditioned.) He also gave us the school ministry with its corresponding properties valued in the millions of pesos. God gave us our own home (fully paid) at Valley Golf in Cainta, Rizal, and he gave me a personal car, a Mercedes Benz E-220. It's an oldie, but it's also a goodie.

In 2016 Gani, our youngest son, passed his bar exams and became a full-fledged attorney. Praise God! Hallelujah! Our God is wonderful, and He is the best Employer ever.

I want to encourage pastors and other ministers who may be going through trials and difficulties, especially in meeting your basic needs. Be patient, be obedient and be faithful in your service to God. He will supply all your need according to His riches in glory by Christ Jesus (see Philippians 4:19)! He guarantees it.   ✄

47

HEAVEN CAN WAIT

Text: John 14:2-3

Today there are many ministers and theologians who proclaim that those who have died (assuming that they are committed Christians) are already in Heaven and are in a better state than we are. This doctrine is based on a belief that the soul survives death and immediately goes to Heaven. When I asked one of the proponents of this doctrine about his definition of *death,* he answered, "Separation."

I followed this with another question: "What separates during death?"

His answer was, "The immaterial from the material."

When I asked him if he could elaborate on that, he declined to answer. What he probably meant was that at death the soul separates from the body and immediately goes to Heaven.

The big questions now is: Are there really people in Heaven now? Or could those ministers of the Gospel be mistaken? Let's find out.

The proponents of this belief cite several verses from the Bible as a basis for their doctrine. Let's just mention two of them. The first one is in Hebrews 11:5, and it alludes to something mentioned in Genesis 5:24. Hebrews 11:5 says this:

By faith Enoch was translated that he should not see death; and was not found, because God had translated him: for before his translation he had this testimony, that he pleased God. (KJV)

Genesis 5:24 says this:

And Enoch walked with God: and he was not; for God took him.

Most Bible translations of Hebrews 11:5 say that Enoch was *taken, taken away* or *taken up*. Only the Living Bible (and the New Living Translation) render the verse to say that God actually took him to Heaven.

Many argue that Enoch did not die, thereby suggesting that he was somehow immortal. Is that right? Did Enoch not die? And is Enoch in Heaven now, as many claim? A careful reading of Hebrews 11 will show that Enoch indeed *did* die. Referring to the heroes of faith mentioned throughout this chapter, verse 13 states: *"THESE ALL DIED in faith, not having received the promises ..."* (Emphasis mine). *ALL* included Enoch, so it is an established biblical fact that Enoch did die.

And the answer to the second question is: No, Enoch is not in Heaven. As a matter of fact, except for Jesus Christ, who is God, no one is in Heaven yet. To say that God took Enoch to Heaven, then, is an error. He is definitely not in Heaven. His body, which decomposed and turned to dust, is still here on Earth. His tomb in Iraq was destroyed by ISIS militants in recent years.

When confronted with seemingly contradictory passages in the Bible, we pastors have a responsibility to seek the guidance and spiritual discernment of the Holy Spirit. We cannot always extract the truth of a certain passage by random reading. For this reason, we have been disciplined to exegete and always consider the context in relation to the text.

Why does Hebrews 11:5 say that *"Enoch was translated that he should not see death?"* No reason is given, so we can make a conjecture relative to Enoch's situation at the time. Probably it was by reason of expediency or emergency. He did not die in the place from where he was translated, but he eventually died in the place he was translated to, as verse 13 suggests.

This word *heaven* in the Bible has three different dimensions: the first, the second and the third heaven. The first heaven is the immediate atmosphere of Earth where there are clouds. The second heaven is outer space, and the third heaven (Heaven) is the abode of God, sometimes referred to as Paradise, a city or a country. It is probable that Enoch was taken up to the first heaven, when he was translated by God. We can cite a similar situation with the prophet Elijah (see 2 Kings 2) and with Philip in New Testament times (see Acts 8:39-40).

Another verse of the Bible that is used to teach that there are people in Heaven now is Luke 23:43:

And Jesus said to him, "Assuredly, I say to you, today you will be with Me in Paradise."

The controversy about this verse is whether the comma should come before the word *today* or after it. That simple act changes the meaning. Did the translators or the printers perhaps make a mistake?

This verse was quoted to me by an opposing minister, who chose to believe that the malefactor, to whom Jesus addressed these words, went to Heaven (Paradise) that very day, when they both died. When I suggested that this was a future promise, he accused me of twisting the Scriptures.

It is my strong and firm conviction, as a follower of Christ, that our Christian life and beliefs are real, rational and logical, never an illusion, so I asked him this question: "Where did Jesus go that day when He died? Did He go to Paradise, together with the malefactor? He did not answer.

The Bible, however, answers this question. Jesus was taken down and buried, and He was in the tomb for the next three days and nights. He did not go to Paradise together with the malefactor that same day.

"If Jesus was in the tomb," I asked the man, "was Paradise in the tomb, or was the tomb a paradise?" There was still no answer.

There is nothing to indicate that the malefactor was put in the tomb together with Jesus. Jesus was buried in one tomb, and the other man was buried in another.

One of the pastors of a large Christian denomination told me that the reason he and others say that those who have died are already in Heaven is just to comfort their loved ones. I thought that was a very poor excuse. The best comfort we can give others is to tell them the truth. And what is the truth about this issue? Because we are unable to reconcile these seemingly conflicting and contradictory passages in the Bible regarding this subject (or any subject, for that matter), we must listen to Jesus. He is the Final Authority, and by His words men will be judged. What did Jesus say?

No one has ascended to heaven but He who came down from heaven, that is, the Son of Man who is in heaven. John 3:13

In My Father's house are many mansions; if it were not so, I would have told you. I go to prepare a place for you. And if I go and prepare a place for you, I will come again and receive you to Myself; that where I am, there you may be also. John 14:2-3

Before anyone goes to Heaven, Christ must come again, for no one goes to Heaven by himself. When Jesus returns, that's the time that He will receive those who died in Christ and the Old Testament saints, together with those who are alive in Christ, those who will be suddenly changed at the time of His return. This was confirmed by Paul in his first letter to the Thessalonians:

Brothers and sisters, we do not want you to be uninformed about those who sleep in death, so that you do not grieve like the rest of mankind, who have no hope. For we believe that Jesus died and rose again, and so we believe that God will bring with Jesus those who have fallen asleep in him. According to the Lord's word, we tell you that we who are still alive, who are left until the coming of the Lord, will certainly not precede those who have fallen asleep. For the Lord himself will come down from heaven, with a loud command, with the voice of the archangel and with the trumpet call of God, and the dead in Christ will rise first. After that, we who are still alive and are left will be caught up together [this is the Rapture] with them in the clouds to meet the Lord in the air. And so we will be with the Lord forever. Therefore encourage one another with these words. 1 Thessalonians 4:13-18, NIV

Personally, I find this teaching to be contrary to the Scriptures. Whereas the Bible says, *"The soul that sinneth, it shall die"* (Ezekiel 18:4), these people say that the soul survives death. Besides, the definition of *death* is "the absence of life," and to me that refers to the soul.

Death is the cessation of all vital functions, and it is the end of life (which is in the soul). So, what soul are they talking about going to Heaven, when it is already dead according to the Bible?

The proponents of this teaching, when proclaiming that the soul lives on after death and goes to Heaven immediately, are resurrecting, in effect, those dead people (souls) and sending them to Heaven by saying, "They are already in Heaven." That is an act of usurpation, for only God has that right. We cannot resurrect people (souls) and send them to Heaven ahead of God's time. Only God has the authority and the power to resurrect people (souls) and take them to Heaven, and it will be done according to His timeline, not ours. So, this is serious error.

Do I mean to say that Christians will not go to Heaven? On the contrary, it is only a matter of when and how. Yes, Heaven can wait!

I urge my fellow pastors and preachers to discard and abandon any erroneous doctrines concerning the life to come. I am convinced that the root of this doctrine goes all the way back to the Garden of Eden, where the devil had the gall to say to Eve, *"You will not surely die"* (Genesis 3:4). She believed that lie, and when one believes a lie, what do we call that? Deceived! ✄

THE IMMORTALITY ISSUE OF THE HUMAN SOUL

Text: Genesis 2:7

This much is clear: When God formed man, He did it with dust from the ground, and then He breathed into man's nostrils the breath of life, and it was at that point that man became a living soul. Still, in mainstream Christianity, there is an issue regarding the soul of man that I find difficult to understand, and I have debated the matter with many well-meaning pastors.

Despite the clear, convincing and overwhelming evidence to the contrary, one pastor insisted that man was created immortal by God even before the Fall. It was God Himself who pronounced to Adam, *"You shall surely die"* (Genesis 2:17), and yet many continue to contradict this truth and, instead, continue to concur with the line of the serpent (the devil) who lied and deceived Eve when he insisted, *"You will not surely die"* (Genesis 3:4). There is clearly a conflict here, and someone is wrong. One side of this argument is the teaching of God, and the other is the teaching of men.

Some err when they connect this soul issue to the issue of the of man. To prove to them that man indeed was created mortal, even before he sinned against God, I told them, "Sin or no sin, man would have eventually died anyway because, by nature, he was mortal." To respond to this, they formed into two threads. The first thread challenged me to a debate on the proposition: "Was sin the cause of the death of man or not?" I was on the negative side and used Genesis 2:16-17 as the basis for my argument.

The lead debater on the opposing side opened by asking me this question: "Do you agree that sin had a consequence on Adam and Eve when they ate the fruit of the forbidden tree? "

I answered,"Yes, I do."

When my turn came to ask a question, I posed this one: "Did Adam and Eve die the same day they disobeyed God?" My opponent could not answer. I asked the same question four times with no response. Finally, I said, "If you are not willing to answer the question, then I'm out of here."

Eventually he answered, and his answer was, "No."

I said, "Then that's it. End of the debate! You just validated my position with your answer."

A definition of terms could be useful here:

- *soul*—life in the physical body
- *mortal*—subject to death
- *immortal*—not subject to death: deathless;
- *death*—the absence of life; the cessation of all vital func-tions of physical/natural life.

The Bible mentions three kinds of death: physical death, spiritual death and the second death. The mortality issue of the soul is connected with physical death. This death is not the annihilation of the soul but simply the temporary absence of life. Sometimes, in lieu of the word *death*, the Bible actually uses the word *sleep*. Jesus used this word (see John 11:11), as did Paul (see 1 Corinthians 11:30) and also Daniel (see Daniel 12:2). This *sleep* is a metaphor which suggests that one day in the future those who have died will be awakened.

Why would Jesus or Paul use this word *sleep* instead of *death*? I believe that they used this word to soften the impact and trauma of death upon bereaved loved ones.

To bring some clarification to this issue, it can help if we first know and understand the nature of man. Based on the psychological point of view, man is composed of two elements: body and soul. From the perspective of theologians, however, man is composed of three elements: spirit, soul and body. Both views are correct! This analysis, or anatomy, of the nature of man is only for the purpose of knowing and understanding the complex structure and the interrelationship of the elements of the human personality.

Man is an integrated being. He is basically a body and soul and either of these human elements is the integral and essential part of his existence. By this, I mean to say: the one can cannot survive without the other. When the word *body* is mentioned in the Bible, it is implied that the body has a soul. Conversely, when the word *soul* is mentioned, it is implicit with a body. The life of the body is the soul, and when the body dies, the soul dies as well.

The proponents of the doctrine that the soul is immortal misconstrue the meaning of Matthew 10:28, which states:

Do not fear those who kill the body but cannot kill the soul. But rather fear Him who is able to destroy both soul and body in hell.

This verse proves that the human soul is mortal and can be killed. When I asked one pastor, who is a proponent of the immortal soul, the question, "What is killed in a body?" he could not answer. This is because what is killed in a body is the soul that gives it life. Therefore, when the body is killed, the soul is also killed, and the result is physical death.

The first part of this verse, which says, *"kill the body,"* is presumed to be a killing done by men. In the second part of the verse, Jesus said, *"but is not able to kill the soul."* What did He mean by this? This part of the verse has an eschatological dimension. At that point, the soul that cannot be killed has already attained immortality. Why? Because it has already been resurrected.

This explains why there are souls in Heaven in Revelation 6:9. They have been resurrected and have become immortal, and so they are now in Heaven.

The Fall of man brought the tragic consequence of spiritual death to all mankind. So, death became a reality of life from then on, as Solomon said:

> *To everything there is a season,*
> *A time for every purpose under heaven:*
> *A time to be born,*
> *And a time to die.*   Ecclesiastes 3:1-2

Death is one appointment that no one can avoid.

261

The issue is whether or not the soul of man survives physical death. In other words: is the human soul immortal? Many pastors disagree with the definition of death I mentioned. They say that death is "separation." When I asked one of them, "What separates during death?" he answered, "The immaterial from the material." When I asked him again to elaborate on this, he did not answer. He probably is referring to the separation of the soul from the body, meaning that the soul survives death.

What is worse: according to this group, after death the soul of man (assuming he is a committed Christian) immediately goes to Heaven. This doctrine is fallacious, and it entangles the subject with much error. There is no evidence in the Bible to support this contention. Instead, this doctrine is based on conjecture and speculation and is misleading. It has no legs to stand on when subjected to direct or collateral challenge.

God is immortal, and angels are immortal too, but not man. The Bible says clearly:

The soul who sins shall die.   Ezekiel 18:4

So, when a man dies, his soul also dies. What soul are they talking about going to Heaven when it is already dead? As a rule, everyone will have to wait for the resurrection before he can attain immortality. This means that those Christians and Old Testament saints who have died already will not be conscious until their time of resurrection. ✄

ର **49** ଛ

ETERNAL AND EVERLASTING LIFE ELABORATED

Text: John 3:14-16

And as Moses lifted up the serpent in the wilderness, even so must the Son of Man be lifted up, that whoever believes in Him should not perish but[a] have eternal life. For God so loved the world that He gave His only begotten Son, that whoever believes in Him should not perish but have everlasting life.

This periscope from the conversation between Jesus and Nicodemus was the culmination of the subject of being born again. Having eternal and everlasting life are consequential blessings and benefits of being born again. Without these, the Christian life is a futile experience.

Who was Nicodemus? He was a man of the Pharisees, a ruler of the Jews, who came to Jesus by night. The Pharisees were a prominent sect of the Jews during the time of Christ. They were opposed to Jesus and His teachings and plotted to kill Him. They were also denounced by Jesus.

Most of the Pharisees were critical of Jesus. They were legalistic and hypocritical, but Nicodemus was curiously intrigued and fascinated by Jesus due to the miracles that He did. So, he clandestinely came to Jesus by night.

When Nicodemus heard the response of Jesus to his opening statements, he was unable to comprehend Jesus' answer. It was mind-boggling to him, as if were a riddle. That is why he asked, *"How can a man be born when he is old? Can he enter the second time into his mother's womb?"* (John 3:4).

After Jesus explained to Nicodemus the process of being born again, with illustration by analogy, he still could not understand the meaning. He then answered and said unto Him, *"How can these things be?"* (John 3:9).

Now Nicodemus was mildly rebuked by Jesus, *"Are you the teacher of Israel, and do not know these things?"* (John 3:10). Jesus was talking to Nicodemus about God's redemptive remedy for man and His statements set the precedent for the salvation of all mankind.

Since Nicodemus could not yet understand what Jesus was talking about, Jesus had to use another illustration of God's redemptive plan, and He told a story that was well-known among the Jews of that time. The story concerned an incident that occurred when the Israelites, in their wilderness journey, were bitten by poisonous snakes and many of them died. It was the Lord who had sent those poisonous snakes, and He had done it because the people had complained against God and against Moses. They said, *"Why have you brought us out of Egypt to die here in the wilderness?"* and *"There is nothing to eat here and nothing to drink. And we hate this horrible manna!"* (Numbers 21:5, NLT).

When the snakes came, the people realized what they had done:

Then the people came to Moses and cried out, "We have sinned by speaking against the Lord and against you. Pray that the Lord will take away the snakes."   Numbers 21:7, NLT

Moses prayed for the people, and the Lord told him what to have the people do to be saved. His instructions were:

Make a replica of a poisonous snake and attach it to a pole. All who are bitten will live if they simply look at it!

Numbers 21:8, NLT

And it worked just as the Lord had said. Those who looked upon the bronze replica of the snakes were spared.

This was what Jesus was alluding to when He said, *"And as Moses in the wilderness lifted up the bronze image of a serpent on a pole, even so I must be lifted up upon a pole, so that anyone who believes in me will have eternal life"* (John 3:14-15, TLB). He was implying that His crucifixion would redeem mankind from sin and punishment. All that was required was that men and women look to Him.

Now, is there a difference between receiving eternal life and everlasting life as a consequence of our faith in Jesus Christ? Or do these two terms mean the same thing? The answer is that they are different and do not mean the same thing.

The secular meaning of eternal life is "life without end or endless life." So, why do Christians die if they already have eternal life after receiving Jesus Christ as their personal Lord and Savior? Eternal life is the God-kind of life which is a privilege imparted to any man or woman who believes in Jesus Christ.

Only God is eternal; we are not. When one is born again what he receives is a qualitative aspect of eternal life. Everlasting life, on the other hand, is the quantitative aspect of the promised eternal life, and it will commence after the Rapture of the Church and the Resurrection of those who have died in Christ.

I believe that the promise of eternal life because of our relationship with our Lord Jesus Christ has two aspects: the qualitative and the quantitative. What we received when we believed in Jesus is the qualitative aspect of eternal life, which is akin to the "likeness" of God in man that he lost when he sinned in the Garden of Eden. Now, that likeness is restored to man through faith in Jesus Christ.

The quantitative aspect, however, is not yet ours; it is for the future. The qualitative eternal life is an earnest of the latter, meaning that it is the assurance of the future quantitative eternal life. This makes the promise of God binding for us.

The big challenge for Christians now is how to nurture and develop this qualitative aspect of eternal life in our daily lives so that we become like Christ. This is the goal of our Christian life here on Earth.

This qualitative eternal life, however, does not guarantee Christians that they will never die. The reason is that we are still mortal. The exception will be when Jesus returns.

This biblical perspective is consistent with the intent of God regarding the natural and spiritual status of man when He created him (even before the Fall). Although man was created *"in the image and likeness of God,"* this did not mean that man would never die.

Man was created mortal. If man were immortal, as many believe and teach, then why did God say to Adam that he would *"surely die"* if he ate fruit from the forbidden tree?

There are two meanings to this pronouncement of God to man: *"You will surely die!"* By the way, what kind of death was God referring to? It was a spiritual death. Sin was not the cause of the physical death of man; it has always been man's nature to die. Why? Because he was created mortal. So, sin or no sin, man was going to die anyway.

The first death is expressed, and the second is implied. The expressed one was punitive, which means that it was a punishment for the violation of God's command. The implied meaning was God's pronouncement of the nature of man, that he was mortal.

The likeness of God in man enabled him to behave like God. Sadly, however, man lost this divine imprint when he disobeyed God. Because God is eternal (qualitatively and quantitatively) and because He in-breathed man, many have come to the conclusion that man was also immortal. This is a serious fallacy that entangles this subject with much error.

When Jesus said, *"I am the resurrection and the life. He who believes in Me, though he may die, he shall live. 26 And whoever lives and believes in Me shall never die"* (John 11:25-26), what He meant in found John 3:16:

> *For God so loved the world that He gave His only begotten Son, that whoever believes in Him should not perish but have everlasting life.*

This *"everlasting life"* is the quantitative eternal life that Jesus was talking about. As the word *everlasting* suggests, it means "a life without ending." So, when will this commence? This will commence at the Second Coming of Jesus Christ! Those who have died in Christ will be resurrected, never to die again. Those who are still alive will be suddenly changed and will then live forever (see 1 Thessalonians 4:13-18), when *"this mortal must put on immortality"* (1 Corinthians 15:53). This is the quantitative eternal life. Praise God! And glory to His name!

It is indispensable that if anyone wants to have eternal life, (qualitative now and everlasting [quantitative] after the Rapture and Resurrection), he must receive Jesus Christ as his personal Lord and Savior, after repenting of his sins because this eternal life is only in Jesus Christ. The Bible says:

For the wages of sin is death, but the gift of God is eternal life in Christ Jesus our Lord. Romans 6:23

Nor is there salvation in any other, for there is no other name under heaven given among men by which we must be saved.

Acts 4:12

Behold, now is the accepted time; behold, now is the day of salvation. 2 Corinthians 6:2

For what profit is it to a man if he gains the whole world, and loses his own soul? Or what will a man give in exchange for his soul? Matthew 16:26

⌘ **50** ⌘

THE IMAGE AND LIKENESS OF GOD IN MAN

Text: Genesis 1:26

Image and *likeness* ... Many believe that when man fell into sin, he lost one of these two divine imprints. The question is: which of the two was lost during the Fall?

I believe that what was lost was the likeness, and my evidence for this position is found in Genesis 9:6:

> *Whoever sheds man's blood,*
> *By man his blood shall be shed;*
> *For in the image of God*
> *He made man.*

Notice that only the phrase *image of God* is used here, not the phrase *likeness of God*. What does this tell us? Regardless of whether or not a person is a follower of Christ, he or she still bears the image of God. That's why we are forbidden by God to commit murder, because, in doing so, we strike the very image of God. The exception, of course, is self-defense.

What, then, is this image that we all have? Besides being a pastor, I am an amateur photographer, and what I know about an image is that it is a photo or a picture of something or someone. On this basis, I believe that you and I look like God, who has a body, with head, hands, feet, eyes, nose, ears and mouth. That is why Jesus, who was and is God, appeared on the Earth looking like a man. In other words, this is the physical and the psychological feature of man which constitutes the human soul.

And what about *likeness*? This is the God-likeness of man which was lost in the Fall. Man was complete before the Fall; he was spirit, soul and body (see 1 Thessalonians 5:23).

The spirit of man is distinct from his soul. The spirit is the human element whereby he is conscious and in contact with God, the true God, Jesus Christ. The soul, which is the self-consciousness of man, has three areas: the mind, the emotions and the will.

The body is the world-consciousness of man: feel, touch and see. It was in the area of the spirit of man that this godlikeness resided, but when man sinned, his spirit died. Since then man has been spiritually dead, even if he is physically alive. Paul explained that before we knew Christ, we were *"dead in [our] trespasses and sins"* (Ephesians 2:1).

The death contemplated as a consequence of sin was not physical but spiritual. Adam and Eve did not die physically at the moment they sinned against God, but they did die spiritually. And spiritual death is much worse than physical death. Spiritual death has eternal consequence, whereas physical death has only temporal consequences.

Have you ever heard someone say, "You look like your father, but you don't behave like him?" This is exactly the spiritual condition of man without Christ.

So how do we recover this likeness of God? Jesus said:

You must be born again. John 3:7

That which is born of the flesh is flesh, and that which is born of the Spirit is spirit. John 3:6

The words that I speak to you are spirit, and they are life. John 6:63

Man shall not live by bread alone, but by every word that proceeds from the mouth of God. Matthew 4:4

I am the bread of life. John 6:35

When the incarnate Word, who is Jesus Christ, is preached to people, the message of that Word is a spiritual seed which germinates in the soul of a man or woman so that they become born again. Thus, everyone who receives Jesus Christ into their lives has been granted the right to be a child of God.

The apostle Peter wrote:

For you have been born again, not of perishable seed, but of imperishable, through the living and enduring word of God. 1 Peter 1:23, NIV

After the new birth, the lost divine imprint of the likeness of God in man is restored to a faithful, obedient and devoted Christian. Thus, the ideal Christian is like Christ. He thinks, speaks, behaves and lives like Jesus Christ, who always delighted to do the will of the father, and he does not continue in sin because God's seed remains in him (see 1 John 3:9).

Question: did some people in the Old Testament also recover the lost divine imprint of the likeness of God? I believe so. Retroactively, the Gospel was also preached to them, and those who believed by faith were justified (saved). One good example was Abraham. He was declared righteous because of his faith in God. When God spoke to him, Abraham was obedient to God, and this obedience was the effect of his spirit being restored to him through faith. That was the reason he responded so positively when God spoke to him.

Another example was David, who was dubbed as *"a man after his [God's] own heart"* (1 Samuel 13:14). David often had struggles and conflicts with his soul, but his spirit, which was restored and thus alive and strong in the Lord, prevailed over his soul.

For example, David said, *"Bless the Lord, O my soul"* (Psalm 103:1). In another instance, he said, *"Why are you cast down, O my soul?"* (Psalm 42:5). Who was talking to David's soul? It was his spirit!

Yes, like Abraham and David, we have our own weaknesses, struggles and conflicts, but we can overcome those—if we are strong in the Lord. And how can we become strong in the Lord? We must remain in Christ and He in us. We must continually and regularly nourish and feed ourselves with the pure spiritual milk of the Word of God so that we will grow up in our salvation. We must not compromise with sin and evil, but we must abhor those and cleave to that which is good.

I say then: Walk in the Spirit, and you shall not fulfill the lust of the flesh [sinful nature].   Ephesians 5:16

In other words, we must not allow our soul to dominate our spirit, but our spirit must be dominant. There is an ongoing conflict between these two. So, if something inside you tells you to get up and go to church, to serve and worship God today because it is Sunday, that's good. It means that your spirit is alive.

If, on the other hand, something inside you tells you, "Sleep on. It's Sunday. Relax, there's no office or work today," that's not good. Either your spirit is dead or your soul is dominating.

What are the acts of the sinful nature? They are sexual immorality, impurity and debauchery, idolatry and witchcraft, hatred, discord, jealousy, fits of rage, envy, drunkenness, orgies and the like (see Galatians 5:19-21). In the Scriptures, this is followed by a serious warning:

I warn you, as I did before, that those who live like this will not inherit the kingdom of God.   Galatians 5:21

And a serious admonition:

Since we live by the Spirit, let us keep in step with the Spirit.

Galatians 5:25

CR **51** ∞

COMPACT AND CONCISE CHRISTIANITY

Text: 1 Corinthians 13:13

Christianity is all about faith, hope and love. These three are intertwined and complement each other. Faith without love is nothing (see 1 Corinthians 13:2). Love always hopes, and faith is the evidence of the things we hope for (see Hebrews 11:1).

What is a Christian's faith? It is one segment of these three Christian doctrines that deal with the Christians' (the followers of Christ's) trust or confidence in God through His Son Jesus Christ. Primarily, it has something to do with the salvation of man through the redemptive work of Christ on the cross of Calvary. We are saved by grace through faith in Jesus Christ (see Ephesians 2:8).

Faith is also the belief in the living God. Although we don't see Him, His power is evident through His creation. The reality of God is bolstered by the revelation of the incarnate Son of God and by the documentary evidence of the Holy Bible, which is the Word of God.

Faith encompasses and governs the entire life of a follower of Christ. The way he thinks or speaks and how he behaves or conducts himself in every relationship or situation is a practice of his faith.

This is not a blind faith, as some suggest, because a Christian is guided by the Word of God and by the Holy Spirit. He has knowledge and understanding of what the will of God is relative to his actions and decisions. It is through faith that we believe in God, and that's why we go to church and worship Him. It is through faith that we pray, because we believe that God answers prayer. It is through faith that we share with others the Good News of salvation in Jesus Christ. It is impossible to please God without faith (see Hebrews 11:6), and God rewards us when we believe.

But the most prominent among these three is love. Why? Because, according to Paul, it is love that validates all other Christian gifts — including faith. Without love, the other gifts would all amount to nothing.

God is love (see 1 John 4:8), and because every Christian is filled with God the Holy Spirit, he is also filled with God's love. This kind of love is more profound than the kind of love everybody is talking about today in our modern world, especially during holidays like Valentine's Day. That is the world's love, but this is the God-kind of love, which is characterized by sacrifice. Jesus went to the cross because God loves every one of us.

The Christian's love acts in two directions. First, it acts toward God (vertically) and then toward our fellow being (horizontally). This is consistent with what Jesus said when He summarized the Ten Commandments into two:

"You shall love the Lord your God with all your heart, with all your soul, and with all your mind." This is the first and great commandment. And the second is like it: "You shall love your neighbor as yourself."   Matthew 22:37-39

The image that is formed from the two directions of a Christian's love forms a cross. I believe this is what Jesus meant when He said:

If anyone desires to come after Me, let him deny himself, and take up his cross, and follow Me.   Matthew 16:24

The Christian's love of God forms his lifetime devotion and dedication, but as followers of Christ, Christians also love one another. In fact, Christians are the most loving, caring, generous, patient and helpful people in the world. The most loving husbands, wives, children and families are Christians. Christians even love their enemies. How do they show this? By doing good to them.

A Christian's hope is something that is expected to happen in the future. We always look forward to something good and positive. Our hope is based on the promises of God in the Bible. There is a temporal hope, and there is an ultimate (eternal) hope. Despite the many trials and hardships of life, Christians are the most hopeful people in the world. They are blessed with perseverance in education, hard work, diligence, honesty, savings and blessings—all through Divine Providence. Christians are always hopeful of a better life, both here in this world and also in the world to come. They live in sufficiency and contentment with peace and joy in the Lord.

Of course, the ultimate Christian hope is otherwise known as *"the Blessed Hope"*:

For the grace of God that brings salvation has appeared to all men, teaching us that, denying ungodliness and worldly lusts, we should live soberly, righteously, and godly in the present age, looking for THE BLESSED HOPE and glorious appearing of our great God and Savior Jesus Christ, who gave Himself for us, that He might redeem us from every lawless deed and purify for Himself His own special people, zealous for good works. Speak these things. Titus 2:11-15, Emphasis Mine

Christ's return will be one of the greatest events in history. It will be at that time when those who have died in Christ will be resurrected, and those who are alive will be changed and given glorified bodies. Then, together, we will all meet the Lord in the air and go to be with Him in Heaven:

For this we say to you by the word of the Lord, that we who are alive and remain until the coming of the Lord will by no means precede those who are asleep. For the Lord Himself will descend from heaven with a shout, with the voice of an archangel, and with the trumpet of God. And the dead in Christ will rise first. Then we who are alive and remain shall be caught up together with them in the clouds to meet the Lord in the air. And thus we shall always be with the Lord. Therefore comfort one another with these words.   1 Thessalonians 4:15-18

This will be the moment John spoke of in Revelation:

And God will wipe away every tear from their eyes; there shall be no more death, nor sorrow, nor crying. There shall be no more pain, for the former things have passed away.   Revelation 21:4

Jesus is coming again—and soon! Are you ready to meet Him? Don't be left behind. If you are not ready yet, then today is your day of salvation. Don't wait for tomorrow, when it may be too late. Call upon the Lord now. Ask His forgiveness for your sins, and receive Him as your Lord and Savior, and you will be saved.

Once you have done that, choose to live for Him the rest of your life, for the best is yet to come!   �֎

CONSTANTLY CONTENTED CHRISTIANS

Text: Hebrews 13:5

One of the moral imperatives for Christians has always been contentment. The writer to the Hebrews advised: *"Be content with such things as you have "* Why? Because God has said that He will never leave us or forsake us.

When John the Baptist preached to the people of his day about God's judgment coming unless they showed fruits of repentance, the people responded by asking him:

What shall we do then?   Luke 3:10

When soldiers who were present asked him that question, he responded:

Do not intimidate anyone or accuse falsely, and be content with your wages.   Luke 3:14

279

The exhortation in Hebrews 13 to Christians to be content is also connected to the issue of money. Paul added to this by stating:

And having food and clothing, with these we shall be content. But those who desire to be rich fall into temptation and a snare, and into many foolish and harmful lusts which drown men in destruction and perdition. For the love of money is a root of all kinds of evil, for which some have strayed from the faith in their greediness, and pierced themselves through with many sorrows.

1 Timothy 6:8-10

This was exactly what happened to Judas, one of the original disciples of our Lord Jesus Christ. Judas loved money, so he betrayed, or sold, Jesus for thirty pieces of silver. In so doing, he plunged himself into perdition.

What is the opposite of contentment? It is covetousness. It is greed. It is the insatiable desire for one to acquire money and things which are not your own, even to the prejudice of other people. The reality of this avarice fills not only the headlines of our media today, but the whole of modern society. Corruption has become the culture of the day. The morality of so many people is all about money, lots of it.

What is disgusting, disgraceful and revolting is when those who are supposed to be respected lawmakers and law-enforcers are the ones who become lawbreakers themselves. For example, here in our country legislators were indicted for plundering government funds in the amount of more than ₱50 million and policemen had to be apprehended because they were suspected of crimes of robbery (*hulidap*), extortion, murder and kidnapping for ransom. Too often, our government systems are filled with corruption, and there is only one reason for all of this systematic hooligan-ism — the love of money.

Followers of Christ are precluded from engaging in or be-ing involved in any form of covetousness. The Bible states emphatically: *"Thou shalt not covet"* (Exodus 20:17, KJV). Why? Because if you covet, you will also cheat, lie and steal.

The tragic story of Achan in the book of Joshua is a stern warning, not only to Christians, but also to all people every-where, of the evil consequences of covetousness. He confessed:

When I saw among the spoils a beautiful Babylonian garment, two hundred shekels of silver, and a wedge of gold weighing fifty shekels, I coveted them and took them. And there they are, hid-den in the earth in the midst of my tent, with the silver under it.

Joshua 7:21

It was a fatal mistake for Achan, for it not only cost him his life, it cost the lives of his children as well. His sin of covetousness also brought defeat to Israel at the hand of her enemies that day.

Christians, whether they are poor or rich, are the most contented people in the world. This means they are satisfied with whatever they have, in terms of money or the things they possess. They do not cheat, lie or steal other people's money or things. They are the most honest and trustworthy people on earth. Whereas covetous people only think of what they can get from other people and how they can get it, Christians are always thinking of what they can give to others and how, especially to the poor and needy. Christians are generous and kind people.

Why are Christians so contented? The answer goes back to our original text. It is because God has said that He will never leave us or forsake us. David knew it and sang:

The LORD is my shepherd;
I shall not want.   Psalm 23:1

One of the names of God is Jehovah Jireh (God who provides). That's why Christians don't worry about what they will eat or drink or what they will wear because our heavenly Father knows our needs (see Matthew 6:25). God has promised to meet all your needs according to His glorious riches in Christ Jesus (see Philippians 4:19).

Jesus said it this way:

But seek first the kingdom of God and His righteousness, and all
these things shall be added to you.   Matthew 6:33

As Paul wrote to Timothy:

Godliness with contentment is great gain.   1 Timothy 6:6

○ʒ **53** ℬ

PRAYERS THAT PREVAIL

Text: Matthew 6:9-13

As Christians, we believe in prayer. This is one of our essential Christian practices. We pray because our God is alive, and He hears and answers our prayers. But why is it that so many of our prayers seem to be ineffective and go unanswered? Let us examine some possible reasons.

One of the reasons our payers may be ineffective and un-answered is because they are lacking in form and substance. Our Lord Jesus Christ taught us how to pray, and this is how a Christian should pray. This prayer is known to many as "The Lord's Prayer," but I prefer to call it "The Christians' Prayer." It is a pattern, or a model, for our prayers.

First of all, we should address God as our Father when we pray. Addressing God as Father in prayers has many far-reaching impli-cations or benefits for us. We must acknowledge Him as Sovereign and as our Creator, etc. It is only then that we should mention our various needs. Some of them are physical, others are financial or material, and there are prayer needs which require supernatural intervention. Finally, all these things must be concluded by asking in the name of Jesus.

Jesus Himself said:

Whatever you ask in My name, that I will do, that the Father may be glorified in the Son. John 14:13

In that day you will ask in My name. John 16:26

We must learn how to properly pray. Just as Jesus taught His disciples to pray, pastors are tasked with teaching their members to pray. We cannot just assume that when a person is already saved they will automatically know how to pray. Most prayers that I hear are copy-cat prayers, improper prayers and prayers full of redundancy and nonsense. Sometimes we wish that the person praying would stop or that they had never prayed at all.

Some people make prayer an art. Their prayers are dotted with much repetition and flowery language that means very little. The truth is that we are precluded by the Lord from using this kind of language in prayer. Jesus taught:

And when you pray, you shall not be like the hypocrites. For they love to pray standing in the synagogues and on the corners of the streets, that they may be seen by men. Matthew 6:5

And when you pray, do not use vain repetitions as the heathen do. For they think that they will be heard for their many words.

Matthew 6:7

Some Christians even shout when they pray. God is not deaf, so you don't need to shout at Him. Speak politely to God.

Others pray without ever opening their mouths or uttering words. This is not prayer; it is meditation. People do this especially when they pray before eating in a restaurant. Are they embarrassed to pray? Or do they simply not know how to pray?

If we want our prayers to be more powerful and more effective, besides the aforementioned proper form and substance, try coupling prayer with fasting. When the disciples of our Lord asked Him why they were unsuccessful in casting out demons, His answer was:

This kind can come out by nothing but prayer and fasting.

Mark 9:9

Try it. You'll be surprised.

∝ **54** ∞

RICH MAN, POOR MAN
(A REVERSAL OF FORTUNES)

Text: Matthew 19:23-24

Why did Jesus pronounce these strong words against the rich? This was His response concerning the rich young man who came to Him asking how he could obtain eternal life. The man was told by Jesus to sell his possessions and give the proceeds to the poor and follow Him, so that he would have treasures in Heaven. But the man was unhappy when he heard this, and he turned away sorrowful. The reason? Because he had great possessions.

What happened to that rich man? He went back to his business, and he had bumper harvests on his farms. He had so much produce that he had to tear down his barns and build larger ones in order to store all of his grain and goods. Then he said to his soul, "Soul, you have plenty of goods laid up for many years. Relax, eat and have a good time" (see Luke 12:16-21).

The rich man was enjoying his success, buying the best clothes and having sumptuous meals every day, but there was also a poor man, and this poor man came to the rich man's house to beg:

> *But there was a certain beggar named Lazarus, full of sores, who was laid at his gate, desiring to be fed with the crumbs which fell from the rich man's table. Moreover the dogs came and licked his sores.* Luke 16:20

Subsequently, Lazarus died and was carried by the angels into Abraham's bosom. The rich man also died:

> *The rich man also died and was buried, and his soul went to the place of the dead. There, in torment, he saw Abraham in the far distance with Lazarus at his side. The rich man shouted, "Father Abraham, have some pity! Send Lazarus over here to dip the tip of his finger in water and cool my tongue. I am in anguish in these flames."*
>
> *But Abraham said to him, "Son, remember that during your lifetime you had everything you wanted, and Lazarus had nothing. So now he is here being comforted, and you are in anguish."* Luke 16:22-25, NLT

What a reversal of fortunes!

As Jesus said:

> *For what will it profit a man if he gains the whole world, and loses his own soul?* Mark 8:36

When Jesus said that it would be difficult for a rich man to enter into the Kingdom of Heaven, the disciples were very surprised and asked Him:

Who then can be saved?   Matthew 19:25

His answer was this:

With men this is impossible; but with God all things are possible.   Matthew 19:26

We all need God to save us. That's why He sent His Son that whoever believes in Him might have eternal life. What must you do? Repent of your sins now and receive Jesus as your personal Lord and Savior. Find a Bible-believing church. Serve God and fellowship with the family of God. Follow Jesus the rest of your life, and you will be saved.

If you are a Christian, do not desire to be rich. Why? Because in order to achieve your desire, you will be tempted to lie, to cheat, to steal and to defraud other people, putting your soul at risk. If a Christian is diligent, industrious and smart, and God blesses him so that he becomes rich, then that is all right.

If you are a rich Christian, do not be proud or trust in your riches, but in God who is the Source of all riches. Be rich in doing charitable works, thereby laying up for yourself treasures in Heaven. These kinds of treasures have eternal values.   ✄

SIGNS, SPECTACLES AND SYMBOLS

Text: Exodus 7:3

The reluctant and hesitant Moses finally decided to return to Egypt and deliver the Israelites out of Egyptian bondage. Prior to this decision, he had made excuses as to why he could not go back there. Two of his excuses were: 1) They will not believe me or listen to me, and 2) I have a speech impediment. So, what convinced Moses and changed his mind? The Lord demonstrated to him miraculous signs in response to his excuses.

For the first sign, the Lord told Moses to throw his staff on the ground. When he did this, it turned into a snake, and he ran from it. Then the Lord told him to take the snake by the tail, and when he did this, it turned into a staff again.

For the second sign, the Lord told Moses to put his hand under his cloak, and when he took his hand out, it had become leprous. When he put his hand back in and then took it out again, it was restored. Then the Lord said to him:

And it shall be, if they do not believe even these two signs, or listen to your voice, that you shall take water from the river and pour it on the dry land. The water which you take from the river will become blood on the dry land. Exodus 4:9

Convinced and confident with these signs, Moses went back to Egypt. He would first have to persuade the Israelites and then persuade Pharaoh, King of Egypt, regarding God's plan of deliverance for His people.

Upon his arrival, Moses was met by his brother Aaron, and they gathered together all the elders of Israel. Aaron relayed to them everything the Lord had said to Moses. He also performed the signs before them, and they believed, bowed down and worshipped.

But when Moses and Aaron went to Pharaoh and told him that God had said, *"Let My people go,"* he refused and, instead, made the labor of the Israelites harsher, imposing even heavier burdens on them. Because of these aggravating circumstances, the Israelites no longer wanted to listen to Moses. They were discouraged by reason of the cruel bondage exacted by Pharaoh.

Moses and Aaron returned to Pharaoh, and they were asked to perform a miracle. Aaron threw his staff in front of Pharaoh, and it became a snake. This was imitated by Pharaoh's magicians, but their snakes were swallowed up by Aaron's snake. Still, the result was disappointing:

And Pharaoh's heart grew hard, and he did not heed them, as the Lord had said. Exodus 7:13

Now God had to demonstrate His spectacle, otherwise known as the Ten Plagues of Egypt. They were the plagues of blood, frogs, gnats, flies, diseased livestock, boils, hail, locusts, darkness and, finally, the plague on the firstborn. In the beginning of these plagues, Pharaoh's magicians tried to imitate them, but soon they gave up and declared: *"This is the finger of God"* (Exodus 8:19).

It is interesting to note that during these calamities, the Lord made a distinction between the Egyptians and the Israelites. While there was tremendous devastation among all of the Egyptians, no one among the Israelites suffered. This was a sign in itself.

Crucial and decisive among these plagues was the death of the firstborn, also known as the Passover. This was the last of the plagues, and it killed all the firstborn of the Egyptians, including the firstborn of Pharaoh, together with their firstborn animals.

The passing of the death angel did not adversely affect the Israelites. The Lord had instructed Moses and Aaron to prepare special lambs, about a year old and without defect, for that particular evening. Each Israelite household must take one of those lambs and kill it at twilight. They were to take some blood from their lamb and put it on the sides and tops of the door frames of the houses, where they would eat the lamb roasted. This blood was to be a sign, and when the Lord saw the blood, no destructive plague would touch His people.

The Lord proceeded to strike down all the firstborn in Egypt that night at the stroke of midnight, including the firstborn of Pharaoh, and so there was death in every Egyptian home that night. Finally, it was too much for Pharaoh to bear, and he released the Israelites and gave them their freedom. This was a day that Israel would commemorate for generations to come—a lasting ordinance, a festival unto the Lord.

What have these Old Testament narratives got to do with us contemporary Christians? Is there any relevance or significance to our Christian faith? What about those signs, the spectacle and the symbols? Are these important or helpful? The answer is affirmative. As followers of Christ, we must understand that the Old and New Testaments are intertwined. Whereas, to the early Christians, the Old Testament was sacred Scripture, to us contemporary Christians, we recognize both the Old and New Testaments as our sacred Scriptures.

Now, are signs or miracles still relevant or significant today? Simply put, does God do miracles or heal people today through His servants? Many people, including many Christians, say that the days of miracles are over, but I still believe in miracles because our God is a God of miracles.

Among the fastest-growing Christian churches during this and the past century have been the various Pentecostal groups. We can observe their phenomenal evangelistic success in North and South America and Europe, but also in Asia and Africa. The reason, I believe, for their dramatic success is their evangelistic strategy. Their Gospel persuasion is coupled with signs and wonders. After preaching the Gospel and challenging people to commit their lives to Christ, they always conclude with prayer for the sick and for miracles. If people do not yet believe their message, then the signs of healing and miracles will validate the veracity of their words.

This was the same predicament Moses faced. He was afraid that his own people, as well as Pharaoh, would not believe him or listen to him. God used the same signs that had convinced Moses to take on the task to convince the Israelites and Pharaoh. Jesus said:

If I do not do the works of My Father, do not believe Me; but if I do, though you do not believe Me, believe the works, that you may know and believe that the Father is in Me, and I in Him.

John 10:37-38

Of course, if there is a genuine miracle, then there is also a fake one, just as there are true prophets and false prophets. The false always wants to copy the true. Fakes are everywhere, even today.

How about symbols? The Bible is filled with many symbols. Some of them are difficult to interpret. Sometimes those symbols are also known as "shadows." For instance, the Passover lamb was a symbol, or shadow, of Jesus Christ, the Lamb of God who takes away the sins of the world. His suffering, His death on the cross and the shedding of His blood were acts of redemption. Peter wrote:

You were not redeemed with corruptible things, like silver or gold, from your aimless conduct received by tradition from your fathers, but with the precious blood of Christ, as of a lamb without blemish and without spot.   1 Peter 1:18-19

Just as the firstborn of the Israelites were spared from death that Passover night because they appropriated the blood of a sacrificial lamb on their door frames, so also everyone who believes in Jesus Christ will not perish but will have eternal life.

We Christians remember the redemptive sacrifice of our Lord Jesus Christ in the Communion, one of our traditional

Christian worship rituals. The bread which is broken and taken by members symbolizes the body of Christ, and the wine symbolizes His blood. Thus, every Christian partakes of Christ's sacrifice in Communion. ✄

❧ **56** ☙

LOVE OR LUST?

Text: 1 John 2:15-16

One of the hallmarks of Christianity is having love toward others. The God whom we Christians worship and serve is a God of love. Followers of Christ are mandated to love God with all their heart, their mind, their soul, their strength and also to love their neighbors as themselves. It is love that validates all the grace of gifts in the Church. Without love, the exercise of gifts mean nothing. That is how important love is to the Christian faith.

Not all love, however, is acceptable to God. There is a wrong kind of love that Christians are precluded from being involved with. This is the *"love of the world."* The word *world* in this passage does not refer to the physical world that God created. And neither does it refer to the world of mankind, because God loves both of these worlds. For example, the Bible shows that we are *in* the world [the physical world and mankind], but we are not *of* this world [the worldly system]. Jesus said:

295

They are not of the world, just as I am not of the world.

John 17:16

This has reference to systems like "the world of entertainment," the "world of sports," the "world of business," etc. It refers to the trends and cultures of the people of this world who are opposed to God and are influenced and inspired by the devil, who is the god of this world. Such systems or lifestyles are contrary to God and His order. These are characterized by lust and wickedness.

The 2014 case of the murder of the Filipino race-car driver, Ferdinand "Enzo" Pastor is relevant to this divine injunction. The "love" of the wife's alleged lover was a wrong kind of love. She was a married woman, so the man had no right to love her. When a man loves a woman who is married, that love is driven by lust—the lust of the flesh and the lust of the eyes. It is immoral, illicit and illegal. In this case, it was also deadly, because the result was that her husband was murdered. This is one situation where divorce (although I personally don't like it) might have been a more acceptable option. It might have been a lesser evil or, as some say, "a necessary evil." Instead of killing a mate, we should live and let live. Let the guilty party stand before the law and before God.

What happened to Enzo is nothing new. There was a similar case of a dangerous love triangle a long time ago in the Bible involving King David, a woman named Bathsheba and her husband Uriah. David lusted after Bathsheba, even after he knew that she was a married woman. In order to legitimize his relationship with her, he devised a sinister plot to murder Uriah. Conveniently, Uriah was killed in the heat of battle against Israel's enemies.

But this thing that David had done displeased the Lord. David's love for the woman trumped his love for God, and through the prophet Nathan, God sternly rebuked David because of his sin. Although David repented of his sin and regretted his actions, the price he paid in pain, agony and untold misery were not worth the pleasure of his misadventure with Bathsheba. His deep remorse for his sin is reflected in Psalm 51, for he was saved by the grace and mercy of God, but four of David's children perished, some of them in a scandalous manner, all as a consequences of his sinful lust.

How can anyone determine the difference between love and lust? When any love for a woman or man has a sign over it which says FORBIDDEN (in Tagalog, *BAWAL*) and you get involved anyway, that is lust.

But how do we know that it is forbidden? It is forbidden when the object of your love, whether a man or a woman, is married. This is a divine injunction, and it also applies to things like money, for example:

For the love of money is a root of all kinds of evil, for which some have strayed from the faith in their greediness, and pierced themselves through with many sorrows. 1 Timothy 6:10

How can anyone avoid lust? The Bible says:

Walk in the Spirit, and you shall not fulfill the lust of the flesh.

Galatians 5:16

This is akin to the command to *"walk by faith and not by sight"* (2 Corinthians 5:7). This means that Christians are motivated by the Word of God. His Word is His Spirit. Jesus said:

> *It is the Spirit who gives life; the flesh profits nothing. The words* *that I speak to you are spirit, and they are life.*   John 6:63

Christians must not be motivated by what they see, feel, think or want. Love or lust? You have been warned! Don't be stupid! Be wise and stay away from trouble—big trouble! �֎

THE FUNDAMENTALS OF OUR CHRISTIAN PRAYER

Text: Matthew 6:7-13

All religions have some form of prayer. It is one of the common ritual practices among all faiths, and that includes our Christian faith.

What is prayer? Prayer is communication with God. For Christians, however, prayer is more than just talking with God. It involves faith, worship, confession, adoration, praise, thanksgiving and dedicated action. Prayer can make a difference in our lives and in the lives of others. That's why we need to know and understand the fundamentals of Christian prayer so that our prayers are acceptable to God and therefore effective.

After Jesus had finished praying one day, one of His disciples asked Him, *"Lord, teach us to pray, as John also taught his disciples"* (Luke 11:1). In response, Jesus first warned the disciples against the futility of copy-cat prayers, which are motivated by hypocrisy and filled with meaningless redundancy.

Sad to say, you can hear prayers like that today in many Christian churches. Even pastors sometimes pray like this. For example, some pray:

- "Lord, I thank You that You brought me to this place." What, are you a robot?

- "Lord, I know that You are a good God because God is good all the time, and all the time God is good. Hallelujah! Praise God!"

- "Lord, heal so and so because You are our healing God! Glory to God!"

- "Lord, I give back all the glory to You. Amen!" What, did you borrow God's glory while you were praying? God will not give His glory to anyone!

It is all right to copy correct prayers, but not when a prayer is wrong! When Jesus taught His disciples to pray, He said:

In this manner, therefore, pray:

Our Father in heaven,

Hallowed be Your name.

Your kingdom come.

Your will be done

On earth as it is in heaven.

Give us this day our daily bread.

And forgive us our debts,

As we forgive our debtors.

And do not lead us into temptation,

But deliver us from the evil one.

For Yours is the kingdom and the power and the glory forever. Amen.

This is commonly called "the Lord's Prayer," but I prefer to call it "The Christian's Prayer" because it is Christians who are to use it.

However, we are not to pray this prayer verbatim. It is not a prayer to be memorized and repeated over and over. Rather it is a model for prayer. In modern terms, this is a *template* for prayer. Jesus said, *"In this manner, therefore, pray,"* meaning "Pray like this."

This prayer pattern is implicit with form and substance, which, when carefully observed, will make our Christian prayers easier and more meaningful. The form is the structure, the skeleton or the framework. Let's simplify this form into Step 1, Step 2 and Step 3.

Step 1 is the beginning of the Christian prayer.

Our Father in heaven: According to Jesus, we must address our prayers to our heavenly Father. It is unfortunate that many Christians do not follow this. Addressing God as *"heavenly Father"* in our prayers has significant implications. First of all, it establishes an intimate relationship between us and God. God is our Father by means of creation, and He is our Father through redemption in Jesus Christ. We must also acknowledge God's sovereignty and power including His will in our lives. This will

301

require knowledge and understanding of our God and also of His Word.

Step 2 is focused on our human needs.

What do we need? What are our basic requirements? Basically, we need food, clothing, shelter, money and good health.

We also need love and forgiveness. We also need peace and freedom from fear. Most of all, we need God. In other words, our needs are physical, emotional and spiritual. This is consistent with our complete human nature, which is composed of body, soul and spirit.

But other people have needs too, so we must pray for them as well.

Prayer is not always asking things from God, but we pray to also give thanks to Him for all His blessings. As far as human need is concerned, our prayers may vary. It could be a petition, an intercession or a prayer of gratitude (thanksgiving).

Step 3 is the conclusion of our prayer.

Christian prayer must be concluded by asking all things in the name of Jesus.

So, what should be the substance of our prayer? It should not be only the contents of Step 2. The words expressed in prayer should include all three steps.

Remember, prayer is your most important conversation. Why? Because you are talking with God Almighty, the King of Kings and the Lord of Lords Himself. So, be careful with your words. The words of your prayer are expressions of what's in your heart. Therefore, be discreet and discerning of your every utterance in prayer. Sometimes you may even want to rehearse your prayers before saying them to be sure they are biblical. Whatever you do, do pray. You will be richly rewarded.

CR **58** ᘓ

THE PRINCE WHO CHOSE TO BE A SLAVE

Text: Hebrews 11:24-26

Moses is one of the most interesting, intriguing and exciting Bible characters. He was an extraordinary person. The circumstances surrounding his life were filled with sensational drama. His decisions and actions were critical to bringing about, not only a turning point in his own life, but also in the whole nation of Israel. The entire nation was delivered from slavery in Egypt by the mighty hand of God revealed through Moses.

God had blessed the Israelites during their sojourn in Egypt, beginning with the time of Joseph, and they had greatly increased in number. But when there arose another Pharaoh who did not know Joseph, he became hostile to and suspicious of them. This Pharaoh, or king, of Egypt, devised a scheme to stop the rapid increase of the Israelite population—the killing of all their male babies. This was achieved by throwing them into the Nile River. It was during these dark and dangerous times that Moses was born.

Moses' mother was courageous and did not fear the king's edict. She hid her son from those who were taking the babies. When she could no longer hide him, she made a basket of papyrus straw and placed her son in it. Then she placed the basket among the reeds along the banks of the Nile, leaving Miriam, Moses' older sister to watch it.

It just so happened that Pharaoh's daughter had gone to the river to bathe that day, and she saw the basket. Curious, she asked for it to be brought to her. When the basket was opened, she saw the baby and immediately knew, "This is one of the Hebrew babies."

About that time Miriam appeared and approached Pharaoh's daughter and asked, "Shall I get one of the Hebrew women to nurse the baby for you?"

"Yes, go," the princess answered, and the girl went and got her own mother.

When Moses' mother had arrived, Pharaoh's daughter said to her, "Take this baby and nurse him for me, and I will pay you." In this way, a godly mother not only saved her child; she was also able to raise him.

Pharaoh's daughter named the child Moses, but when he was grown, he refused to be known as the son of Pharaoh's daughter. Instead, he chose to be mistreated, along with the people of God, rather than enjoy the pleasure of sin for a short time. The book of Hebrews tells us that Moses regarded disgrace for the sake of Christ as of greater value than the treasures of Egypt, and he did it because he was looking ahead to his reward.

Moses then left Egypt, not fearing the king's anger:

By faith he forsook Egypt, not fearing the wrath of the king; for he endured as seeing Him who is invisible. Hebrews 11:27

How did Moses persevere, being chased by the most powerful man on earth? He saw *"Him who is invisible."*

Why did Moses decline to be a prince and abandon even the potential of becoming king of Egypt? Why did he abandon the comfort, the power, the prestige, the popularity and the pleasure of the palace in Egypt? Why did he decide, instead, to suffer, be mistreated, be disgraced and be humiliated with his people—the Israelites? These are mind-boggling questions, especially to an ordinary person. Most people cannot understand why Moses would have made such a decision. Some say that it was foolish of him to give up his life in the palace. Yes, it may have seemed foolishness to men, but for Moses, it was the wisdom of God.

What was the reason Moses chose to be identified with his people? The answer is: *"for he looked to the reward."* What is a reward? It is something given after one has reached some achievement. And what was Moses' reward? It was seeing *"Him who is invisible."*

How could Moses have seen someone who was invisible? This is a paradox. He perceived the reality of God by faith.

What is faith? The Bible says, *"Faith is being sure of what we hope for and certain of what we do not see"* (Hebrews 11:1, NIV). How did Moses get that kind of faith? Again, the Bible says, *"faith comes by hearing, and hearing by the word of God"* (Romans 10:17). It was apparent that Moses heard the Word of God from his mother who raised him. Although he was educated in all the wisdom of the Egyptians, the faith that his mother taught him was dominant in his thinking. For Moses, *"seeing Him who is invisible"* was far more valuable than enjoying the pleasures of sin temporarily at the palace, and suffering for Christ was greater riches than the treasures of Egypt.

The Bible says:

Eye has not seen, nor ear heard,

Nor have entered into the heart of man

The things which God has prepared for those who love Him.

1 Corinthians 2:9

Therefore we do not lose heart. Even though our outward man is perishing, yet the inward man is being renewed day by day. For our light affliction, which is but for a moment, is working for us a far more exceeding and eternal weight of glory, while we do not look at the things which are seen, but at the things which are not seen. For the things which are seen are temporary, but the things which are not seen are eternal.   1 Corinthians 4:16-18

CB **59** BO

THE TWO ADAMS

Text: 1 Corinthians 15:45

The Bible speaks of two Adams. Are they the same person? No! They are two different people. What's the difference between the two? It is immense, very immense. It is the difference between Earth and Heaven.

The first man called Adam was created by God in His image and likeness. He was taken from the Earth (terrestrial) and then formed and, finally, he was inbreathed by God. Thus, Adam became *"a living soul"* (Genesis 2:7). But this Adam, despite having been inbreathed by God, was mortal not immortal, as many Christians suggest and believe. His mortality was indicated by God when he was warned not to eat from the forbidden tree because if he did, he would *"surely die."* Unfortunately, Adam disobeyed God, so the first Adam died, and the legacy that he left for the rest of mankind was one of death.

The second man called Adam was also said to be the *"last Adam."* He was God incarnate. He was none other than Jesus Christ, and He was the *"express image"* of the invisible God (Hebrews 1:3). He was the Lord of Heaven (celestial). He is eternal and is a *"quickening [or life-giving] spirit."* He was the obedient Son of God who died on the cross to redeem us from the curse of sin and death. He rose again from the dead, to give all of us who believe in Him the hope of resurrection and immortality in Heaven.

What do these two Adams have to do with us today? Well, regarding the first Adam, we are stuck with his Adamic nature. As the saying goes, "We cannot choose our parents." We die like Adam, and we also face judgment and condemnation thereafter.

But, wait a minute! We can now choose and change our eternal destiny. That choice is in Jesus, *"the last Adam,"* who died to redeem us all from our sins and promised us all forgiveness of sins and eternal life. This is Good News indeed!

In the first Adam, we all die, but in the last Adam (Jesus Christ), we will live again. How wonderful!

Now, the big question is this: What will we do with Jesus Christ? If we ignore and reject Him, we will die in our sins without hope. This is why, in our evangelistic challenge to unsaved people and during our altar calls, we convince and persuade the lost that, besides turning away from sin, they should receive Jesus Christ as their personal Lord and Savior. Jesus Christ is indispensable to our salvation because there is *"no other name under heaven given among men by which we must be saved"* (Acts 4:12).

Yes, you can escape judgment and Hell right now. Repent and be sorry for your sins. Receive Jesus Christ into your heart, and your name will be written in the Book of Life in Heaven. Abide in Him, in His Word, the Bible, and in His Church. He is even now preparing us a place in Heaven, and He will come back to take us to Heaven to be with Him forever.

CR **60** &

THE THREE DEATHS OF MAN

Text: Romans 5:12-15

As a consequence of Adam's disobedience, man began to die. The death contemplated in the Bible is of three kinds: namely, spiritual death, physical death and the second death.

WHAT IS DEATH?

What is death? Death is the absence of life. It is the cessation of all vital functions of physical life. It is the extinction and the end of man's existence on earth. There are some issues, however, with regards to this definition relative to the death of man. To give some clarification to this issue, it will help if we first know and understand the nature of man. Based on the psychological point of view, man is composed of two elements: body and soul. From the perspective of theologians, however, man is composed of three elements: spirit, soul and body. Both views are correct.

310

The Three Deaths of Man

This analysis, or anatomy, of the nature of man is only for the purpose of knowing and understanding the complex structure and the interrelations of the elements of the human personality. Man is an integrated being. He is basically a body and soul and both of these human elements are an integral and essential part of man's existence. This means that one cannot survive without the other. When the word *body* is mentioned in the Bible, it is implied that the body has a soul. Conversely, when the word *soul* is mentioned, it is understood that this soul has a body. The life of the body is the soul, and when the body dies, the soul dies as well.

What Is Spiritual Death?

Now, what is spiritual death? It is the death of the spirit part of man. The spirit of man, in contradistinction to his soul, is his conscious connection with God. Man was complete when he was created by God, with spirit, soul and body. But when man sinned against God, his spirit died. Since then, men are spiritually dead, even if they are religious.

People who are without Christ are spiritual zombies; they are walking dead. That's why they need to be born again through faith in Christ, so that they can become spiritually alive again.

What Is Physical Death?

How about physical death? This is the death which is commonly experienced by human beings, both sinners and saints (unbelievers or followers of Christ). Will there be people who will not experience this kind of death? The answer is yes. This is the exception to the rule that everybody dies. According to Paul, in 1 Thessalonians 4 and 1 Corinthians 15, those who are alive when Jesus Christ returns to earth *"will all be changed"* (1 Corinthians 15:51, NIV), receiving glorified bodies, to join those who are resurrected to meet the Lord in the air and be with the Lord forever.

What happens to those who have died in Christ? Are they in Heaven now? No, not yet! Then where are they? They are in their graves. (RIP, Rest In Peace). Are they going to Heaven? Yes! When? At the Rapture, when Jesus Christ returns. They will be resurrected and will meet the Lord in the air to be forever with Him in Heaven.

WHAT IS THE SECOND DEATH?

How about those who have died without Christ? Are they in Hell now? No, not yet. Are they going to Hell? Definitely, yes. When? After the millennial reign of Jesus Christ, those who died without Him will be resurrected to face judgment. Then they will be thrown into the Lake of Fire, which is the *"second death"* (Revelation 20:14). This concept of death is rather extraordinary, peculiar and ironic compared with physical death. Whereas, in physical death, life (the body and soul) is ended, in the *"second death,"* life (the body and soul) is restored. For what purpose? Judgment in absentia is ruled out.

Proponents of the doctrine that the soul survives death miscon-strue the meaning of Matthew 10:28, which says:

And do not fear those who kill the body but cannot kill the soul. But rather fear Him who is able to destroy both soul and body in hell.

This is one verse that proves that the human soul is mortal; it can be killed. When I asked one pastor who is a proponent of an immortal soul the question, What is killed in a body?, he could not answer. It is because what is killed in a body is the soul that gives life to that body. Therefore, when the body is killed, the soul is also killed, and the result is physical death.

The first part of this verse which says, *"kill the body"* is presumed to be a killing done by men. The second part of this verse which says, *"kill the soul"* is the killing done by God.

The latter part of the verse has an eschatological dimension. This has reference to the time of the Great White Throne Judgment, when sinners and unbelievers will be thrown into the Lake of Fire. This is *"the second death."* We can avoid this. Repent of your sins, and receive Jesus Christ as your personal Lord and Savior, and you will be saved. �֎

❧ **61** ❧

JUDGMENTS IN THE AFTERLIFE

Text: Hebrews 9:27

The Bible tells us that there will be two judgments in the hereafter. They are 1) The Judgment Seat of Christ and 2) The Great White Throne Judgment.

Question: Will all the followers of Christ appear at the judgment? The answer is yes, all Christians will appear before the Judgment Seat of Christ.

Will they be punished? Absolutely not!

Then why will they be judged? This judgment is not punitive; it is more of a rewards ceremony for those servants of God who have been faithful in serving Him while here on Earth. Jesus said that we should *"lay up ... treasures in Heaven"* (Matthew 6:20) and not on Earth because treasures in Heaven are lasting, while earthly treasures are temporary. I believe that the Judgment Seat of Christ will be the time when faithful servants of God will receive their rewards, and the venue of this event is Heaven.

As the old saying goes:

Only one life, 'twill soon be past,
Only what's done for Christ will last. [1]

The things of this world will soon pass away,
But there is coming a judgment day.

The other judgment, the Great White Throne Judgment, will transpire after the millennial reign of Jesus Christ on Earth. This will be the judgment for sinners, unbelievers and all liars. This judgment is punitive.

In his vision recorded in the book of Revelation, the apostle John saw the dead standing before God. They will be judged according to their works, which are all recorded in a book. Yes, God has a record book of the works of sinners and unbelievers.

Wait a minute! Why are these condemned dead standing before God to be judged? Isn't it true that the dead are nonexistent when they die? That's true! But they will also be resurrected to face judgment. This is consistent with what Jesus declared:

Do not marvel at this; for the hour is coming in which all who are in the graves will hear His voice and come forth—those who have done good, to the resurrection of life, and those who have done evil, to the resurrection of condemnation.   John 5:28-29

---

1. From the poem by C.T. Studd

This will be a dreadful scenario:

And anyone not found written in the Book of Life was cast into the lake of fire. Revelation 20:15

Actually, man is already judged while he is still alive, and the verdict is "GUILTY." According to the writings of Paul:

For all have sinned and fall short of the glory of God.

Romans 3:23

For the wages of sin is death, but the gift of God is eternal life in Christ Jesus our Lord. Romans 6:23

Jesus said that those who do not believe in Him are *"condemned already"* (John 3:18) . But, while man is still alive, he has a chance to reverse the guilty verdict, be exonerated and escape punishment. How? As with our criminal justice system today, an accused person has a period after the judge has already rendered judgment during which they can exhaust other available remedies. This period of time—usually about fifteen days, depending on the case—is called, here in our country, a reglementary period. During that period, a person can appeal the decision of the judge. He still has potential remedies. But, if the accused is negligent and does not act in time, and the reglementary period is allowed to elapse, the judgment then becomes final and executory.

God has given man a lifetime reglementary period during which he can invoke the only remedy, and that is the substitutionary act of Christ on the cross of Calvary on our behalf. When a man dies without acting on or invoking the remedy, the judgment becomes final and executory, and there is no more remedy.

So, act now, while you are still alive. *"Now is the day of salvation"* (2 Corinthians 6:2). On your knees, repent of your sins. Open your heart and invite Jesus to come in. Then follow Him the rest of your life, and you will be saved!

THE RESURRECTION OF THE DEAD

Text: 1 Corinthians 15:12-20

The subject of the resurrection is essential to the Christian faith. All Christian practices would be futile without a belief in resurrection. Summing up all his arguments in defence of the resurrection, Paul concluded, *"If in this life only we have hope in Christ, we are of all men most miserable"* (KJV). This is how important the doctrine of resurrection is to every believer.

I am convinced that Paul expressed two of the most important quests of his lifetime when he wrote to the Philippian believers:

That I may know Him and the power of His resurrection.

Philippians 3:10

What is resurrection? It is the extraordinary bringing back to life of one who has been dead. It is the raising of the dead to life. This means that the body, which is resurrected, has become

318

immortal and imperishable. This domain of power is exclusive to God alone.

Sometimes this word *resurrection* is misunderstood and inappropriately used as meaning resuscitation. Those who were brought back to life in the Bible were not resurrected but simply resuscitated. They died again later.

The resurrection of Jesus Christ is a historical fact that validates the Christians' belief in resurrection. His resurrection set a precedent. The evidence establishing the truth and the matter of fact of the resurrection of Jesus were undeniable, overwhelming and beyond any shadow of a doubt.

First, there is no argument that Jesus Christ died and was buried, just as the Bible says. This was corroborated by many witnesses. Then His resurrection was also affirmed by many eyewitnesses, including Peter and other disciples, some women, and more than five hundred other followers. Then he was also seen by Paul (see 1 Corinthians 15:5-8).

According to Jesus, there are two general resurrections. They are: 1) The resurrection to life and 2) The resurrection to damnation. This is in concurrence with the Old Testament prophecy of Daniel:

And many of those who sleep in the dust of the earth shall awake,

Some to everlasting life,

Some to shame and everlasting contempt.   Daniel 12:2

The time difference between these two resurrections is of eschatological dimensions. The first resurrection, which is the resurrection to life, is of several different phases. The resurrection of Jesus Christ is called the firstfruits. This will be followed by the Rapture, when those who have died in Christ will be resurrected at the Second Coming of Christ. Then, together with those Christians who are still alive and who will be changed in the twinkling of an eye during this unprecedented event in the history of mankind, they will meet the Lord in the air simultaneously, to be with Him in Heaven:

> *For the Lord Himself will descend from heaven with a shout, with the voice of an archangel, and with the trumpet of God. And the dead in Christ will rise first. Then we who are alive and remain shall be caught up together with them in the clouds to meet the Lord in the air. And thus we shall always be with the Lord.*
>
> 1 Thessalonians 4:16-17

Prior to the establishment of the millennial Kingdom of Jesus Christ, there will be Tribulation saints and the two witnesses, among others, who will also be resurrected.

The second general resurrection, which is the resurrection to damnation, will take place after the millennial Kingdom of Jesus Christ:

> *But the rest of the dead did not live again until the thousand years were finished.*
>
> Revelation 20:5

The purpose of this second resurrection is for the unbelieving to face judgment. Afterward, they will be cast into the Lake of Fire.

We can escape this dreadful Lake of Fire, and this is the Good News. Through faith in Jesus Christ, we will be spared and, instead, be included among those who will be in the first resurrection. Repent of your sins today and receive Jesus Christ as your personal Lord and Savior, and you will be saved. Live for God, and whether you live or die, you have the assurance of salvation! ✄

CHANGING OUR WORLD

Text: Jeremiah 18:1-4

God told the prophet Jeremiah to go down to the local potter's house, and there He would give him His message. So, Jeremiah went, and there he saw the potter working at the wheel. The vessel the potter was shaping from the clay was marred in his hands, so he turned it into another vessel, shaping it as seemed best to him.

Perhaps you and I can relate to and identify with the story of the vessel in the potter's hand before and after our conversion to Christ. Before Christ came into our lives, we were like the vessel which was *"marred."* The word *marred* denotes that something was wrong with the vessel, even as the potter was shaping it from the clay. Maybe a foreign object got into the clay and contaminated it. That would compromise and alter the outcome.

The potter's intention was for the vessel to be perfect. The potter here is God, and we are that vessel He was shaping:

And the LORD God formed man of the dust of the ground, and breathed into his nostrils the breath of life; and man became a living being. Genesis 2:7

When we think about the potter Jeremiah encountered and his intentions for the vessel he was shaping, our minds go back to the dawn of Creation. After God created man, His evaluation of him was no less than perfect. He declared His creation, man, to be *"very good"*:

Then God saw everything that He had made, and indeed it was very good. Genesis 1:31

Before Christ came into my life, I was like that marred vessel. My life was broken, shattered and fragmented. My wife and I were separated, and it was all my fault. I was being controlled by an irresistible force called *sin*.

I even contemplated ending my life. Before that happened, thank God, two Filipina lady missionaries witnessed to me about the Gospel of Jesus Christ. I repented of my sins and accepted Jesus into my life, as my Lord and Savior.

When I told my wife about my conversion experience with Christ, she also believed, and we were reconciled. Praise God! Hallelujah! As our gratitude to God, we both entered the Bible school in preparation for our commitment and dedication to serve God.

After our graduation from Bible school, my wife and I, as a team, traveled to many provinces of the Philippines preaching and sharing the Gospel of Jesus Christ in schools, plazas and churches.

Eventually, when our family had grown, we settled for the more stationary ministry of church establishment and pastoring. Until now, we have established four congregations.

Then God sent us some wonderful Swedish partners, and with their help our work expanded to social, relief and educational ministries by putting up pre-school, elementary and high schools. Today we have more than two thousand children studying in our two schools in Taytay and Infanta. The purpose of these schools is to help provide quality and affordable basic education to the children of poor families, especially those living in the poor colonies. Since we put up these schools, more than 80,000 children have studied there, and more than 13,000 of those graduated. Many of them are now professionals in their own fields of endeavor.

A well-known story goes like this: a pastor was studying his Bible one Saturday morning, preparing his message for the church the following day. His wife opened the door of the room where he was studying and said to him, "Honey, can you please look after Junior (their son who was about six years old) because I'm going to the market to buy food."

The pastor had not yet finished preparing his message, so he tried to think of some game that might keep Junior occupied while he continued his studies. He noticed a world map on the wall, and an idea came to him. Taking it down, he showed it to Junior and said, "Let's play a game, son. I will tear this world map in pieces, and you go into the other room and see if you can put it back together again. Okay?"

"Okay, Papa," Junior answered.

The pastor thought it would take his son at least an hour to get the map back together, and that would give him sufficient time to finish his preparations. However, after only ten minutes, there was a knock on the door. He was sure his wife could not be back from the market so soon, as it was quite a distance away. When he opened the door, he was amazed to see his son standing there proudly holding the completed world map. "Wow! How did you do that so fast, son?" he asked.

Junior answered, "While you were tearing up the map of the world, I saw a figure of a man at the back of the map. I don't know much about the world, but I know the parts of a man—where to put his head, his hands and his feet. So, I figured out that if I could make the man all right, his world would also be all right!"

"Oh, you are so right, Junior," his father said. "You have just given me the message for tomorrow."

Yes, before Jesus came, man was not right, and his world was not right either. That's why Jesus said:

"Come to Me, all you who labor and are heavy laden, and I will give you rest. Take My yoke upon you and learn from Me, for I am gentle and lowly in heart, and you will find rest for your souls. For My yoke is easy and My burden is light."

Matthew 11:28-30

The apostle Paul added to this:

Therefore, if anyone is in Christ, he is a new creation; old things have passed away; behold, all things have become new.

2 Corinthians 5:17

This change in our lives, effected by our faith in the Lord Jesus Christ, has a ripple effect in the water of humanity. Our salvation has an impact and an influence upon the people around us that will also result in change to their lives.

Christians are catalysts, which means they are agents for change—God's agents for change. If Christians are committed, dedicated and obedient to the will of God, they can become instruments of change for the better.

We may not be able to change the whole world, but we can surely change our own world. Hallelujah! The best is yet to come! Glory to God! Praise His holy name! ✄

ᘓ **64** ᘔ

LOVE SUBLIME

Text: Matthew 22:37-40

This divine dictum was the answer of our Lord Jesus Christ to the question of one of the teachers of the Law regarding the most important of all the commandments. This, therefore, is the highest of all the Christian's moral imperatives.

Jesus quoted the ten commandments in a capsulated compendium, plus one. What is this "plus one?" It is to "love ourselves," after loving God and our neighbors. This was not included in the original Ten Commandments. So, for Christians, we might say, there are now eleven commandments.

The question of the teacher of the Law relative to this issue was rather interesting. Apparently he just wanted to follow one of the Ten Commandments, and that was why he asked which one was the most important. But the decalogue is essentially a unit, meaning to say, one commandment cannot be separated from the rest of the commandments. They are integrated just like the human soul that cannot be separated from the human body, even by physical death.

Now, the big question is this: As Christians, are we still obligated to follow or obey the decalogue? The answer is yes, plus one. This responsibility was not abrogated, even though we are now under grace and no more under the Law. We are to follow this divine dictum, not to be saved, because we are already saved through faith in the Lord Jesus Christ. We follow the Decalogue plus one because this is our code of conduct, our standard of Christian and personal behavior based on this moral principle. It is characteristic of a Christian to love God, his fellow being and himself.

When, why and how do we love God? Our love affair with God begins when we are saved and have been born again. We love God because He first loved us. It is a reciprocal and mutual love relationship between God and man that develops when man is saved. And how should we love God? Answer: with all of our heart, soul, mind and strength.

The Israelites were reminded by God of this divine dictum and told that they should pass it on to their children as a legacy of faith. It should be part of a majority of their conversations. As a symbol of their love and obedience to God, they were to tie these commandments to their foreheads and arms (see Deuteronomy 6).

The Jewish concept of the heart and mind is that the two are integrated. For example:

For as he thinks in his heart, so is he.   Proverbs 23:7

The two can, however, be distinguished by way of rhetorical function. This means that man's love of God must involve his total being, both his abstract and physical elements.

A closer look at this divine dictum will reveal that when God gave it to His people, the Israelites, and when Jesus pronounced it, both were in the imperative mode. This means that the commandments were mandates, not options. When God says something to His people and then He repeats it, we'd better pay attention. This is much more true when He repeats it three times. In that case, we can know that it is something very serious indeed.

As parents, when we discipline our children over some of their misbehaviors, we sometimes warn them by counting: one, two, three. After three, if they have not listened, then they get the corresponding punishment.

How do we love God with our whole being? The first mention is loving God with all our heart. The human heart is the seat of emotion. We get emotional when we are in love. It is an exciting, powerful and wonderful feeling. Someone in love will defy reason, ignore ridicule and suffer all sorts of mistreatment just to be with the person they love. It is a feeling of "you and me against the world."

Do we love God like that? Do we get emotional with our love for Him? I do. Every time I think of how Jesus Christ suffered on the cross to redeem me and save me from my sins, I get emotional—very emotional. Tears run freely down my cheeks. Every time I remember how God lifted me up from a life of poverty to a life of plenty, I burst into tears, just thinking about God's goodness and faithfulness to me and my family. Every time I worship God in church, lifting up my hands and singing songs of praise to Him, I get emotional. This emotion is the expression of my love for God, and I know full well what I am doing because my mind tells me so. My love of God is with ardent and fervent dedication, devotion and obedience to His will.

The next question is: How do we love our fellow being? Aside from the profound illustration given by our Lord Jesus Christ in answer to the question by one expert of the Law, *"And who is my neighbor?"*(Luke 10:29), the apostle Paul gave a wonderful exposition and elaboration on this subject of sublime love (see 1 Corinthians 13). This love emanates from God, for *"God is love"* (1 John 4:8 and 16).

Love for our neighbor is characterized by patience and kindness and an absence of envy, pride, rudeness or selfishness. Godly love is *"not easily angered,"* and *"keeps no record of wrongs"* (1 Corinthians 13:5, NIV). It *"does not delight in evil but rejoices with the truth"* (verse 6). *"It always protects, always trusts, always hopes, always perseveres"* (verse 7). *"Love never fails"* (verse 8).

One of the characteristics of love is sacrifice. God loves us so much that He sacrificed His own Son. Sacrifice is the act of offering someone or something precious to God or to someone else. To sacrifice also means "to surrender or give up at a loss" or "to endure." We all know that Jesus Christ did this when He suffered on the cross. This was a cruel love, and sometimes love can be cruel. Jesus said:

> *If anyone desires to come after Me, let him deny himself, and take up his cross, and follow Me.*　　　　　Matthew 16:24

Does this mean that we have to take up a literal wooden cross and carry it around? I have seen some Christians do that. But I believe that the meaning of what Jesus said is part of the Divine Dictum we are considering here. It demands our love for God and our fellow being, and when we do love in this way, we deny ourselves. One direction of this act of love is vertical, toward God, and the other is horizontal, toward our fellow being. The image formed in this act of love is a cross.

Of course, we must not neglect or ignore to love ourselves. This is the eleventh commandment, according to our Lord Jesus Christ. In one sense, it is human nature that everyone loves himself or herself, so I need not elaborate on this point, but many hate themselves.

Also, the order or sequence of our loves is very important. It must be: first, love Jesus, then love others, and then yourself. That is:

Jesus

Others

Yourself

This spells JOY, which is constant happiness, whether the circumstances in our lives are good or bad. Yes, love sublime will bring you joy unspeakable and full of glory!   �֍

⚛ **65** ⚛

THE CHRISTIANS' VIEW AND VALUE OF WORK

Text: Genesis 2:2-3

Work occupies at least a third of our lifetime. In each day, we allocate eight hours to work, eight hours to sleep and eight hours to leisure or recreation.

To many people, work is a boring routine and a drudgery of activity, but to others, especially Christians, work is an essential and significant part and purpose of our life. Through our work (some call it a job), we help support ourselves and sustain our families, render service to others and our society, to our government and, ultimately, to God. Besides, work gives a person a sense of dignity, fulfillment, self-esteem and financial and economic security.

There are different kinds of work and many varied areas of endeavor. There are, for example, those who are engaged in agricultural work (farmers), in industrial work (factory workers), in commercial and business work, in construction, in transportation, in maritime work (seamen), in medical work, in the legal profession, in church work, in government, in education, etc. There are those whose work involves mostly mental exertion and others whose work requires manual labor.

There are those who are involved in what we consider to be dirty work, like garbage collecting, sewage control and sanitation management. Although these dirty and stinky manual jobs seem to some to be demeaning to the workers, we must be very thankful to those who maintain the hygiene of our towns and cities. Without sanitation workers, we would be vulnerable to outbreaks and epidemics of all sorts of sicknesses and diseases.

How do we render services to others through our work? Through the goods and services we produce. Other people are benefited, and this adds to the compensation we receive, which helps with the sustenance of ourselves and our family.

Let's take the example of farmers. What they produce not only feeds their own family but also many others. Another example would be those who are involved in the construction industry. We have infrastructures like roads, bridges and buildings in our communities and cities because of construction workers. We all benefit from their labors.

Also the taxes derived from the sale of the many goods and services provided serve as funds to finance our government systems. In this way, our individual and corporate work contributes to the stability, sustainability, symbiosis and dynamics of our society and its government.

God is a worker, and when He created man, He intended for him to become a worker also. The Divine imprint in man, who is created in the image and likeness of God, suggests and implies this intention and purpose.

Who can doubt that God is a worker? He worked six days in creating the universe and all that is in it, and He wants man to be a worker, too, a partner in work that is:

Then the LORD God took the man and put him in the garden of Eden to tend and keep it. Genesis 2:15

God wants man to be like Him, to be active, creative and productive. Contrary to the belief of many that work is part of the curse, here we see that before the fall, work had already been instituted by God for man. God provided nature through His creation, but He placed man to be the cultivator of that nature, and so work has become the cultural mandate for man.

It is God who provides the land, the seed and growth to that seed, but it is man who has to do the work of cultivating, sowing and reaping. God gives life to the fetus in the mother's womb, but when the baby is born, it is the mother's responsibility to look after that baby. A doctor puts a bandage on the wound of a patient, but it is God who does the healing. This is a universal working partnership principle between God and man.

Understanding the essence and significance of work and seeing our work as our human cultural mandate will make our work satisfactory and never a drudgery, even though it may be a routine activity. God was satisfied with His work. After He saw all that He had made, He said, *"It was very good"* (Genesis 1:31). We should mimic this kind of work attitude and take satisfaction from our work.

This is what I do personally. I am satisfied with my work. In fact, I enjoy it. When we have this kind of work attitude, our work will never be boring or seem like a drudgery of activity.

Many workers, including Christian workers, frequently change jobs. Usually it is because they are not satisfied either with their work or their salary (although there may be other reasons). God has promised His people that if they are fully obedient to Him, He will make them the head and not the tail (see Deuteronomy 28:13), but sometimes we have to start at the tail and work our way up to becoming the head. But if we keep jumping from one job to another because we hate work, without spending enough time in any one position, we are doomed to always remain the tail and will never be the head.

There are rules, serious rules, in the New Testament governing our Christian work attitude. They are tantamount to Christian Work Ethics. First, there is the rule which says:

If anyone will not work, neither shall he eat.

2 Thessalonians 3:10

This is clearly an injunction against lazy Christians. Paul rebuked the lazy among the Thessalonians for being idle and going around depending on other Christians for their sustenance, although they were quite capable of working. That entire passage is worth quoting:

But we command you, brethren, in the name of our Lord Jesus Christ, that you withdraw from every brother who walks disorderly and not according to the tradition which he received from us. For

335

you yourselves know how you ought to follow us, for we were not disorderly among you; nor did we eat anyone's bread free of charge, but worked with labor and toil night and day, that we might not be a burden to any of you, not because we do not have authority, but to make ourselves an example of how you should follow us.

For even when we were with you, we commanded you this: If anyone will not work, neither shall he eat. For we hear that there are some who walk among you in a disorderly manner, not working at all, but are busybodies. Now those who are such we command and exhort through our Lord Jesus Christ that they work in quietness and eat their own bread. 2 Thessalonians 3:6-12

Paul also warned the Philippian Christians not to gain their income from illicit means, and he taught them to share with those who had genuine needs.

With every rule, there is an exception. Who is exempt from work? Children, for one, should be exempt from work so that they can go to school and learn. They also require time for play if they are to develop properly. Parents should work and support their growing children.

The elderly, especially the weak and the sick, are also exempt from work, so their children should look after their well-being. This charitable work toward the elderly is consistent with the biblical admonition to children:

Honor your father and your mother, that your days may be long upon the land which the LORD your God is giving you.

Exodus 20:11

Yes, it's payback time. They supported you, and now it's your turn to support them.

We must be thankful to God if we have work, and we must do our job without complaining and murmuring. And, finally, whatever we do, let us do it all for His glory:

Do all things without complaining and disputing, that you may become blameless and harmless, children of God without fault in the midst of a crooked and perverse generation, among whom you shine as lights in the world, holding fast the word of life, so that I may rejoice in the day of Christ that I have not run in vain or labored in vain. Philippians 2:14-16

What does it mean for us to do our jobs without complaining or murmuring? These usually occur when we are dissatisfied with our work. It may have to do with our working conditions, with the attitude of our superiors or with our compensation. Instead of rebelling against an employer or reviling them, it is better to just quietly resign and look for another job.

As Christians, we have another consideration: We must keep intact and protect our Christian testimony, our integrity and our convictions, sometimes under very difficult circumstances. We must always find ways to glorify God with our work.

Then, just as God rested after six days of work, we also must rest, and we must honor God on the seventh day by going to His House, the church. In church, we Christians acknowledge the blessings and favor of God over the past days and express thanks through worship and thanksgiving. This includes the giving of our tithes and offerings.

The pattern for this was set by God Himself. For six days He labored, and then He rested on the seventh day. This mandate to God's people has not been abrogated; it still stands and is in effect. Obedience to this mandate has nothing to do with our salvation because we have been saved through faith in Christ Jesus, but it is still a matter of obligation. Don't be an ingrate! God gave us life, salvation, strength, sound mind, resources and work opportunities, so we owe Him a lot. Glorify God in your work, and then go to His House to give Him thanks. ✖

$\mathscr{C}$ **66** $\mathscr{D}$

TRAGIC LOVE

Text: Judges 2:11, 3:7, 4:1 and 6:1

This phrase, *"the children of Israel did evil in the sight of the Lord,"* is repeated several times in the book of Judges. What was this evil that provoked the Lord to anger against His people? They forsook and forgot the Lord, the God of their fathers, who had brought them out of Egypt. What was worse: they followed and worshipped various gods of the people around them, like Baal and the Ashtoreths. Why were they always backsliding in this way? It was because these were new generations of Israelites who had come along after the death of Joshua, and they did not know the Lord or the great things He had done for their nation.

Because these new generations refused to give up their evil practices and stubborn ways, God allowed the enemies surrounding them, like the Philistines, to afflict and oppress them. When they cried out to the Lord because of their afflictions at the hand of these oppressive enemies, the Lord had compassion on them and raised up deliverers who set therm free again. These deliverers were also called judges, and they were men and women who knew God, and He was with them and often gave them extraordinary powers.

God had warned the Israelites before they entered into Canaan, the land of promise, not to follow other gods, the gods of the people around them. They were also precluded from intermarrying with the people of Canaan. They must not give their daughters to the sons of Canaan or take Canaanite daughters for their sons. Why? Because the daughters of Canaan would turn away their sons from following the Lord to serve other gods, and the Lord's anger would burn against them as a result.

Samson was among these godly judges and deliverers whom the Lord gave to the Israelites when they cried out to Him by reason of the oppression of their enemies. Samson was an extraordinary man. He had lived under the vow of a Nazarite from birth. This special vow was for the purpose of separating oneself unto the Lord. A Nazarite must abstain from wine and other fermented drink. He must not go near a dead body, and during the entire period of his vow, no razor could be used on his head. He must let his hair grow. But, alas, this man's life was also a reflection and representation of the condition and moral reality of the nation of Israel during this period. Samson had his ups and his downs.

Samson had supernatural strength. Where did that strength come from? Some say that it came from his long hair, but others say that his strength came from the Lord, when His Spirit came upon Samson in power. Personally, I think the two are related.

At one point, Samson killed a young lion with his bare hands. With a jawbone of a donkey, he killed a thousand of the Philistines. It seemed that Samson was invincible against his Philistine enemies. But he did have one weakness, and that weakness proved to be his undoing. He loved women, especially, it seems, Philistine women.

TRAGIC LOVE

One day, Samson saw a young Philistine woman in Timnah, and he wanted her. When he returned home, he said to his parents, *"I have seen a woman in Timnah of the daughters of the Philistines; now therefore, get her for me as a wife"* (Judges 14:2).

His parents objected: *"Is there no woman among the daughters of your brethren, or among all my people, that you must go and get a wife from the uncircumcised Philistines?"* (verse 3).

Samson remained unmoved. He was convinced that this was the right woman for him. *"Get her for me, for she pleases me well"* he insisted (verse 3).

Who was right? Samson or his parents? The Bible states emphatically:

> *Children, obey your parents in the Lord, for this is right.*
>
> Ephesians 6:1

It doesn't say that parents are always right, but it says that it is always right to obey your parents. The book of Proverbs teaches:

> *There is a way that seems right to a man,*
> *But its end is the way of death.*   Proverbs 14:12

Sure enough, Samson's marriage to the Philistine woman ended in tragedy. She and her father were burned to death by the Philistines, and Samson had to flee from his enemies.

But Samson didn't learn his lesson. Now he went to Gaza and slept with a prostitute, further lowering his standards and his taste in women. He always seemed to be in the wrong place at a wrong time.

Next, he fell in love with a woman named Delilah. This woman was not only dangerous; she was treacherous. She didn't love Samson; she was just after his money. What was worse: she was in cahoots with the Philistines to learn where his real strength lay.

When she nagged him incessantly, Samson finally gave in and told Delilah that if his hair was cut, he would become as weak as any other man. The next thing he knew he was waking up, and his head had been shaved while he was sleeping. He wasn't concerned, convinced that he could escape as before. This time, however, it was different:

So he awoke from his sleep, and said, "I will go out as before, at other times, and shake myself free!" But he did not know that the LORD had departed from him. Judges 16:20

What happened to Samson next is very sad:

Then the Philistines took him and put out his eyes, and brought him down to Gaza. They bound him with bronze fetters, and he became a grinder in the prison. Judges 16:21

Now Samson was forced to get serious. With extreme remorse, he prayed to God to once more restore to him his supernatural strength in order to exact revenge against his Philistine enemies. God heard that plea:

And Samson took hold of the two middle pillars which supported the temple, and he braced himself against them, one on his right and the other on his left. Then Samson said, "Let me die with the Philistines!" And he pushed with all his might, and the temple fell on the lords and all the people who were in it. So the dead that he killed at his death were more than he had killed in his life.

Judges 16:29-30

At the end of his life, Samson met tragedy, and it was all his fault. What was the cause of this tragedy? It was love, the love of women who don't belong to the same community of faith. Love's story is supposed to end with the words *happily ever after*, not with such tragedy.

This is a serious warning to all Christians, both men and women, but especially to those who are single. If you don't want your love life to turn to tragedy, don't be unequally yoked together with unbelievers:

Do not be unequally yoked together with unbelievers. For what fellowship has righteousness with lawlessness? And what communion has light with darkness? And what accord has Christ with Belial? Or what part has a believer with an unbeliever? And what agreement has the temple of God with idols? For you are the temple of the living God. As God has said:

"I will dwell in them
And walk among them.
I will be their God,

343

And they shall be My people."

Therefore

"Come out from among them

And be separate, says the Lord.

Do not touch what is unclean,

And I will receive you.

I will be a Father to you,

And you shall be My sons and daughters,

Says the Lord Almighty."   2 Corinthians 6:14-18

Save yourself from tremendous trouble and tragedy. Don't become romantically involved with unbelievers.   �֍

cs **67** so

A Christian's Personal Perspective

Text: Philippians 3:13-14

At the end of each year, many evaluate their achievements during the past year and assess what they should do in the coming year. Then they make a "New Year's resolution." In this way, they hope to avoid the mistakes and blunders they committed in the past. In fact, they resolve not to repeat them. Through the mistakes of the past, some have learned valuable, albeit expensive, lessons that will make them more cautious in the days ahead.

Some have health issues and may want to slow down on their food intake and discipline their bodies to do more exercise. These are commendable resolutions.

For most of us, New Years is always a good time to save more money and prioritize our expenses and purchases so as to have more left over for the emergencies of life. These are all good and beneficial to us, if we are committed to resolve our personal issues.

But what about our Christian life and testimony? Do we have personal issues that we need to resolve in the new year? How will we tackle these issues? What are our priorities as Christians, whether we work in the sacred or in the secular? To answer these questions, I would like to adopt Paul's perspective on his personal life and service to God. He said, *"One thing I do, forgetting those things which are behind and reaching forward to those things which are ahead, I press toward the goal for the prize of the upward call of God in Christ Jesus."* What was he talking about? He was talking about the hindsight, the insight and the foresight of his life and service to God as a Christian. He was focused on doing *"one thing,"* and that one thing was forgetting the past and reaching out for the future.

What were the things that Paul was forgetting? I believe that he was referring to his zeal for his former religion. Paul, just like so many people, had been sincere, but he was sincerely wrong. He declared:

> *But what things were gain to me, these I have counted loss for Christ. Yet indeed I also count all things loss for the excellence of the knowledge of Christ Jesus my Lord, for whom I have suffered the loss of all things, and count them as rubbish, that I may gain Christ and be found in Him, not having my own righteousness, which is from the law, but that which is through faith in Christ, the righteousness which is from God by faith; that I may know Him and the power of His resurrection, and the fellowship of His sufferings, being conformed to His death, if, by any means, I may attain to the resurrection from the dead.* Philippians 3:7-11

Using commercial terms, Paul had thought that he had profit or gain from his former religion and activities, but when he met and came to know Christ Jesus, what he had thought was gain now became *"loss"* for him and worthless compared with the majesty of the knowledge of Christ. He had thought that he had righteousness by the Law, but that was insufficient and insignificant compared with the righteousness by faith in Christ Jesus. In fact, now he treated all those past things as *"rubbish."* The King James Version of the Bible translates this word as *"dung,"* which means "manure." That's about as worthless as you can get.

What did Paul mean by *"forgetting"* past things? He meant that past things must not influence or affect our present and future Christian life. I have heard many Christians, when they testify, seem to magnify their past above their present life in Christ. They revel in the fact that were murderers, rapists, robbers, swindlers or drug addicts. I believe that this is unnecessary and inappropriate. Sometimes it is scary to get close to such people. You never know if there might be a recurrence of their former life.

We believe that Christians should not tell a lie, but we also don't have to tell all the gory details of our past lives. There are good truths, and there are bad truths. We don't have to tell the bad truths, especially when they are self-incriminating and will besmirch our name and our family's reputation. No one is asking anyway, and we're not under oath in a court of law. I believe that our sinful past has been covered and erased by the precious blood of Jesus Christ. That is enough to know.

What is the *"one thing"* that we should be focused on doing with each new year? The answer to this question is a serious challenge to Christians, especially to Christian workers. I always advise and encourage my fellow pastors to focus on their work. We must not compromise our commitment, dedication and devotion to God and His calling for us with the things of this world. We need things in order to exist, but our priority must be to pursue God and be faithful in His service.

I have often received invitations to speak outside of our church, but if these invitations conflict with our church services, I decline them because I am committed to serving our congregation. I must be loyal to that commitment.

During the early years of our ministry, I was a very poor pastor, and most of our members were also poor because they came from a squatters colony. Many times I was forced to do some moon-lighting in order augment our income and feed my wife and three children. I did not like to squeeze our members for money because they were poor too, so I bought and sold items of clothing and cars.

Then I discovered how to be financially stable through the economic principles espoused by Joseph in the Bible. As a result, with capital gathered through years of savings (and loans I was able to secure) I ventured into some real estate transactions. I was able to acquire two properties and build two houses, and that set me on a course of action. I was about to get seriously into buying land, building houses and selling those houses when suddenly I realized that this business was sucking me out of the ministry. My focus had been diverted from ministry to business. The result was that I quit the business and refocused on my pastoral ministry.

Let us remember, as the song says:

Only one life, it will soon be past,
Only what's done for Christ will last.

Things in this world will soon pass away

And there is coming a judgment day.

Jesus said:

For what will it profit a man if he gains the whole world, and loses his own soul? Mark 8:36

But seek first the kingdom of God and His righteousness, and all these things shall be added to you. Matthew 6:33

Since I refocused my life in pursuit of and service to God, I haven't had to worry about our sustenance, shelter, education for our children and money for whatever else we needed, because He promised:

And my God shall supply all your need according to His riches in glory by Christ Jesus. Philippians 4:19

Praise God! Hallelujah!

❧ **68** ❨

THE REMEDY OF REDEMPTION

Text: Genesis 3:6-12

The ramifications of Adam's disobedience in the Garden of Eden were direct and collateral. His offence brought death to himself and also to the rest of mankind. Besides that, it brought destruction, damage and hostility, undermining the harmony of God's created order.

Added to this sad and tragic episode of the human and divine drama was the behind-the-scenes divine trauma. I believe (I can only conjecture or speculate) that God was deeply hurt by this horrendous action of Adam. God is also an emotional God. At one time He said, *"I am a jealous God"* (Exodus 20:5). Others have called the offence of Adam "treason" or "a crime." Most theologians call it sin, but I call it betrayal. After all that God had done for Adam—He gave him life, gave him love and fellowship, gave him the Garden of Eden and gave him Eve—the man betrayed Him. This, of course, was caused by the Intruder, the devil, who did nothing good for Adam and Eve, but lied to them, and they believed him and not God.

Do you know how it feels to be betrayed? Ask a husband whose wife has given her body to another man. Ask a pastor about members who have left him and gone to a mega-church. Can we ask God how He felt when He was betrayed by Adam? Of course you can, but I'm not sure if you will get an answer. When we are betrayed, we feel humiliated and rejected. It's a very painful feeling.

Let's look at Adam's side of the story. There was tremendous tension created when Eve offered him the forbidden fruit and asked him to eat it. He was in a dilemma. If he refused to eat the forbidden fruit, he might lose Eve, and he didn't want to be alone and lonely or unhappy as before. So, he decided to take a bite and die with Eve instead.

But what did Adam really do that day? He was being selfish. He was only thinking of himself. He was not thinking this thing through to its logical conclusion. He had allowed his emotions to overrule his reason. And that was the source of all of human misery. Blame it on Adam, folks.

For his part, Adam passed the blame along to Eve, and Eve blamed the serpent. This is what we have come to call "the blame game." Doesn't it sounds typical of people even today? This was, as a matter of fact, a love story and a love triangle—Adam's love for God pitted against his love for Eve.

God is a God of love, but His love is not like that of Adam's. God's love is a sacrificial love. He is also an understanding and forgiving God. So, instead of imposing and implementing the perpetual penalty for sin, He mitigated it Himself. It was God Himself who devised the remedy for man's sin, and that remedy is called "the plan of redemption."

What is that plan? God sent His Son incarnate in the flesh to do this job. His name is Jesus. He shed His blood and died on the cross to provide redemption for fallen man. He arose from the dead (resurrection) to give all of us the assurance of salvation.

If anyone may ask, "How can I be saved?" it is simple and free. Right now, repent of your sins, open your heart, invite Jesus to come in, and accept Him as your Lord and Savior. Get yourself a Bible and start reading from the New Testament. Find a Christian church where you can fellowship with God's people and grow spiritually. Then, you will have the assurance of the salvation by faith that Jesus paid for.

POOR BUT PROSPEROUS

Text: Luke 6:20

How relevant is the Gospel of our Lord Jesus Christ to the poor today? One sister in the Lord answered with a question: "Who are the poor?"

I said, "Good question. Do you know?"

She did not answer.

A pastor answered and said, "Very relevant." I asked him to elaborate, but he, likewise, did not answer.

During the early ministry of Jesus, many, if not most, of those who followed Him were poor people. They were the sick, the outcasts, the slaves and the children. Categorized, they were the spiritually poor, the physically poor, the materially and financially poor and also the socially and politically poor.

What were the indicators that these groups of people could be considered poor? First, they had been reduced to begging, and second, they were dependant upon the welfare of others. That's why children are included, because they depend on their parents to sustain them. Without that support from their parents, many children would perish.

Poor people beg because their survival and existence depend on the generosity of their benefactors. Such was the case with Lazarus who begged at the rich man's table. Unfortunately, the rich man was unwilling to share with him, so Lazarus died (see Luke 16).

Actually, all people—whether poor or rich—are spiritually poor in the eyes of God, even though most of them don't realize their spiritual condition. When Jesus said, *"Blessed are the poor ... ,"* He was not inferring that spiritual, physical or economic poverty was a blessing. The blessedness of those poor was in begging for and depending on the grace and mercy of God.

True Christians have this kind of attitude from the time they are saved. Then this attitude continues because they are forever dependent upon God for spiritual sustenance. This is why Paul, even though he had already met Christ, wrote, *"That I may know him ..."* (Philippians 3:10).

The spiritually poor who beg and children have one thing in common: they are both heirs of the Kingdom of Heaven. Jesus said:

Assuredly, I say to you, unless you are converted and become as little children, you will by no means enter the kingdom of heaven. Matthew 18:3

Today prosperity, as promised by God to the followers of Christ in the Bible, has become quite a controversial issue among pastors and preachers. This prosperity promise is comprehensive, covering spiritual and physical, as well as economic. God, through the pages of the Bible, says it this way:

> *Beloved, I wish above all things that thou mayest prosper and be in health, even as thy soul prospereth.*   3 John 2, KJV

What a wonderful promise!

First, God calls us beloved, and then He says He wants us to prosper. I believe that, and I have experienced it. I was once a very poor pastor, but God has prospered me. Yes, we can be spiritually poor, as I have explained, and still be prosperous.

There are pastors and preachers who attribute the wonderful prosperity promise of God to the devil. To my way of thinking, they are themselves agents and advocates of the devil. Because they preach the bad news of unbelief, they have no business being pastors or preachers in the Church of the Lord Jesus Christ. Let them be part of the media, where they, no doubt, will continue to broadcast their bad news. You and I must believe the truth and prosper.   �֎

❦ 70 ❧

THE GOD OF BLESSINGS

Text: Genesis 1:22 and 28

Our God is a God of blessing. This was one of His intentions when He created the world that we live in, including us human beings. In fact, the Bible shows that God pronounced these blessings twice. That's a double blessing.

Our God is also a God of order. He has established certain laws and principles, in keeping with His divine purpose, in order to set in motion and harmony His created system. Breaking these laws and principles would cause derailment and derangement of the order and harmony, not only of the relationship between God and man, but also the created Earth itself. This was an offence against God. The other word we use for it is *sin*.

Sin has two sides to its coin—the sin of commission and the sin of omission. When a person is precluded by God from doing a certain thing, and he goes ahead and does it anyway, that's a sin of commission. When one is ordered by God to do something, and he fails to do it, that's a sin of omission.

356

THE GOD OF BLESSINGS

The incident that occurred in the Garden of Eden, as described in Genesis 3, is not only a sad and sorry one, but also a tragic one. Instead of living a life with the blessings of God, Adam and Eve brought a curse upon themselves and upon the whole Earth because of their disobedience to God's law. This curse has permeated the entire human race and caused untold misery, hardship, disaster, suffering, sickness, sorrow, pain and death.

The Old Testament ends with the word *curse* because that is the legacy man left. However, God's people, through His grace and mercy, can reverse the curse and regain His blessings. How? By obeying God's Word and His will.

Abraham was an example. God said to Abraham (formerly Abram):

"Get out of your country,
From your family
And from your father's house,
To a land that I will show you.
I will make you a great nation;
I will bless you
And make your name great;
And you shall be a blessing.
I will bless those who bless you,
And I will curse him who curses you;
And in you all the families of the earth shall be blessed."

Genesis 12:1-3

Another example was God's promise of blessing to the children of Israel after they had come out of Egypt. God said to them:

Now it shall come to pass, if you diligently obey the voice of the LORD your God, to observe carefully all His commandments which I command you today, that the LORD your God will set you high above all nations of the earth. And all these blessings shall come upon you and overtake you, because you obey the voice of the LORD your God:

Blessed shall you be in the city, and blessed shall you be in the country.

Blessed shall be the fruit of your body, the produce of your ground and the increase of your herds, the increase of your cattle and the offspring of your flocks.

Blessed shall be your basket and your kneading bowl.

Blessed shall you be when you come in, and blessed shall you be when you go out.

The LORD will cause your enemies who rise against you to be defeated before your face; they shall come out against you one way and flee before you seven ways.

The LORD will command the blessing on you in your storehouses and in all to which you set your hand, and He will bless you in the land which the LORD your God is giving you.

Deuteronomy 28:1-8

The birth of Jesus Christ in the New Testament was the highest of God's blessings. Jesus was to be a blessing to all mankind, not just for God's chosen nation or a select few people. He was to bring the blessing of salvation, if we believe in Him and accept Him as our Lord and Savior. This blessing far exceeds any earthly blessings, which are only temporal.

Now, through Jesus Christ, we can even gain heavenly blessings, and these will be good for all eternity. Hallelujah! Praise God!

Our Lord Jesus commenced His ministry by pronouncing blessings upon the unblessed:

Blessed are the poor in spirit ... .   Matthew 5:3

Blessed are those who mourn ... .   Matthew 5:4

Blessed are the meek ... .   Matthew 5:5

Blessed are those who hunger and thirst for righteousness ... .
                                                 Matthew 5:6

Blessed are the merciful ... .   Matthew 5:7

Blessed are the pure in heart ... .   Matthew 5:8

Blessed are the peacemakers ... .   Matthew 5:9

Blessed are those who are persecuted for righteousness' sake ... .   Matthew 5:10

Blessed are you ... .   Matthew 5:11

God has blessed us *"with all spiritual blessings in heavenly places in Christ"* (Ephesians 1:3). So, Christians, let us obey the Lord and be faithful. Stop feeling self-pity and feeling poor and miserable, and start praising and thanking God. Claim and count your blessings now. His Word declares:

The blessing of the LORD makes one rich,
And He adds no sorrow with it.   Proverbs 10:22

Dreadful, Destructive and Deadly Demons

Text: John 10:10

Through stealth (disguised as a serpent), the chief of all demons, called the devil, lured Eve into a death trap, by enticing her to eat of the forbidden tree. His specialty is deceit, temptation, destruction and death. Jesus described him well in John 10:10. Far too often we are unaware that the cause of our misery, misfortunes and mishaps is the devil himself.

Where did demons come from? Demons are fallen angels. The Bible shows that the devil was once an archangel whose name was Lucifer. He was created perfect, but he later sinned. The particular sin found in him was pride (see Isaiah 14).

Lucifer, together with a third of all the angelic hosts of Heaven, rebelled against God. As a result, they were cast out of Heaven. Jesus confirmed this when He said, *"I saw Satan [another name for the devil, which means "enemy of God and man"]) fall like lightning from heaven"* (Luke 10:18).

There are two kinds of demons (as far as their status is concerned): 1) those demons that roam around free, and 2) those demons that are incarcerated in the abyss. The name of the leader of the incarcerated demons is Abaddon, also known as Apollyon. These demons look hideous, grotesque, bizarre and terrifying. They will be unleashed in the apocalyptic future to wreck havoc upon the people of the Earth. Their sting will torment people with excruciating pain, so much so that men will seek death, but death will elude them for five months. One third of the total population of the Earth will eventually be killed by these demons from Hell (see Revelation 9).

During His earthly ministry, Jesus delivered many people who were possessed by demons. For instance, one day a demoniac who lived among the tombs came out to meet Him. Some had attempted to bind this man with chains, but he was so strong that he broke the chains. No one could control him. People were afraid to pass by the place where he lived because he was always shouting and cutting himself with stones. He recognized Jesus and, in fact, worshipped Him. He begged Jesus not to torment him before the time, but Jesus commanded the demons to come out of the man, and the man was instantly delivered. Afterward he was found sitting with Jesus, clothed and in his right mind (see Mark 5).

Mary Magdalene was among those whom Jesus delivered from the captivity and control of demons. She'd had seven demons. Can you imagine having seven demons? No wonder she loved Jesus so much that she followed Him, even to Calvary.

Mary Magdalene was still there when Jesus was resurrected. He said:

DREADFUL, DESTRUCTIVE AND DEADLY DEMONS

But if I cast out demons by the Spirit of God, surely the kingdom of God has come upon you.   Matthew 12:28

Therefore if the Son makes you free, you shall be free indeed.

John 8:36

Warning: If you have been delivered from demon possession and you are now clean and empty, don't remain empty for long. Otherwise, the demon who was ejected will come back to visit you, and if he finds you empty, he will invite more demons to join him in possessing you again, so that your situation will become much worse than before (see Matthew 12:43-45).

To fill yourself with God, find a good Bible-believing church and fellowship with God's people. Fill yourself with God's Word and His Spirit, and don't give the devil any place in your life. When he tempts you, resist him, and he will flee from you, in the name of Jesus! ✖

ɕ **72** ɞ

HOW THE MIGHTY BECAME MEEK

Text: Acts 7:22

In spite of his royal upbringing, Moses, when he was grown, began to identify with His Israelite people. One day when he visited
them he saw one of them being mistreated by an Egyptian. Going
to the man's defense, Moses killed the Egyptian. He thought that
surely his people would realize that God wanted to use him to
rescue them from their terrible slavery, but they did not.

The next day Moses came upon two Israelites who were fighting.
He tried to reconcile them by saying, "Men, you are brothers. Why
do you want to hurt each other?" But the man who was mistreating
the other pushed Moses aside and said, "Who made you ruler and
judge over us? Do you want to kill me, as you killed the Egyptian
yesterday?" (see Exodus 2:14). When Pharaoh, the king of Egypt,
heard about this, he tried to kill Moses, and Moses was forced to
flee to Midian, where he remained for the next forty years.

In Midian, Moses married Zipporah, one of the daughters of
Jethro, the priest of Midian. Zipporah bore Moses a son, and he

364

was named Gershom, which meant, *"I have been a stranger in a foreign land"* (Exodus 2:22).

During that long period, Moses worked as a shepherd, tending the flocks of his father-in law near Mount Horeb, the mountain of God. Then one day, the Angel of the Lord appeared there on that mountain in flames of fire coming from within a bush. When Moses went up to see this extraordinary phenomenon, he was amazed to see that the bush appeared to be on fire, but it did not burn up. What could this mean?

As Moses approached the burning bush, God called to him from within the bush, *"Moses, Moses!"* (Exodus 3:4).

Moses answered, *"Here I am"* (verse 4).

"Do not draw near this place," God said. *"Take your sandals off your feet, for the place where you stand is holy ground"* (Exodus 3:5). Moses was in the presence of God, and God was talking to him.

God continued: *"I am the God of your father—the God of Abraham, the God of Isaac, and the God of Jacob"* (Exodus 3:6).

For his part, Moses hid his face because he was afraid to look at God.

It was God's turn again:

And the LORD said. *"I have surely seen the oppression of My people who are in Egypt, and have heard their cry because of their taskmasters, for I know their sorrows. So I have come down to deliver them out of the hand of the Egyptians, and to bring them up from that land to a good and large land, to a land flowing with milk and honey, to the place of the Canaanites and the Hittites and the Amorites and the Perizzites and the Hivites and the*

Jebusites. Now therefore, behold, the cry of the children of Israel has come to Me, and I have also seen the oppression with which the Egyptians oppress them. Come now, therefore, and I will send you to Pharaoh that you may bring My people, the children of Israel, out of Egypt."   Exodus 3:7-10

Moses objected: *"Who am I that I should go to Pharaoh, and that I should bring the children of Israel out of Egypt?"* (Exodus 3:11).

God's answer was: *"I will certainly be with you"* (Exodus 3:12).

Between Moses' life in Egypt and his life in Midian, forty more years had now gone by. That made him eighty years old when he talked with God on Mt. Horeb. While most ministers of the Gospel today retire at sixty-five, Moses was just getting starting at eighty. Hallelujah!

What happened to Moses during those forty years in Midian? He did the seemingly mundane task of shepherding his father-in-law's flocks. What must have gone through his mind during those forty years? Did he regret his decision to renounce his Egyptian privileges? What was his feeling toward his fellow Israelites in Egypt? Had he lost faith and hope in God? Was he now a total failure, as far as the mission of delivering his people from Egyptian slavery and oppression was concerned? These are interesting and intriguing questions, and the Bible does not reveal most of the answers. We can only imagine. Only God and Moses know for sure.

But perhaps you and I, if we try to put ourselves in Moses' shoes (or sandals, in his case), can answer some of these questions. What would be the answer based on our personal experiences? If you asked me, I would say, "Of course, it would have been a normal and expected reaction to feel like a failure and to lose faith and hope after so many years of waiting. I, personally, would have been deeply disappointed and hurt that, after all the sacrifices I had made and my well-intentioned motives to help my people, I had become disgraced and rejected. It was an extreme degradation.

Quite honestly, I don't know what I would have done or how I would have reacted. It is a difficult question for us to answer, as we are only spectators in this narrative of Moses' ordeal. Would we feel like a total failure? Would we feel self-pity? Oh, yes, I think so.

And yet, through it all, the faith of Moses developed and became a living reality. In Egypt, he had endured as seeing the invisible God through the eyes of faith (probably by means of his mother's teachings). Now, at Mount Horeb, Moses was able to actually see God face-to-face. So he clearly had no problem with his relationship with God.

Moses' troubles were with himself, with the people of God and with Pharaoh, King of Egypt. These brought him disappointment and failure. But Moses overcame all of these troubles through a change of attitude. In Egypt, he was mighty, but with God at Mount Horeb, he became meek. What changed Moses? Was it his troubles? Or was it his forty years in Midian? I believe that it was seeing God face-to-face and being in His presence. If we want to succeed in our service to God, we must not only rely on our own thoughts or what other people think, but we must totally depend on and rely on God. We must never use God, but, instead, allow Him to use us. ✼

NONE OF THESE DISEASES

Text: Exodus 15:26

Following the crossing of the Red Sea by the Israelites, Moses led them through the Desert of Shur. They traveled for three days without finding water, and when they came to a place called Marah, they could not drink the water there because it was bitter. The people grumbled against Moses, so he cried out to the Lord, and the Lord showed him a piece of wood. He threw that piece of wood into the water, and the water became sweet. It was there that God gave His people the promise: *NONE OF THESE DISEASES*.

This was the first decree or law given to the Israelites by God after they came out of Egypt. But the object of the law, healing and freedom from disease, was incumbent upon their obedience to God's Word. This was a quasi-contract, and the two parties involved were God and the Israelites. The stipulated conditions of the contract were as follows: for the Israelites, they had to listen to God, do what was right in His sight, obey and keep His commands. The obligation of God was not to put any of *these diseases* upon them but, instead, to be their Healer.

Before we go any further, let us ask this question: do all diseases come from God? The answer is no, not all diseases come from God. It is obvious in this case, however, that it was God who put certain diseases upon the Egyptians. Those diseases were some sort of punishment for the fact that the Egyptians had defied God's commands. Disobeying God's commands brings consequences and has a punitive effect. Allowing the Egyptians to suffer sickness was divine justice, and that is God's sovereign prerogative.

More often than not, disease comes from the devil. The case of Job is a good example:

> So Satan [another name for the devil] went out from the presence of the LORD and afflicted Job with painful sores from the soles of his feet to the crown of his head.   Job 2:7

The devil always has bad intentions, and his motives for inflicting diseases on people are based on envy, his whims, pure caprice and his delight in doing evil. As Jesus said, " *The thief does not come except to steal, and to kill, and to destroy*" (John 10:10).

So, why did God say that He would heal His people and, at the same time promise *"none of these diseases"*? This principle of divine healing does not apply in the first instance. It applies to the second and the third instances, when the diseases comes from the devil and when God's people are vulnerable to disease by reason of their careless or promiscuous living. The sins of the past can bring diseases, even though we have already repented of those sins.

Who do you think healed Job of his diseases inflicted by the devil? Of course, it was God who healed him. So, in these last two instances, God is the Healer of His people.

Being human, however, makes us vulnerable to sickness and disease, so sometimes we can't blame either God or the devil for our diseases. Careless and promiscuous living and a disregard for proper hygiene can bring on self-invited sicknesses. The old saying, "Cleanliness is next to godliness" is true.

Not too long ago, the major health concern in the world was AIDS. Now, at this writing, it is the Ebola virus. This deadly disease has killed more than six thousand in three West African countries in recent years, and cases have been diagnosed in several other countries. Nations are terrified of this disease reaching their borders.

But the Ebola outbreak is nothing compared with the great wave of Bubonic Plague, also known as the Black Death, that reached pandemic proportions during the Middle Ages. The disease swept China, Europe and India and killed more than one hundred million people. It was the biggest killer of all times. What was the Black Death? It was an infection thought to be carried by the fleas on rats. These rats boarded ships and were carried all over the world, thus spreading the infection far and wide.

One of the ministry strategies of our Lord Jesus Christ during His evangelistic outreaches was healing the people's diseases:

Then Jesus went about all the cities and villages, teaching in their synagogues, preaching the gospel of the kingdom, and healing every sickness and every disease among the people.

Matthew 9:35

The people brought to Jesus were those who were ill with various diseases, those suffering severe pain, the demon-possessed, those having seizures, and the paralyzed, and He healed them all. In this way, Jesus practically wiped out sickness and disease in the Palestine of His day. His earthly ministry envisioned a time when there would be: *"none of these diseases."*

The subject of divine healing relative to human diseases is very relevant and material in our contemporary Christian life. God has promised divine healing then and now, since the time of Moses and the Israelites until today:

Jesus Christ is the same yesterday, today, and forever.

Hebrews 13:8

He honors those who fear the LORD*;*
He who swears to his own hurt and does not change.

Psalm 15:4

Several of God's promises regarding divine healing are:

I am the LORD *[Jehovah Rapha] who heals you.*   Exodus 15:26

Who Himself bore our sins in His own body on the tree, that we, having died to sins, might live for righteousness — by whose stripes you were healed.   1 Peter 2:24

371

For with God nothing will be impossible.   Luke 1:37

I believe in divine healing. Our eldest son had epilepsy when he was a little boy. My wife and I prayed for his healing, and God healed him. That was the last seizure he ever had.

My wife had a stroke a couple of years ago. Her face was disfigured, and she could hardly move her arm. She prayed to God by herself, invoking His promise of divine healing, and she was healed. Now, her face looks beautiful again, and she can move her arm normally.

Glory to God! Hallelujah! Have faith in God!   ✂

A PRELUDE TO CHRISTMAS

Text: Luke 1:5-13

Whereas the Old Testament ends with the word *curse*, the New Testament commences with blessings, double blessings as a matter of fact. These blessings were foretold in an announcement by no ordinary herald, but by the angel Gabriel who stands in the presence of God. Gabriel was sent to godly and devout people to inform them of the extraordinary births of two infants. The first announcement concerned the birth of John the Baptist and the second the birth of Jesus Himself. John the Baptist was to be the forerunner of our Lord Jesus Christ, to pave the way for His earthly ministry.

The first appearance of Gabriel was to Zacharias in the Temple in Jerusalem. When Zacharias saw the angel, standing at the right side of the altar of incense, he was startled and even gripped with fear. The angel told him not to be afraid. His prayer had been heard. His wife Elizabeth would bear a son. He was to name him John.

The angel went on:

373

And you will have joy and gladness, and many will rejoice at his birth. For he will be great in the sight of the Lord, and shall drink neither wine nor strong drink. He will also be filled with the Holy Spirit, even from his mother's womb. And he will turn many of the children of Israel to the Lord their God. He will also go before Him in the spirit and power of Elijah, "to turn the hearts of the fathers to the children," and the disobedient to the wisdom of the just, to make ready a people prepared for the Lord.

Luke 1:14-17

Zacharias and Elizabeth had no children because she was barren. Added to this was the fact that they were both growing old. Both of these individuals were descendants of the priestly line, and the Bible says that they were upright in the sight of God, observing all the commandments and regulations blamelessly.

Zacharias doubted the words of the angel Gabriel that day regarding the good news of the birth of a son in his old age, and as a result, he was struck dumb, meaning that he could no longer speak. This continued to be his condition until the birth of his son John. When he had completed his temple service that day and went home, Zacharias could only express himself through gestures.

Nevertheless, a miracle happened. Elizabeth was soon pregnant, and she remained in seclusion for the next five months. She was a happy woman. She declared:

The Lord has done this for me. In these days he has shown his favor and taken away my disgrace among the people.

Luke 1:25, NIV

374

Then, in Elizabeth's sixth month, God sent the angel Gabriel on another similar assignment. This time he went to Nazareth, a small town in Galilee, to visit a virgin named Mary:

> *The angel went to her and said, "Greetings, you who are highly favored! The Lord is with you."*
>
> *Mary was greatly troubled at his words and wondered what kind of greeting this might be. But the angel said to her, "Do not be afraid, Mary; you have found favor with God. You will conceive and give birth to a son, and you are to call him Jesus. He will be great and will be called the Son of the Most High. The Lord God will give him the throne of his father David, and he will reign over Jacob's descendants forever; his kingdom will never end."*
>
> *"How will this be," Mary asked the angel, "since I am a virgin?"*
>
> *The angel answered. "The Holy Spirit will come on you, and the power of the Most High will overshadow you. So the holy one to be born will be called the Son of God. Even Elizabeth your relative is going to have a child in her old age, and she who was said to be unable to conceive is in her sixth month. For no word from God will ever fail."*
>
> *"I am the Lord's servant," Mary answered. "May your word to me be fulfilled." Then the angel left her.*   Luke 1:28-38, NIV

These two remarkable and extraordinary events leading up to the birth of Jesus were characterized by the miraculous. Zacharias and Elizabeth were beyond childbearing age, and Elizabeth was barren. They must have been praying for a child because the angel said to them, *"Your prayer has been heard."* The answer to their prayer was a miracle baby, John the Baptist.

Mary was a virgin, and it would take a miracle for her to become impregnated. Through divine intervention, she also received a miracle baby—Jesus. All of these miracles were covered in one statement by the angel Gabriel:

For with God nothing will be impossible.　　　Luke 1:37

Is this message still relevant and material to us as Christians even in our contemporary times? Does God still do miracles? Does God still answer prayer? These are good questions, and they are relevant and material. I don't know about you, but I believe that God still does miracles today, and He still answers prayer. Maybe we're not having miracle babies these days, as did Elizabeth and Mary, but we have many other miraculous blessings.

Maybe the miracle you need is money. As the managing director of a mission and school, I have an enormous responsibility, especially in the area of finances. Our school, with more than two thousand children enrolled in both the elementary and high school, is a non-profit educational institution. Many of those children are not able to pay because they are from very poor families. We have more than ninety teachers and employees who expect their regular salaries and benefits twice each month.

My biggest financial burden comes each December. During that month, we are mandated by law to provide an extra month's pay for all of our teachers and workers. That alone requires ₱1 million. I can say that in twenty-five years of operation of our Star of

Hope in the Philippines, God has never failed us. He has always provided that extra ₱1 million every December. Praise the Lord! And glory to God! He has angels from many places who send in the money just in time. Hallelujah! So we always have a blessed and merry Christmas. ✂

❧ **75** ❧

REMEMBER LOT'S WIFE!

Text: Luke 17:32

One of the shortest verses in the Bible, these words were uttered by our Lord Jesus Christ, and they have serious warning implications still today.

The context of this passage speaks of two unprecedented cataclysmic events in the history of mankind. The first catastrophe was the universal deluge during the time of Noah, when all flesh perished (including every man who was not in the ark), in a watery grave. Only eight people survived the flood, together with the various animals that were in the ark.

The second catastrophe referred to here was the destruction of Sodom and Gomorrah with the other cities of the plain. All the inhabitants of those cities were incinerated with fire and brimstone, and only three souls escaped. These were God's early judgments on sinful mankind and a grim reality indeed.

When Jesus expounded these two terrifying Old Testament events, He was validating them as historical facts, and He was saying that the same type of devastating destruction will reoccur during the *"day of the Lord,"* which will transpire in the end times.

A repetition of a worldwide catastrophic flood has been already ruled out. In his covenant with Noah, God promised that He would never again destroy all of mankind by means of a universal flood. There is a probability, however, that the next divine judgment to be visited upon mankind will come by fire, as hinted at by Jesus when He cited the tragic incident at Sodom and Gomorrah.

Now who was Lot's wife? And, for that matter, who was Lot? The book of Genesis tells us that Lot was Abraham's nephew, who joined him when God called Abraham to go to Canaan. In time, Lot and his Uncle Abraham had a disagreement because of a skirmish between their respective herdsmen, and Abraham suggested that they part ways in order to avoid further misunderstanding. Abraham remained in Canaan, while Lot settled in Sodom.

With regards to Lot's wife, there is no indication in the book of Genesis that she was from the same country as Lot, so there is a strong probability that she was actually from Sodom itself. Sodom was a prosperous place at the time, but the men of Sodom were said to be *"exceedingly wicked and sinful against the* LORD*"* (Genesis 13:13).

Two angels, appearing as humans, came to Sodom and Gomorrah in order to execute God's judgment upon those places because of the gross sinfulness and sexual perversion (sodomy) of their citizens. Lot, his wife and two daughters were commanded to get out with haste from the city and escape for their lives because the time had come that the Lord would destroy those cities. The angels emphatically warned them not to look back:

Escape for your life! Do not look behind you nor stay anywhere in the plain. Escape to the mountains, lest you be destroyed.

Genesis 19:17

When Lot, his wife and his daughters were out of Sodom and on their way to a designated place of refuge, the Lord rained down fire and brimstone from Heaven and destroyed those cities with their inhabitants. But Lot's wife could not help herself; she looked back:

But his wife looked back behind him, and she became a pillar of salt. Genesis 19:26

Lost's wife was out of Sodom, but Sodom was not yet out of her. Jesus said:

You are the salt of the earth; but if the salt loses its flavor, how shall it be seasoned? It is then good for nothing but to be thrown out and trampled underfoot by men. Matthew 5:13

Don't look back to your sin and your old sinful life, but rather, look to Jesus, the Author and Finisher of our faith. He invites you now to come to Him. Receive Him as your Lord and Savior, and you will be saved. He said:

Come to Me, all you who labor and are heavy laden, and I will give you rest. Take My yoke upon you and learn from Me, for I am gentle and lowly in heart, and you will find rest for your souls. Matthew 11:28-29

ೞ **76** ൦

THE AGGRAVATING CIRCUMSTANCES OF SIN

Text: Romans 6:23

There are several judicial aspects that are analogous to sin, which was the consequence of Adam's disobedience. In political law, the violation of Adam and Eve was tantamount to treason. In civil law, it was an offense. The closest thing we can compare the sin of Adam and Eve to in criminal law is a crime. The apostle Paul did substantial explanation and elaboration in his writings regarding this judicial aspect, especially in the book of Romans. I presume that Paul was a lawyer before he was converted to Christ because he used legal terminology to explain our spiritual status before and after we accept Christ as our personal Lord and Savior.

The sin of Adam and Eve was a criminal act. It was a *mala prohibita*, in contradistinction to a *mala en se*, which act, by nature, is evil. An example of this crime is murder. Although there is nothing inherently evil in eating, it became evil when God precluded Adam and Eve from eating the fruit of the forbidden tree. God's command to them was this:

But of the tree of the knowledge of good and evil you shall not eat, for in the day that you eat of it you shall surely die.

Genesis 2:17

This included a punitive effect, meaning to say that Adam and Eve would be punished if they disobeyed God. What was their punishment? It was death, spiritual death. So it was capital punishment.

The punishment of Adam and Eve was clearly not physical death, as many Christians believe—including some pastors and theologians. How do we know this? By nature, they were already mortal, so even if they had not sinned, they would have died eventually. So there is a distinction between their nature and their act. Proof of this is that when Adam and Eve ate of the fruit anyway, they did not die (at least physically). They died spiritually.

Sin did not kill Adam and Eve physically, and conversely, when a person has Christ in him, that does not yet make him immortal. He will still die, awaiting resurrection to attain immortality.

The penalty for sin was fixed. It was spiritual death, the maximum penalty. Spiritual death implies separation from God, which is worse than physical death.

In criminal law, the circumstances surrounding the act of the crime may add burden to or make the penalty more severe. Spiritual death is what is called an accessory penalty, and it carries what is known as aggravating circumstances.

There are several elements to consider in order to determine that a crime committed carries with it a penalty that includes aggravating circumstances. Only one of these elements is required for an additional penalty to be imposed. So, what was the aggravating circumstance in the case of the sin of Adam and Eve? Their sin (the crime committed) was an insult, in contempt of and disregard for the respect due to the Sovereign Authority, none other than God Himself! And how was this accessory penalty imposed? It was imposed on the physical life of Adam and Eve, as well as upon all mankind through them.

To the woman, God said:

> *I will greatly multiply your sorrow and your conception;*
> *In pain you shall bring forth children;*
> *Your desire shall be for your husband,*
> *And he shall rule over you.*   Genesis 3:16

To Adam, God said:

> *Cursed is the ground for your sake;*
> *In toil you shall eat of it*
> *All the days of your life.*
> *Both thorns and thistles it shall bring forth for you,*
> *And you shall eat the herb of the field.*
> *In the sweat of your face you shall eat bread*
> *Till you return to the ground,*
> *For out of it you were taken;*
> *For dust you are,*
> *And to dust you shall return.*   Genesis 3:17-19

What is the opposite of aggravating circumstances? It is mitigating circumstances. In the case of mitigating circumstances, the penalty imposed is alleviated or made less severe. Was there an element of mitigating circumstance in the crime of Adam and Eve? I see at least one element, and it is that their crime, or sin, was instigated by an outside force, and he seemed to them to be irresistible.

How were the mitigating circumstance implemented? They were implemented by implication, when the Lord God made garments of skin for Adam and Eve and clothed them Himself. Later, in the New Testament, our Lord Jesus Christ expressed that mitigating circumstance, when He said:

> *Come to Me, all you who labor and are heavy laden, and I will give you rest. Take My yoke upon you and learn from Me, for I am gentle and lowly in heart, and you will find rest for your souls. For My yoke is easy and My burden is light.*
>
> Matthew 11:28-30

This is good news indeed!

Since I responded to the call of Jesus through the Gospel, came to Him and accepted Him as my Lord and Savior, my life has been changed for the better. I no longer have to struggle with the burden of living in sin and the guilt of it because God has already forgiven me, and He has provided all my needs.

As the pastor of a church, I don't receive much salary, but I have never complained about it. Somehow God always compensates me, not only in terms of having money and material things, but also in having good health and a loving and supportive wife and family. God has also given us favor with people who trusted us with ministry. We have sufficiency in Christ and more than enough, so that we are able to share with others and help the needy. Therefore, I am not a pauper pastor; I am living a mitigated Christian life.

Modesty aside, I have noticed that others who earn more money seem to always be in need. I have never understood why, in spite of their sizable income, they are in debt and are always borrowing money. Besides this, they are also miserable. Someone suggested that this might be due to a curse on them. If that is the case, their curse can be reversed and become a blessing. How? Right now, open your heart to God. Repent of your sins. Invite Jesus Christ into your heart and accept Him as your personal Lord and Savior. If you do this, your life will be changed into a blessed one.

God is a God of blessings. Even though you don't have much in terms of money or material possessions, as the saying goes: *"Little is much when God is in it."* The Scriptures teach:

The blessing of the LORD makes one rich,
And He adds no sorrow with it.　　　　　　Proverbs 10:22

The most wonderful news of all is that there exist justifying circumstances. This means that we will not incur criminal liability. We are absolved from the punishment of spiritual death and Hell. We will no longer be separated from God. Instead, we are reconciled to Him. Wow! How did that happen? Was there any element of justifying circumstance in the sinful (criminal) act of Adam and Eve to warrant this? No, there was none.

What then? Justifying circumstances are available to us through a judicial act of the sovereign God. He provided it through the sacrificial death of His Son, Jesus Christ, on the cross of Calvary. We call this act grace and mercy. This is what

Paul was talking all about in the book of Romans. Among other things, he wrote:

> *Therefore, having been justified by faith, we have peace with God through our Lord Jesus Christ, through whom also we have access by faith into this grace in which we stand, and rejoice in hope of the glory of God.* Romans 5:1-2

> *There is therefore now no condemnation to those who are in Christ Jesus, who do not walk according to the flesh, but according to the Spirit.* Romans 8:1

> *Therefore if the Son makes you free, you shall be free indeed.*
>
> Romans 8:36

✂

ဆ **77** ဘ

THE ESSENTIAL RIGHTEOUSNESS

Text: Matthew 5:20

There are two kinds of righteousness that Jesus was talking about here. The first was the righteousness of the Pharisees and teachers of the Law, and the second was a greater righteousness. This second type of righteousness is the key to entering the Kingdom of Heaven. This is the heart of the Sermon on the Mount, and this second righteousness is a condition precedent that must be in place before anyone can enter God's Kingdom.

What is this second righteousness? It is the righteousness of God imputed, or credited, to man as a consequence of his faith in God and in His Son Jesus Christ. The first righteousness is ruled out, as far as justification is concerned, because it is the righteousness of man, which, in the standard of God, is *"like filthy rags"* in His sight:

> *But we are all like an unclean thing,*
> *And all our righteousnesses are like filthy rags;*
> *We all fade as a leaf,*

387

And our iniquities, like the wind,
Have taken us away.   Isaiah 64:6

What is righteousness? It is "holy and upright living, in accordance with God's standard." It is a moral concept, which literally means "straightness." Righteousness is the consequence of obedience to the laws of God.

In the Old Testament, the term *righteousness* was used to define man's relationship with God and with others. Although the Pharisees and the teachers of the Law were the most devout and pious of all men, when it came to the observance of the Law, they fell short because they did not satisfy God's demand for righteousness. Paul confirmed this when he said:

There is none righteous, no, not one;
There is none who understands;
There is none who seeks after God.
They have all turned aside;
They have together become unprofitable;
There is none who does good, no, not one.   Romans 3:10-12

Paul meant that no one was able to fulfil the laws of God. Man could not be righteous in the sight of God on his own merits.

Is man hopeless then, with regards to obtaining the righteousness needed to enter the Kingdom of Heaven? The answer is no. Abraham, in the Old Testament, is a good example of how to obtain this acceptable righteousness. He was the forerunner of all believers. In the book of Romans, Paul presented an extensive commentary on Abraham obtaining this acceptable righteousness. There he said that Abraham had believed God, and that his faith had been credited to him as righteousness:

He did not waver at the promise of God through unbelief, but was strengthened in faith, giving glory to God, and being fully convinced that what He had promised He was also able to perform. And therefore "it was accounted to him for righteousness."

Now it was not written for his sake alone that it was imputed to him, but also for us. It shall be imputed to us who believe in Him who raised up Jesus our Lord from the dead, who was delivered up because of our offenses, and was raised because of our justification.

Romans 4:20-25

Nowadays, in New Testament times, the only way a man or woman can obtain the acceptable righteousness is through faith in Jesus Christ. He is the righteousness from God revealed to us. He is our righteousness.

In His Sermon on the Mount, Jesus said that He had come to fulfil the Law, something no one else could do. Therefore, when we believe in Jesus Christ, it is as if we had already fulfilled the Law in and through Him.

For this reason, it is always indispensable for us, in our evangelistic challenges to others to be saved, to make it clear to them that every person must receive Jesus Christ as personal Lord and Savior after repenting of their sins. It is in this way, one receives the righteousness of God in his life, which righteousness is the only way one can become acceptable to God.

When we accept Christ and His righteousness, God then sees us as righteous because of our identification, by faith, with His Son Jesus Christ. This gift of righteousness becomes the door that will open for anyone who is willing to enter the Kingdom of Heaven. Jesus also told His followers:

Blessed are those who hunger and thirst for righteousness,
For they shall be filled.   Matthew 5:6

 G3 **78** 80

THE GREATEST ESCAPE

Text: Exodus 14:2 and 9

After Moses and the Israelites had come out of Egypt, the Lord told them to camp by the sea. But when the King of Egypt was told that his Hebrew slaves had fled, he and his other officials changed their minds about releasing them. So he had his chariots made ready and took an army with six hundred of his best chariots along to pursue the Israelites. Thus Pharaoh, with all of his horses and chariots, went after the Israelites and soon overtook them at their camp by the sea.

As Pharaoh approached, the Israelites looked up, and there were the Egyptians, marching after them. They were terrified and cried out to the Lord. They said to Moses:

Because there were no graves in Egypt, have you taken us away to die in the wilderness? Why have you so dealt with us, to bring us up out of Egypt? Is this not the word that we told you in Egypt, saying, "Let us alone that we may serve the Egyptians"? For it would have been better for us to serve the Egyptians than that we should die in the wilderness. Exodus 14:11-12

Moses answered them:

Do not be afraid. Stand still, and see the salvation of the Lord, which He will accomplish for you today. For the Egyptians whom you see today, you shall see again no more forever. The Lord will fight for you, and you shall hold your peace.

Exodus 14:13-14

Then the Lord spoke to Moses:

Why do you cry to Me? Tell the children of Israel to go forward. But lift up your rod, and stretch out your hand over the sea and divide it. And the children of Israel shall go on dry ground through the midst of the sea. Exodus 14:15-16

Moses stretched out his hand over the sea, and all that night the Lord drove the waters back with a strong east wind, until the bottom of the sea had turned into dry land. The waters were divided, and the Israelites went through the sea on dry ground, with one wall of water on their right and another on their left. Undaunted, the Egyptians pursued, and all of Pharaoh's horses and chariots and horsemen followed into the sea.

Then the Lord spoke to Moses again to stretch out his hand over the sea so that the waters would flow back over the Egyptians and their chariots and horsemen. Moses did this, and at daybreak the sea flowed back into its place.

As the water flowed back, it covered the chariots and horsemen — the entire army of Pharaoh that had followed the Israelites into the sea. Not one Egyptian soldier survived that day. In this way, the Lord saved the Israelites from the hands of the Egyptians. When the Israelites saw the great power the Lord displayed against the Egyptians, they feared the Lord and put their trust in Him and in Moses His servant (see Exodus 14 31).

The exodus of the Israelites from Egypt was one of the most amazing, extraordinary, dramatic and fantastic events in the history of mankind. More than six hundred thousand men, besides women and children, were involved in this mass departure. They also brought along with them their livestock and their other belongings. The sheer number of people to guide and the volume of property to transport must have been a logistical nightmare for Moses, Aaron and the other elders. It was an immense task and responsibility for the leaders to bring these people through the desert and on to the Promise Land, said to be *"flowing with milk and honey"* (Exodus 3:8).

How did the Israelites know which way to go to reach their destination? They had no compasses yet. Did Moses or any of the other leaders know the way? The Bible shows that the Lord Himself was their Guide. By day He went ahead of them in a pillar of cloud, to guide them on their way, and by night He appeared to them in a pillar of fire to give them light and warmth. So the Israelites were able to travel by day and also by night. In all their journeying, neither the pillar of cloud by day nor the pillar of fire by night left its place before them.

Why did Pharaoh and his officials change their minds and pursue the Israelites into the desert? Was their motive to avenge the deaths of all the Egyptian firstborn? Were they bent on killing all the Israelites? No, Pharaoh and the Egyptians needed the Israelites alive, and the Israelites would have been no use to them dead. Life would now be very hard for the Egyptians without the accustomed services of their Israelite slaves. So, they wanted them alive, and they wanted to bring them back to Egypt.

Unfortunately for the Israelites, they actually felt they would rather go back to Egypt and continue serving the Egyptians, even under these cruel circumstances, rather than die in the desert. God knew this from the beginning. Rather than face their enemy, they would prefer to go back to Egypt and become slaves again. The Israelites were out of Egypt, but Egypt was not out of them yet. All they were thinking about was dying rather than depending on the Lord.

Did God want the Israelites to go back to Egypt? Absolutely not! Although there was a shorter route to the Promised Land, God led them through the desert, which was definitely a longer route. The reason was: if they had taken a shorter route, they might have encountered warlike inhabitants, and they might have changed their minds and gone back to Egypt.

God did not want His people to return to Egypt and be enslaved again by their former taskmasters. In fact, I believe that God helped the Israelites cross the Red Sea as on a dry ground, to keep them from turning back. Once the Israelites were on the other side of the sea, there was no way they could have returned to Egypt. They now had no other recourse than to proceed to the Promised Land, just as God had planned. This was God's purpose for the greatest escape ever, that His people would not return to Egypt.

Our Christian life is analogous to the life of the Israelites. It has been said that Christians are the spiritual Israelites. The journey of the Israelites to the Promised Land is similar in many aspects to our spiritual experiences, which are filled with many difficult challenges and testings. Christians are besieged with temptations, which are often recurring. We are surrounded with pressures from multiple perils, some of which are trials involving our physical health, finances, work and even relationships. Sometimes we are confused by all of this, and we don't know what to do. The Bible says that these temptations and trials are common to all followers of Christ (see 1 Corinthians 10:13).

What is most reassuring in our journey of faith is this: just as the Lord was with the Israelites in their journey to the Promised Land, He is also with us—always. His providence and power will help us escape or overcome all obstacles and will give us victory in the name of Jesus Christ our Lord! Praise the Lord! Glory to His name! Hallelujah!

THE RELEVANCE AND REALITY OF ANGELS

Text: Genesis 3:24 and Hebrews 1:13-14

Throughout the Bible, from the book of Genesis to the book of Revelation, we see the active involvement of angels in the affairs of God and man. We first see these heavenly beings in the Garden of Eden, standing guard with a flaming sword. They were tasked to preclude Adam and Eve from the tree of life after man had sinned against God.

Who or what are angels? We know very little about the origin of these heavenly beings. The Bible, however, does reveal that angels were also created and that they are spirit beings. They already existed before the Earth was created. Sometimes they were referred to as *"son[s] of the morning"* (Isaiah 14:12) or *"sons of God"* (Job 1:6, 2:1 and 38:7). They were created immortal, and therefore they cannot die. They are superior, compared with man, in terms of power and intelligence, but they are not all-powerful, and they are not omniscient.

At one time, an angel of the Lord massacred 185,000 Assyrian soldiers in one night. That's how powerful an angel is, so don't mess with them. They are also innumerable.

396

There are orders and ranks of angels according to the Bible. There are, for instance, the seraphim, the cherubim and the four living creatures. The main duty of these three orders of angels is to proclaim the holiness and the glory of God. They are constantly praising God around His throne. These are winged angels, but not all angels are winged. Some angels even appear in human form. There are the archangels—Michael and Gabriel—and the rest of the angels are guardian, guiding and protecting beings.

Angels were active participants before and during the birth of Christ. They announced the Good News of His birth first to Mary and, later, to the shepherds. An angel appeared to Joseph in a dream, clarifying some issues about Mary and warned Joseph of the impending danger to the child Jesus from the plotting of Herod, the current king.

Multitudes of angels came down from Heaven and sang praises to God at the birth of Jesus. Angels came and ministered to Jesus after His severe temptation in the wilderness. Thousands of angels were at the disposition of Jesus if He wanted to escape the death on the cross, but He did not.

The first herald of Jesus' resurrection was an angel as well, and angels proclaimed the return of Jesus to the disciples who were looking up as He was taken into Heaven.

Besides our protection and guidance, angels are also interested in the salvation of the lost. In fact, they rejoice when a soul gets saved.

I believe that every follower of Christ, being an *"heir of salva-tion,"* has a guardian angel dispatched by God to keep watch over them. This is good news! More good news is that God will elevate all followers of Christ at the resurrection to be *"as the angels"* in Heaven (Mark 12:25)!

397

In these dangerous times, security is a paramount concern for people the world over. We, as followers of Christ, need not worry because we have angels to guard us. Some years ago, I had a car accident while on my way up to Baguio City. [2] My car sustained serious damage in the accident, and it was thrown to the other side of the road. Miraculously, in all of this, I was unhurt. I believe that my guardian angel protected me. Praise God!

Can anyone avail themselves of a guardian angel? No, guardian angels are exclusively dispatched and assigned to those who are the *"heirs of salvation."* How can a person become an heir of salvation? It is easy, but it is also hard. Repent of your sins and receive Jesus Christ as your Lord and Savior. Then, live for God and follow Christ, and you will become an heir of salvation. ✄

---

2. For those who are not familiar with Baguio City, it is the largest city in Northern Luzon, it sits high in the mountains, and the road leading there is winding and can be treacherous. The population of this once-small mountain town has now soared to over 300,000.

ೞ **80** ೞ

THE SIGNIFICANCE OF TEN RIGHTEOUS

Text: Genesis 18:1-5

One of the theophanies [3] in the Old Testament occurred when Abraham invited three persons to visit with him in his tent. These three visitors were no ordinary beings. Two of them were angels, and the third was the Lord Himself. Many theologians believe that He was the pre-incarnate Christ.

That day the Lord brought Abraham two pieces of news. The first one was good news, and the second one was bad news. The good news was that Sarah, Abraham's wife, would bear him a child, even though she was past the childbearing age. This would be a miracle. The second bit of news concerned the imminent destruction of Sodom and Gomorrah, together with the cities of the plains, because of their exceeding wickedness.

It is interesting to note that a sovereign God would reveal His plans ahead of time to one of His created beings such as Abraham. It was a great honor and privilege for Abraham that God Almighty would disclose to him His will. But, then, Abraham was a special

---

3. A visible appearance of God, usually in human form

person in the eyes of God. He was, in fact, *"the Friend of God"* (James 2:23).

While the two angels proceeded to Sodom and Gomorrah to execute the judgment of God upon those cities, the Lord remained with Abraham. Knowing that his nephew Lot and his family were in the city of Sodom, Abraham began to intercede for Lot through an extraordinary and remarkable prayer. In approaching God on this subject, Abraham began with a question:

Would You also destroy the righteous with the wicked? Suppose there were fifty righteous within the city; would You also destroy the place and not spare it for the fifty righteous that were in it?

Genesis 18:23-24

God answered:

If I find in Sodom fifty righteous within the city, then I will spare all the place for their sakes. Genesis 18:25

Abraham now apologized for his boldness, but he had to ask a similar question? Suppose there were forty-five righteous in the city. Would God still destroy it? God answered:

If I find there forty-five, I will not destroy it. Genesis 18:28

But Abraham was not satisfied. He felt compelled to ask about forty, about thirty, about twenty and then about ten. God was consistent with His answers to this passionate prayer of Abraham. He would not destroy Sodom and Gomorrah for the sake of forty righteous, or thirty, or twenty or even ten. Unfortunately, Abraham stopped interceding at that point, and apparently there were not even ten righteous people to be found in all of Sodom and Gomorrah, and because of it, those cities were destroyed.

How unbelievable that out of the thousands of inhabitants of Sodom and Gomorrah, together with the cities of the plain, there was to be found only one righteous person, and that person was Abraham's nephew Lot. If there had been even ten righteous people there, Sodom and Gomorrah would not have been obliterated.

This all teaches us a divine principle of judgment: God will not destroy the righteous with the wicked. This means that the whole world owes a lot to the Christians. Why? Because we are *"the salt [or preservative] of the earth"* (Matthew 5:3). If anyone alive values human life, it is the Christian. Christians build more hospitals and more schools than anyone else. They have more involvement in humanitarian aid than anyone else, and they are very much into the preservation of our environment. The world as a whole is ripe for divine judgment, but because of the Christians in it, this judgment is yet averted.

How can we become righteous? Will our own righteousness suffice? No, our own righteousness is not acceptable to God. It is *"like filthy rags"* (Isaiah 64:6). The only acceptable righteousness to God is to be found in Jesus Christ. That's why it is indispensable that we receive Jesus Christ as our Lord and Savior.

We must first repent of our sins and receive Jesus Christ into our hearts by faith. Then and only then can we become righteous. In Christ, righteousness is imputed to us. Praise God! Glory to His holy name!

❧ **81** ☙

WHEN GOD BECAME A MAN

Text: John 1:1-5

This was the foreword to John's Gospel. He continued with this:

He was in the world, and the world was made through Him, and the world did not know Him. He came to His own, and His own did not receive Him. But as many as received Him, to them He gave the right to become children of God, to those who believe in His name: who were born, not of blood, nor of the will of the flesh, nor of the will of man, but of God.　　　　John 1:10-13

If that was not wonderful enough, he added:

And the Word became flesh and dwelt among us, and we beheld His glory, the glory as of the only begotten of the Father, full of grace and truth.　　　　John 1:14

This foreword to John's gospel is a paraphrase of Genesis 1, the first chapter of the first book of the Bible. Notice the similarities between the first phrases of each of the two books. Moses [4] opened his book with the words *"in the beginning"* (Genesis 1:1), and John opened his gospel with the same words.

Moses continued, *"In the beginning God"* and, in the same way, John wrote, *"In the beginning was the Word."* Both God and the Word were *"in the beginning,"* according to Moses and John.

John added that *"the Word was God"* and that He was *"with God"* in the beginning. There is no doubt that he was referring to Jesus as the Word and was showing us that He was and is God. As proof of this fact, John referred to Jesus as the One who created the world: *"All things were made through Him [Jesus], and without Him [Jesus] nothing was made that was made."*

Just as Genesis was the book of beginnings of the Old Testament, the gospel of John is the book of beginnings for the New Testament, the beginnings of the life and ministry of Jesus Christ, the Son of God, sent to redeem mankind.

It is also interesting to note that in Genesis 1:2, after God created the heavens and the earth, the earth was *"formless and empty,"* and *"darkness was over the surface of the deep"* (NIV). Some Bible scholars believe that between verses 1 and 2 a cataclysmic event occurred that rendered the earth empty and in darkness. They speculate that the earth had once been inhabited by angels who rebelled against God, and that this rebellion resulted in the destruction, emptiness and darkness of the earth. [5] These scholars may be speculating, but they have several biblical references to back up their theory. If

4. Most Bible scholars agree that Moses was the author of the book of Genesis.
5. Could this have been the time when dinosaurs and other giant animals roamed the earth?

they are right, then what Genesis 1:3 relays is actually a re-creation of the earth, not the original creation.

Both Moses and John mention light:

And God said, "Let there be light," and there was light.

Genesis 1:3, NIV

John also mentioned the light, but he said that Jesus Christ is the light of men and that He shines in darkness.

Now, several questions must be asked: How did God become a man? Why did God become a man? Where did this happen? And when did this happen?

Maybe it would be logical to start with the second question: Why did God become a man? I can think of at least two reasons given by the Bible. The first is that He did it to save mankind from sin and destruction:

For God so loved the world that he gave his one and only Son, that whoever believes in him shall not perish but have eternal life. For God did not send his Son into the world to condemn the world, but to save the world through him. Whoever believes in him is not condemned, but whoever does not believe stands condemned already because they have not believed in the name of God's one and only Son.   John 3:16-18

The second reason, I believe, why God became a man was to show people everywhere who He was. Before He became a man, people didn't know the one true and living God. They worshipped many different gods, even unknown gods. This is one reason why there are so many different religions in the world. In Jesus Christ, we see, know and understand the true and living God, because He is God. He is *"the express image"* of the invisible God (Hebrews 1:3). Besides the other innumerable witnesses and His own words and miraculous works, God the Father Himself affirmed the deity of Jesus.

How did God become a man? The Bible says, *"The Word became flesh and made His dwelling among us"* (NIV). The modern word for this miracle is *incarnation.* Mary was instrumental in this divine process. This is the doctrine that the eternal Son of God became human and that He did so without, in any manner or degree, diminishing His divine nature.

This divine condescension is also relative to the other questions I mentioned: Where and when did this happen? It happened in a little town called Bethlehem (where King David was from). Joseph had taken Mary and gone to Bethlehem to register for the census because he was of the lineage of David. While they were there, Jesus was born. They had found lodging in a stable, and now Mary wrapped the baby Jesus in cloths and placed Him in a manger.

This momentous and historical event happened this way because Caesar Augustus had issued a decree that a census should be taken of the entire Roman world, and everyone was sent to their hometown to register. Was it just a coincidence? Definitely not. It was divine providence.

That God became man is the basis of the Christmas story. Christ, the Son of God, was born in Bethlehem of Judea, and His birth was welcomed by multitudes of angelic hosts, who all sang in jubilation:

Glory to God in the highest,

And on earth peace, goodwill toward men! Luke 2:14

Unfortunately, only a handful of people welcomed Jesus' birth. These were led by Mary and Joseph and the shepherds, but they also included some of those who heard the news the shepherds offered. Most of those who heard about His birth were indifferent, but not the shepherds:

Then the shepherds returned, glorifying and praising God for all the things that they had heard and seen, as it was told them.

Luke 2:20

At Christmas time and every day of the year, let us welcome Jesus Christ by receiving Him into our hearts, our homes, our churches and our communities with joy and gladness, just like Mary, Joseph and the shepherds did that first Christmas day. Let Christ's birth be the center and the focus of our Christmas celebrations and our daily walk. Let us know and understand the significance and the true meaning of God becoming a man. In this way, we will have a truly blessed and merry Christmas and can count on a happy and prosperous New Year to come—every year.

✾

When God Gave Up

Text: Romans 1:24-26 and 32

Does God run out of patience with sinful and wicked people? Yes, it is apparent that He does. In this passage, such people are clearly warned of the impending wrath of God from Heaven:

God gave them up.   Verse 24

God gave them up.   Verse 26

This phrase *"god gave them up"* is used twice in quick succession in this first chapter of Romans. This suggests a seriousness and a heartfelt concern with regards to the judgment to be visited upon rebellious people, whether individually or as a nation. God said:

Because I have called and you refused,
I have stretched out my hand and no one regarded,

Because you disdained all my counsel,
And would have none of my rebuke,
I also will laugh at your calamity;
I will mock when your terror comes,
When your terror comes like a storm,
And your destruction comes like a whirlwind,
When distress and anguish come upon you.
Then they will call on me, but I will not answer;
They will seek me diligently, but they will not find me.
Because they hated knowledge
And did not choose the fear of the LORD,
They would have none of my counsel
And despised my every rebuke.
Therefore they shall eat the fruit of their own way,
And be filled to the full with their own fancies.
For the turning away of the simple will slay them,
And the complacency of fools will destroy them;
But whoever listens to me will dwell safely,
And will be secure, without fear of evil.   Proverbs 1:24-33

There are two specific sins which are foremost among the causes of God's pronouncement of judgment upon certain people: idolatry and sexual immorality. Other sins are mentioned—like murder, covetousness, disobedience to parents, wickedness, hatred of God, lawbreaking, boastfulness and the lack of mercy—but two are shown to be of the utmost importance.

What is idolatry? It is "worshipping something created rather than the Creator Himself." This is a violation of the second commandment concerning the making and worshipping of images. This religious practice was prevalent from the time of Abraham on down through the Old Testament and then into New Testament times. The Greeks and Romans were idolaters, and the early Church was contaminated with their idolatry after Christianity was declared the state religion of the Roman Empire. Ever since then, many have been blinded to idolatrous worship, which God detests and abhors.

What is sexual immorality? It is "the promiscuous practice and relationships between two persons of the same sex." Other names for it are sodomy and homosexuality. Whereas, in the old days, to be gay was "taboo," nowadays, it is accepted. Gays are now proud to proclaim to the world that they are gay and that "gay is okay." No matter what justifications or arguments these people might put forward, in the sight of God it is *not* okay. According to many medical experts, the proliferation of the deadly disease known as AIDS (Auto Immune Deficiency Syndrome) is the consequence of this unnatural sexual practice. AIDS leaves a Sword of Damocles hanging over the heads of those who practice unnatural sex.

What was the effect when God gave these people up to a reprobate mind? The destruction of the inhabitants of Sodom and Gomorrah is one very good Bible answer. Despite the intercessory prayers of the righteous Abraham, the wickedness of the people was so overwhelming that finally God decided to annihilate them with fire and brimstone from Heaven.

Is that scary? Yes, it certainly is! Is there a remedy? Yes! Can God reverse His impending judgment? Yes! The case of the people of Nineveh in the Old Testament is a very good example. God sent His prophet Jonah to announce impending doom to the people of Nineveh because of their wickedness. The result was that from the greatest to the least, the people of Nineveh believed God and repented, and God spared them from judgment.

God is *"no respecter of persons"* (Acts 10:34, KJV), and He is *"the same yesterday, today and forever"* (Hebrews 13:8). If you are willing to repent and turn from your wicked ways, you can save yourself from the wrath of God to come. Open your heart in prayer and receive Jesus Christ as your personal Lord and Savior, and you will be saved. Then follow God and live for Him the rest of your life.

❈

WHO WERE THE WISE MEN OF CHRISTMAS?

Text: Matthew 2:1-2

Several mysterious men called *magi* or *wise men* came to Jerusalem looking for Jesus. The circumstances surrounding them and their visit have been shrouded in controversy ever since. Who were they? And where were they from?

One of our traditional Christmas carols says:

We three kings of Orient are;
Bearing gifts we traverse afar,
Field and fountain, moor and mountain,
Following yonder star. [6]

Were these visitors really kings? Were there really three of them? Were they really riding on camels, as they have been depicted in many popular artistic conceptions? Were they really from the Orient? There are many things yet to be clarified concerning these mysterious guests.

6. John Henry Hopkins, Jr., 1857

411

First, the Bible does not call them kings, but, rather, magi or wise men. Next, there were probably more than three of them. In those days it was very dangerous to travel in small groups, especially that far because thieves waited along the known travel routes to steal anything they could. So these men were probably part of a brigade of magi.

Were they riding camels? Probably not. Something about the wise men caused Herod and the people of Jerusalem to fear, so some have wondered if they might not have been mounted on powerful steeds outfitted for war.

Matthew described the wise men as having come from *"the east,"* not necessarily from the Orient.

Several places in the Bible speak of wise men. The first was during the time of Joseph, when Pharaoh, the king of Egypt, had a dream and was troubled about the dream. When he woke up, he sent for men he thought might be able to explain his dream:

> *Now it came to pass in the morning that his spirit was troubled, and he sent and called for all the magicians of Egypt and all its wise men. And Pharaoh told them his dreams, but there was no one who could interpret them for Pharaoh.*   Genesis 41:8

Pharaoh told these respected men his dreams, but not one of them was able to interpret it. This was what led to Joseph being called from the prison, and with wisdom and favor from God, he was able to interpret the dream.

The second mention of wise men was during the time of Moses. This also took place in Pharaoh's court, but it was a different time and a different Pharaoh. When Aaron, Moses' brother, threw his staff in front of Pharaoh and it became a snake, Pharaoh then summoned men called wise men, sorcerers and magicians, and they seemingly were able to do the same thing by their magic arts:

> *But Pharaoh also called the wise men and the sorcerers; so the magicians of Egypt, they also did in like manner with their enchantments. For every man threw down his rod, and they became serpents. But Aaron's rod swallowed up their rods. And Pharaoh's heart grew hard, and he did not heed them, as the LORD had said.* Exodus 7:11-13

The third mention of wise men also involved a dream. This time it was King Nebuchadnezzar of Babylon who had dreamed, and again he was troubled by his dreams and could no longer sleep. Like the Pharaoh before him, King Nebuchadnezzar summoned men whom he thought might be able to help him interpret his dreams. The problem was that he had forgotten the dreams, so now he expected them to first tell him the dreams and then tell him the interpretation:

> *Then the king gave the command to call the magicians, the astrologers, the sorcerers, and the Chaldeans to tell the king his dreams.* Daniel 2:2

Here, for the first time, we can see a possible connection to our magi of Matthew 2. These men were learned and prominent. They were employed at the King's court, possibly as advisers or consultants to the king. Many historians suggest that although these men were not kings themselves, they were almost certainly kingmakers. One of them was named Daniel, and he was a Jewish exile in the land.

During the Babylonian captivity of the Jews, sometime around 586 B.C., Daniel was found among those who had been carried away captive into Babylon. By Providence, he was chosen and trained as a member of this group of magi, due to the exceptional talents God had given him. He could understand visions and dreams of all kinds, and when examined, he was found *"ten times better"* than all the magicians and enchanters in the whole of the kingdom (Daniel 1:20).

When the first group of magicians and astrologers called were unable to tell the king his dreams and their interpretation, he was so furious that he ordered the execution of all the wise men in Babylon. The decree of death which was issued as a result included Daniel and his friends.

When Daniel received this notice, he quickly went to the palace to ask the king for a little more time. He then returned home and told his friends what was happening, and they all began to pray for wisdom. The clock was ticking.

After prayer, Daniel was very confident:

> *Then Daniel went to Arioch, whom the king had appointed to execute the wise men of Babylon, and said to him, "Do not execute the wise men of Babylon. Take me to the king, and I will interpret his dream for him."*
> Daniel 2:24

That confidence was not misplaced. Daniel was indeed able to interpret the king's dreams. In doing this, Daniel was able, not only to save himself and his friends, but also all of the wise men of the land.

Because Daniel saved these men from certain death, I believe he was given the opportunity to share with them his faith in God, and many were converted. There is also no doubt in my mind that Daniel told them about the prophecies concerning the coming Messiah. Because of their Daniel connection, these magi or wise men embraced the God of Daniel.

It seems apparent to me that the magi or wise men who came to Jerusalem seeking the newborn King of the Jews were descendants of the group of people whom Daniel had converted to his Jewish faith. How else could these Magi know about the birth of the Messiah, unless someone had told them this information? Daniel was the link. He gave them this information.

What about the star that the wise men saw in the east and that guided them until it rested over the place where the infant Jesus was? Was it a heavenly body as many suggest? I don't believe that this star was a heavenly body, otherwise the place where it rested would have burned. I believe that this star was the glory of Jesus, which He temporarily relinquished. This is what the Magi saw in the east, and it guided them to the place where the infant Jesus was.

If we look at a map of the land in those days and trace back to where the magi might have come from, *"the east"* was just about where present-day Iraq is located. That is also where ancient Babylon was located, so it was a logical base for our Daniel connection.

The magi of Matthew 2, after finding Jesus and fulfilling their mission of worshipping Him and giving Him their gifts, returned to their own country with new faith in the Lord. This explains why there are many Christians in Iraq. I believe that the Christians there are descendants of the magi who found the baby Jesus in Bethlehem of Judea.

Oh, how amazing and wonderful are the grace and mercy of God! This group of people, who were of the priestly caste of the Medes and who practiced astrology, divination, sorcery and magic, were once detestable in the sight of God. In fact, God warned and precluded the Israelites from involving themselves in any of these detestable practices when they entered Canaan. But through the Daniel connection, these magi became the first gentile witnesses of Christmas and eventually became the first gentile converts to Christianity.

The big challenge for us Christians today, relative to this Christmas episode, is to be more like Daniel. Let us be bold in our witness for Christ and share our faith in God with unbelievers wherever and whenever we have the opportunity. Jesus said:

But you will receive power when the Holy Spirit comes on you; and you will be my witnesses in Jerusalem, and in all Judea and Samaria, and to the ends of the earth. Acts 1:8

❧ 84 ❧

WHY DO BAD THINGS HAPPEN TO GOOD AND GODLY PEOPLE?

Text: Psalm 37:23-24

There is a saying: "If there is an effect, then there must be a cause." This can be expressed conversely: "With every cause, there is an effect." Are there always causes to the bad things that happen to good and godly people? Maybe if those same bad things happened to bad people, we might not question them. We might even concur with many that bad things happen to bad people as a consequence of their bad behavior. Why? And what are the causes of the bad things that happen to good and godly people? To find the answer to these questions, let us look at examples of good and godly people in the Bible who experienced bad things in their lives.

First, let us look at Samson in the book of Judges. Samson was a good man. As a matter of fact, he was extraordinarily gifted. When the Spirit of God came upon him, he had superhuman strength. With this strength, he became a deliverer of his people, the Israelites, against the oppression and affliction of their enemies,

417

the Philistines. At one time, Samson killed a thousand Philistines using only the jawbone of a donkey. But some bad things also happened to Samson, despite his previous victories against his enemies. Eventually he suffered defeat and humiliation at their hands, and his life ended in tragedy. Why?

The causes of the bad things that happened to Samson are not hard to find. He unwisely involved himself with bad women, and those bad women were from among his enemies, the Philistines. The greater reason was that the Lord had left him, and Samson failed to recognize that fact until it was too late.

Another example was David. He was a good man and one of God's favorite people. In fact, he was dubbed: *"a man after his [God's] own heart"* (1 Samuel 13:14). David taught us much about worship and left us his powerful psalms as an example to follow. In one of those many powerful psalms, he sang these words: *"The steps of a good man are ordered by the LORD, and He delights in his way."* Unfortunately, bad things happened to David and his family. His son Absalom rebelled against him and was killed. Including Absalom, four of David's children died tragic deaths.

David also suffered terrible shame and scandal. Why? What was the cause? The answer is not hard to find. He had no business engaging in an adulterous relationship with a married woman named Bathsheba. He got so obsessed with this woman that he hatched a sinister plot to murder her husband, and that plot was carried out. It goes without saying that these things strongly displeased the Lord.

On the other hand, Daniel had some friends who escaped the effects of the bad things that seemed destined to destroy them. Their names were Shadrach, Meshach and Abednego, and they were also among the Jewish exiles in Babylon.

WHY DO BAD THINGS HAPPEN TO GOOD AND GODLY PEOPLE?

The king made a decree that everyone must bow down and worship the golden image he had set up, and anyone who refused would be instantly thrown into a blazing furnace. For their part, these three men decided not to obey, and when the time came to bow down, they refused. When they were drug before the king, and he reminded them of the consequences of their actions, they responded:

O Nebuchadnezzar, we have no need to answer you in this matter. If that is the case, our God whom we serve is able to deliver us from the burning fiery furnace, and He will deliver us from your hand, O king. But if not, let it be known to you, O king, that we do not serve your gods, nor will we worship the gold image which you have set up. Daniel 3:16-18

Nebuchadnezzar was furious with such insolence, and he ordered the furnace to be heated seven times hotter than usual. Then he commanded the strongest of his soldiers to tie these three men up and throw them into the blazing furnace. The fire was so intense that even the soldiers who took up Meshach, Shadrach and Abednego were killed.

When the three fell into the blazing furnace, the king leaped to his feet in amazement at what he saw before him and asked:

Did we not cast three men bound into the midst of the fire?...

Look! ... I see four men loose, walking in the midst of the fire; and they are not hurt, and the form of the fourth is like the Son of God. Daniel 3:24-25

419

Those three Hebrew young men came out of the fire, and the king's officer saw that the fire had not harmed their bodies Their hair and clothes had no smell of fire on them. In this ways, God was glorified, and the king declared that no one in his kingdom would be allowed to speak a word against the God of Meshach, Shadrach and Abednego, who were then promoted.

Another example of this effect was Daniel himself. When King Darius promoted Daniel to the top position in the kingdom, other officials became jealous of him. They tried to find any charge or accusation of corruption or negligence against him they could make, but could not, because he was so trustworthy. So they devised a scheme and persuaded the king to issue an edict that anyone who prayed to any god besides the king would be thrown into a lions' den.

Daniel was not intimidated by the king's decree, and he remained resolute in his faith in God—the true God, the God of Israel. As was his regular practice, he got down on his knees and prayed, giving thanks to God every day in his house. Soon Daniel's enemies went to the king and told him that Daniel was violating his decree. Although the king was hesitant, he ordered that Daniel be thrown into the lions' den. Because he knew Daniel, he expected God to help him. He said to Daniel:

Your God, whom you serve continually, He will deliver you.

Daniel 6:16

That night the king was restless and could not sleep. Early the next morning, he hurriedly went to the lions' den. When he came near the entrance, he called out to Daniel in an anguished voice:

Daniel, servant of the living God, has your God, whom you serve continually, been able to deliver you from the lions?

Daniel 6:20

He was relieved to hear Daniel answer:

O king, live forever! My God sent His angel and shut the lions' mouths, so that they have not hurt me, because I was found innocent before Him; and also, O king, I have done no wrong before you. Daniel 6:21-22

When Daniel was lifted out of the lions' den, no wound was found on him. He had trusted in His God, and God had protected him.

So what are the causes and effects of why bad things happen to good and godly people? In our first two examples of people who experienced bad things in their lives, we found that the causes of the bad things originated from their own bad behavior, and the effects of those bad things on them was suffering. So, these were self-invited troubles. On the other hand, in the last two examples, the bad things that happened did not originate from their own bad behavior, but the behavior of other people. When it happened, they did not compromise their faith, so God protected them from harm, and they did not suffer.

Always remember:

Do not be deceived, God is not mocked; for whatever a man sows, that he will also reap. Galatians 6:7

I believe that the Lord's promise, *"Lo, I will be with you always"* (Matthew 28:20), is not absolute. Two Christians were in a car, and the driver was driving too fast. The passenger said, "Brother, I think you're driving too fast!"

The driver answered, "Don't worry! The Lord is with us."

"You're wrong," the other man answered. "He left when you exceeded the speed limit!" So keep safe by staying away from troubles:

Abhor what is evil. Cling to what is good.   Romans 12:9

�֎

ൠ **85** ൡ

IN THE MATTER OF JUDGING

Text: Matthew 7:1-5

"Do not judge!" These are the opening words of Chapter 7 of the Gospel according to Matthew. The tone of these words is in the imperative and negative mode. In other words, it is a command.

Why did Jesus command us not to judge? The answer to this question can be broad, but we can find an immediate answer right here in the text itself. *"For with the judgment you pronounce you will be judged"* (RSV). This is the serious consequence of being judgmental of others.

Next, by way of illustration, Jesus gave us the reason we should not judge others:

> *Why do you see the speck that is in your brother's eye but do not notice the log that is in your own eye? Or how can you say to your brother, "Let me take the speck out of your eye," when there is the log in your own eye? You hypocrite, first take the log out of your own eye, and then you will see clearly to take the speck out of your brother's eye.* Verses 3-5, RSV

Is this command not to judge absolute? The answer is no. It is a general rule or command, and with every rule, there is an exception. So what is the exception in this case? Jesus said, in another instance, *"Judge righteous judgement"* (John 7:24, ASV). What He was saying was that not everyone has the right or the authority to judge others. This is indicated in His illustration when He said there was *"a log"* in the eye of the one judging his brother and that had to be removed before he could have the right to judge others. Jesus called this person a *"hypocrite."*

What is a hypocrite? A hypocrite is a person who affects virtues or qualities he does not personally possess. In other words, he is a pretender. The legal term for this is *usurper*. A usurper is a person who uses or exercises power by force without having the proper right or authority.

Who, then, has the right to judge? There are two situations in which certain people clearly have a right to judge: a judge in a court of law and parents involving their children in a domestic proceeding.

Usually, when we talk of judging, we are referring to the pronouncements of a judge in a decision, whether to exonerate the accused or to punish him. It is essential that upon arrival at a judgement or decision, the judge must consider the ambit of the law and the facts of the case. These are the substantive and the procedural aspects of the proceedings. Otherwise, the judge's decision can be arbitrary, which can result in error of jurisdiction or error in judgment.

Fundamental to all in a judicial proceeding is that the accused is accorded the "due process of the law." In the law, it is provided that: "No person shall be deprived of life, liberty or property without the due process of law."

What is *due process* or *the due process of law*? Due process of the law means that before any man can be deprived of his life, liberty or property, he must be given an opportunity to defend himself. This contemplates notice and opportunity to be heard before judgment is rendered affecting one's person, liberty or property. In a general sense, it means the right to be heard before some tribunal having jurisdiction to determine the question in dispute. This procedure fully protects the life, liberty and property of the citizen of the state. More simply put, due process means, "Hear me first before you strike."

God is the originator of the "due process of law." Before He meted out punishment on Adam and Eve, after they have sinned, He heard them out first. Let's look back at their trial in the Garden of Eden after the fall:

> But the Lord God called to the man, and said to him, "Where are you?"
>
> And he said, I heard the sound of thee in the garden, and I was afraid because I was naked; and I hid myself."
>
> He said, "Who told you that you were naked? Have you eaten of the tree of which I commanded you not to eat?"
>
> The man said, "The woman whom thou gavest to be with me, she gave me fruit of the tree, and I ate."
>
> Then the Lord God said to the woman, "What is this that you have done?"
>
> The woman said, "The serpent beguiled me, and I ate."
>
> Genesis 3:9-13, RSV

It was only after hearing Adam and Eve that God imposed punishment on them. Their punishments were as follows:

To the woman He said, "I will greatly multiply your pain in childbearing; in pain you shall bring forth children, yet your desire shall be for your husband, and he shall rule over you"

To Adam He said, "Because you have listened to the voice of your wife, and have eaten of the tree of which I commanded you, 'You shall not eat of it,' cursed is the ground because of you; in toil you shall eat of it all the days of your life; thorns and thistles it shall bring forth for you; and you shall eat the plants of the field. In the sweat of your face you shall eat bread till you return to the ground, for out of it you were taken; you are dust, and to dust you shall return." Genesis 3:16-19, RSV

Due process must also be observed when disciplining children in the home. God has placed upon the parents the right and authority to discipline their children, but without the observance of due process, this parental authority is often misused or abused. Too often parents spank, or beat, their children for their supposed mischief or misconduct especially when it is reported to them by other people without first investigating the child's circumstances or giving them the chance to tell their side of the story.

Why is it that some parents believe the bad reports of other people involving their children rather than believing their own children? This is wrong, and any resulting punishment is unjust and without due process.

What did Jesus indicate as the liabilities for those who violate this rule *"Judge not?"* Those who violate this rule are liable, first of all, according to Jesus, to suffer the same judgment they have pronounced on others.

Judging too quickly, without knowing the circumstances, is wrong. There could be some aggravating circumstances. When we point a finger at others, three fingers are pointed back at ourselves. And, if we do not have the right and authority to judge a particular person, Jesus said that we are hypocrites to do so. The law agrees, finding us guilty of usurpation.

Usurpation, under our law, is a punishable crime. The victim of this offence can file a case of either slander or libel, as the case may be and the courts will hear them.

Sadly, these days there is a rampant and indiscriminate habit and practice by many people of judging others, especially on social media. This is not only trial by publicity, but judgment by publicity.

Photos of the victims of these unjust and unfair judgments are also posted on social media. Some say that pastors who are rich are all corrupt and thieves. In this way, people not only accuse others, but have already judged them guilty without any fair trial.

What motivates these hypocrites to slander people in this way? I have observed that these usurpers tend to make these unfounded and baseless judgments whenever any pastor becomes well off, prospers and is financially blessed. They never seem to criticize poor pastors in this way.

If you are guilty of this, please repent without delay. Even if you have personal knowledge or evidence of wrongdoing on the part of another person (especially a pastor), you must refrain from judging them. Why? Because you are not a qualified or authorized judge. Even those who are authorized judges are to render righteous judgment, with appropriate jurisdiction according to law, the facts of the case being fully explored and due process being given.

If you have been prejudiced by people who are judgmental, there is always proper recourse, the settlement of disputes between or among parties.

Finally, we must learn to control our tongue and our emotions in order to avoid and prevent injury and damage to other people and to ourselves. �֍

cs **86** &

HEAVEN, THE ABODE OF GOD

Text: Genesis 1:1

As Christians, we believe in Heaven. In fact, Heaven is one of the essential elements of our faith, and both the Old and New Testaments are replete with the subject. The Bible even opens with the statement that in the beginning God created Heaven and Earth.

As Christians, Heaven is our hope and ultimate destiny. We believe that those Christians who have already died will go to Heaven. We sing about Heaven in our worship services and are admonished in the Scriptures to ponder it.

For His part, Jesus said:

> *Do not lay up for yourselves treasures on earth, where moth and rust destroy and where thieves break in and steal; but lay up for yourselves treasures in heaven, where neither moth nor rust destroys and where thieves do not break in and steal. For where your treasure is, there your heart will be also.*

Matthew 6:19-21

429

When the Bible refers to *"the heavens,"* the meaning is different. *Heaven* is one thing, and *the heavens* are something else entirely. There are three places referred to in the Scriptures as *heaven* or *heavens*. We might call them the first heaven, the second heaven and the third Heaven. The first heaven is the expanse and firmament surrounding the Earth's atmosphere, where clouds are gathered. This was the area mentioned in the Old Testament when the people built a tower in Babel that they wanted to reached up to *"the heavens"* (Genesis 11:4). It was the first heaven that Enoch and Elijah were translated into, as well as Philip in the New Testament.

The second heaven is outer space, beyond the Earth's atmosphere, where the other planets are located.

The third Heaven is the dwelling place of God. In his second letter to the Corinthian believers, Paul actually called it *"the third heaven"* (2 Corinthians 12:2).

Is Heaven real or just imaginary? Personally, I believe that Heaven is real. Just as the Earth that God created is real, so also is the Heaven that He created.

What is Heaven like? The Bible shows that Heaven is a paradise. It is a place of exquisite beauty and eternal bliss. It is a Garden of Eden. Jesus, while hanging on the cross of Calvary, promised the repentant malefactor that he would be with Him *"in paradise"* (Luke 23:43).

The Bible also calls Heaven *"a country"* (Hebrews 11:16). This means that Heaven has a defined territory, a population, a government and a sovereignty. Heaven is also likened to *"a city"* where there are lots of inhabitants and a rather complex and highly urbanized political subdivision (Revelation 21:10-). Finally, Heaven is *"a kingdom"* where there is a King and His subjects (Matthew

18:23-35). The phrase the Kingdom of Heaven means the same as the Kingdom of God.

Although no eye has seen, no ear has heard and no mind has conceived of what God has prepared for those who love Him, He has chosen to reveal it to us by His Spirit (see 1 Corinthians 2:9-10). The latter part of the Book of Revelation gives us a glimpse of the physical description of Heaven.

Someday the dwelling of God (Heaven) will be with His people, and God Himself will dwell among us (see Revelation 21:1-3). He will wipe away every tear from our eyes. There will be no more death or mourning or crying or pain, for the old order has passed away (see verse 4). The Holy City, the New Jerusalem, by allegory, describes Heaven as a city of pure gold which shines with the glory of God, and its brilliance is like that of a very precious jewel. The foundations of the City are made of precious stones (see verse 19), the gates are made of pearl (see verse 21), and the great street was of pure gold, like transparent glass (see verse 18).

There is a river flowing through Heaven which is the water of life, as clear as crystal, flowing from the throne of God and of the Lamb down the middle of the great street of the city (see Revelation 22:1). On each side of the river stands the tree of life, bearing twelve crops of fruit, yielding its fruit every month. And the leaves of the tree are for the healing of the nations (see Revelation 22:2). There will be no more curses.

The throne of God and of the Lamb will be in the city, and His servants will serve Him (see Revelation 22:3). They will see His face, and His name will be on their foreheads (see Revelation 22 4).

There will be no more night. They will not need the light of a lamp or the light of the sun, for the Lord God will give them light. And they will reign for ever and ever (see Revelation 22: 5).

Who will not be allowed to enter Heaven? The answer is: those who are cowardly, the unbelieving, the vile, the murderers, the sexually immoral, those who practice magic arts, the idolaters, those who are impure, the deceitful and all liars (see Revelation 21:8).

Who will be allowed to enter Heaven? The answer is: only those whose names are written in the Lamb's book of life (see Revelation 21:27).

How can our names be written in the Lamb's book of life? We must repent of our sins, open our hearts and receive Jesus Christ into our life as our personal Lord and Savior. Then, God will give us the right to become His children. To those who believe in Him and follow Him, Jesus said:

In My Father's house are many mansions; if it were not so, I would have told you. I go to prepare a place for you. And if I go and prepare a place for you, I will come again and receive you to Myself; that where I am, there you may be also.   John 14:2-3

What a promise! Hallelujah!   ✄

GOD STILL DOES MIRACLES TODAY!

Text: Hebrews 13:8

A few years ago, my wife, my beautiful Liling, had a stroke. She was immediately rushed to the hospital and into the ICU (intensive care unit). Her right eye and mouth had collapsed, and her face looked disfigured. The doctors also found a lump in her ear, which, they said, was dangerous and required immediate surgery.

The operation was successful, but Liling's face remained disfigured. The hospitalization and the operation were very expensive. The total hospital bill amounted to hundreds of thousands of pesos, but God provided the money to pay it.

When Liling left the hospital, she was still on a maintenance medication, and the doctors also recommended therapy for her disfigured face and a hearing aid for her ear.

Shortly after that, one day she locked herself in our bathroom and didn't come out for two hours. Worried and concerned for her welfare, I forced opened the bathroom door. I'm not sure what I was expecting to see, but what I did see was her prostrate on the floor, weeping. I asked her, "What happened?"

She replied, "Leave me alone. I'm praying to God!"

When Liling came out of the bathroom that day, her face was restored, and she was beautiful again. She said that while she was praying, she had heard three sounds in her head: "Clack! Clack! Clack!" When she looked in the mirror, her face was restored.

She went back to the doctor for her hearing aid appointment, and the doctor was surprised that she could already hear well enough without the need for a hearing aid. He said, "Well, we do our best, and God does the rest!" Now, who says that the days of miracles are over?

Jesus Christ is the same yesterday, today and forever.

He is our God who heals us and, by the stripes of Jesus, we are healed! Our God is powerful and wonderful! Praise God! Glory to His name! ✿

cs **88** so

A Demon at Our Window

Text: Mark 16:17

After we had finished the classroom portion of our Bible school training, Liling and I were sent on our first missionary assignment, this one to the Province of Zambales. We were to go to schools, churches and plazas and preach the Gospel of our Lord Jesus Christ wherever we found hungry hearts. After preaching and praying with the people, we were to give out copies of the Gospel of John. Our first stop was the town of Botolan.

Besides our bus ticket, we had been given just 100 pesos pocket money, and it was night when we arrived there, and we had no contact and nowhere to sleep. To complicate things, Liling was pregnant again, and our two-year-old son Norman was tagging along. I had to carry the box of gospel portions, so he had to get along the best he could.

Before long, some local policemen came along, wanting to know what we intended to do in their town. When we told them that we were missionaries, they were very kind and helped us, taking us

435

to a Catholic convent run by some sisters, and those sisters took good care of us. They gave us a place to sleep and fed us well.

We shared our personal testimonies with the nuns, and they allowed us to preach in their schools, as well as in their churches. It was a wonderful opportunity for us to reach out to hungry hearts. Being so wonderfully received was a great miracle, as the Catholics and Protestants had a long history of animosity toward each other. Later, we stayed in a Methodist pastoral house, and we had a phenomenal experience there.

In the middle of the night we suddenly heard the moaning and crying of a woman. Then there was the clanking sound of chains, as if somebody was dragging fetters. It was a bright, moonlit night, and there was also an incessant howling of dogs outside. Then Liling was startled to see a woman in the window. But how could she have gotten there? We were sleeping on the second floor of a two-story house.

We had opened the window because it was so hot, and Liling now saw this woman smiling at her through the window and attempting to reach her bulging tummy with her seemingly-elastic hand. Paralyzed with fright, Liling was unable to move her body, but in her mind she kept rebuking the woman, "In the name of Jesus."

I woke up, hearing Liling struggling, and immediately stood up. My body was covered with goose bumps, but our faith in God was strong. I, too, rebuked that evil spirit. With a loud voice, I said, "In the name of Jesus, go away, you evil spirit."

That was the end of the noise and the appearances and we were able to go back to sleep and sleep soundly, that night, the next night, and all the succeeding nights. Hallelujah! Our God is powerful! Glory to God!

The next morning, while having breakfast with our host pastor in another house (in this case, it happened to be a lady pastor), she told us that she had heard some commotion in the night. We told her of our experience, and she said that she had deliberately put us in that house, which was known to be haunted, in order to test us and see if we were really servants of God. Now she knew that we were, and that gave us more open doors in local churches and schools, to preach the Gospel of our Lord Jesus Christ. There is power in the name of Jesus! Glory to God! Hallelujah!

ଔ **89** ଓ

JOSEPH'S ECONOMIC FORMULA FOR FINANCIAL SUCCESS AND STABILITY

Text: Genesis 41:25-36

I was reading through the Bible, from the Old Testament to the New Testament. during our days of financial difficulty, and the story of Joseph in the book of Genesis really inspired me, especially with regards to how God lifted him up from his difficulty. The drama of his life was so sensational, and I found myself weeping as I was reading his most trying episodes. I somehow felt that I could identify with him in his situations.

Then, suddenly, God helped Joseph to graduate from his school of hard trials and gave him an amazing transition into a life that could only be summarized as: "From the Prison to the Palace." Joseph got to the palace because God gave him the knowledge and wisdom to know what to do and how to do it in preparation for the coming famine.

The seven years leading up to the famine, Joseph gathered twenty percent of all the harvests and stored the resulting grain in each of the major cities of Egypt. In the days to come, food would be the most valuable commodity. And that is still true today.

When it came, the famine was so severe in the regions of Canaan and Egypt that people came to Joseph to buy food, and Joseph gave all the proceeds to the ruling Pharaoh. When people no longer had money to buy food, they came to Joseph and traded him their livestock for food. Then, after another year of famine, the people came back to Joseph again, begging him to give them food and seed to plant so that they would not perish. Now they gave their bodies as slaves and their land in exchange for food and seed. In this way, Joseph was able to purchase most of the land in Egypt for the Pharaoh. Then he made a decree that the people of Egypt would give Pharaoh twenty percent of the yields of their crops, and the people gladly complied.

When I read the interpretation of Pharaoh's dream and the solution that Joseph offered to Pharaoh, something jumped within me, and I got very excited. "Seven years of plenty followed by seven years of famine" seemed to me like an economic cycle, and I saw in it a principle that would serve an individual, a family, a business or even a nation.

There is at least one time in the economic life of a person that everything seems to comes easily, and they prosper. Businesses experience wind-fall profits at some time, and farmers have bumper crops. But there are also times when everything seems to be so difficult that it is depressing. No matter how hard one tries to get ahead, everything seems to converge to drag him down. He may be doing his best, but circumstances seem to be arrayed against him. So, what should he do? Joseph showed us that during times of plenty we must set aside a certain percentage of our income in anticipation of years of famine (economic depression)By adopting this economic formula, I was convinced that I could break the cycle of poverty in my life and get out of financial difficulty.

My wife and I decided that, although we were staying rent free at the parsonage of the church we were pastoring, we would set aside money in savings as if we were paying monthly rent. From that point on, financial blessings just kept coming. We didn't even know some of the people who were giving to us.

One day a Christian doctor from the U.S. appeared at our door. He was looking for someone to accompany him on a personal mission to the Visayas and Mindanao, so I agreed to go with him, and we did some evangelistic missions there. Before the man went back to the States, he gave us US $1,000.00. I later learned that this man was the brother of the founder of a well-known accounting firm in Manila. His name was Doctor Sycip, brother of Washington Sycip of Sycip, Gorres, Velayo and Company. God sent him to us to bless us.

Once I had accumulated sufficient capital I did some moonlighting in business to bring in more funds for our family. One of my ventures was buying and selling used cars. I also did some small-time real estate deals. When I saw how blessed we were in all of this, I began teaching this practical economic principle to the members of our church, many of them also poor.

It works. I may not be the Prime Minister of Egypt, as Joseph of the Bible, but God lifted me from my life of poverty to a life of plenty. I may not ride the Pharaoh's chariot, like Joseph, but at least, I have my own ride now—a 1994 Mercedes Benze E-220. I may not live in a palace like Joseph, but I have my own home now, and it is fully paid. It has been said that "a man's home is his palace." Well, I was dreaming of this kind of life and all these things when I was young, and now, praise God, He has made my dreams come true. God is good, generous and kind indeed. Jesus said:

But seek first the kingdom of God and His righteousness, and all these things shall be added to you. Matthew 6:33

Yes! We can have abundant life in Jesus Christ. Hallelujah! Blessed be His holy name!

cs **90** so

SAMSON'S SOUR SAGA
(LOVE GONE WRONG)

Text: Judges 16

The book of Judges in the Old Testament is characterized by the repeated and recurring refrain, *"Again the Israelites did evil in the eyes of the Lord."* What was this evil that the Israelites did that provoked the Lord to anger? They forsook and forgot the Lord, the God of their fathers, who brought them out of Egypt. They followed and worshipped various gods of the people around them, like Baal and the Astoreths. Why were they always backsliding? The new generation of Israelites born after the death of Joshua did not know the Lord or what He had done for Israel.

Because this new generation of the Israelites refused to give up their evil practices and stubborn ways, God allowed their enemies around them, like the nation of the Philistines, to afflict and oppress them. When they cried out to the Lord, as they groaned under the oppression and affliction of their enemies, the Lord had compassion on them and raised up deliverers who saved them out of the hands of their oppressors. These deliverers were also called judges, and the Lord was with them. To some of them, the Lord gave extraordinary power.

God had warned the Israelites before they entered Canaan, the land of promise, not to follow other gods, the gods of the peoples around them. Besides, they were also precluded from intermarrying with the people of Canaan. They must not give their daughters to the sons of Canaan or take the daughters of Canaan for their sons. Why? Because they would turn away their sons and daughters from following the Lord to serve other gods, and the Lord's anger would burn against them.

Samson was among the judges and deliverers that the Lord gave to the Israelites when they cried out to Him by reason of the oppression of their enemies. Samson was an extraordinary man. He had made the vow of a Nazarite, which vow was from birth. This special vow was for the purpose of separation unto the Lord. He must abstain from wine and fermented drink. He must not go near a dead body. And, during the entire period of his vow, no razor could be used on his head. He must let the hair of his head grow long. But Samson's life was also a reflection and representation of the condition and moral reality of the nation of Israel during that period, and that was his problem.

Samson had supernatural strength. Where did this strength come from? Some have said that it came from his long hair, but others have said that his strength came from the Lord when His Spirit came upon Samson in power. I think that these two are related.

One time Samson killed a young lion with his bare hands. With a jawbone of a donkey, he killed a thousand of the Philistines. He seemed to be invincible against his Philistine enemies. But ... he had one weakness, a serious one, the love of women. He had a particular desire for Philistine women.

On one occasion, Samson saw a young Philistine woman in Timnah. When he returned home, he said to his father and mother, *"I have seen a Philistine woman in Timnah; now get her for me as my wife"* (Judges 14:2). His father and mother replied, *"Is there no woman among the daughters of your brethren, or among all my people, that you must go and get a wife from the uncircumcised Philistines?"* (Judges 14:3). But Samson insisted, *"Get her for me, for she pleases me well"* (same verse). Who was right in this case? Samson or his parents? The Bible says, *"Obey your parents in the Lord, for this is right"* (Ephesians 6:1). Not because they are right, but because *"this is right!"*

The Scriptures declare:

There is a way that seems right to a man,
But its end is the way of death.   Proverbs 14:12

Samson's marriage to this Philistine woman ended in tragedy. She and her father were burned to death by the Philistines, and Samson was hunted down by his enemies.

But Samson failed to learn his lesson. On another occasion, he went to Gaza and slept with a prostitute, thus lowering his standards of taste in women. He always seemed to be in the wrong place at a wrong time. Eventually he fell in love with a woman named Delilah. This woman was treacherously dangerous. She did not love Samson. She was just in the relationship for the money. Actually she was in cahoots with the Philistines to find out where the strength of Samson really lay.

After constant and incessant nagging by Delilah, Samson finally gave in and told her that if his hair was cut, he would become as weak as any other man. They shaved his hair off while he slept on Delilah's knees, and when he awoke, a surprising thing happened:

> *So he awoke from his sleep, and said, "I will go out as before, at other times, and shake myself free!" But he did not know that the LORD had departed from him.*   Judges 16:20

The sad result was that the Philistines seized him, gouged his eyes out, took him to Gaza, bound him with bronze shackles and set him to grinding in their prison. With extreme remorse, Samson prayed to God to once more restore to him his supernatural strength in order to exact revenge against his Philistine enemies. God heard his cry and he was able to push over the supporting columns of the coliseum where the Philistine were gathered making sport of him. The entire structure collapsed, and he died together with some three thousand of his enemies.

It was a tragic end to the life of Samson, and the tragedy was on him. The cause of this disaster was love—love of women, love of the wrong women, women who did not belong to his community of faith.

Love is supposed to end with the words "happily ever after," not with tragedy. This is a serious warning to all Christian men and women, especially those who are single and still young. If you don't want your love life to turn into a disaster or tragedy, obey the Scriptures:

> *Do not be unequally yoked together with unbelievers. For what fellowship has righteousness with lawlessness? And what communion has light with darkness?*   2 Corinthians 6:14

What harmony can there be between Christ and the devil? What does a believer have in common with an unbeliever? Save yourself from tremendous trouble and tragedy by not getting romantically involved with unbelievers. ✄

03 **91** 80

THE BLESSINGS OF CHRISTMAS

Text: Genesis 1:28

Our God is a God of blessings. This was one of His intentions when He created the world that we live in, including us, human beings. In fact, the Bible says that God pronounced blessings twice upon His creation:

> *And God blessed them, saying, "Be fruitful and multiply ... ."*
>
> Genesis 1:21

> *Then God blessed them, and God said to them, "Be fruitful and multiply ... ."*
> Genesis 1:28

That's a double blessing!

Our God is also a God of order. He has established certain laws and principles according to His divine purpose in order to set in

447

motion and in harmony His created system. Breaking these laws and principles will cause derailment and derange the order and harmony, not only the relationship between God and man, but also of the created Earth itself. This is an offense to God, and another term for it is *sin*.

Sin has two sides of the coin. There is a sin of commission, and there is a sin of omission. When a person is told by God not to do a certain thing and he does it anyway, that's a sin of commission. When one is ordered by God to do something and he fails to do it, that's a sin of omission.

The incident in the Garden of Eden in Genesis chapter 3 is not only a sad and sorry one but also a tragedy. Instead of living a life with the blessings of God, Adam and Eve brought a curse upon themselves and upon the whole the Earth because of their disobedience of God's law:

Then to Adam He said, "Because you have heeded the voice of your wife, and have eaten from the tree of which I commanded you, saying, 'You shall not eat of it':

"Cursed is the ground for your sake;
In toil you shall eat of it
All the days of your life.
Both thorns and thistles it shall bring forth for you,
And you shall eat the herb of the field.
In the sweat of your face you shall eat bread
Till you return to the ground,

For out of it you were taken;

For dust you are,

And to dust you shall return."   Genesis 3:17-19

This curse has permeated the entire human race ever since with untold misery, hardships, disasters, suffering, sickness, sorrow, pain and death. The result was that the Old Testament ended with the word *curse*.

God's people, through the grace and mercy of our loving God, however, can reverse the curse and regain the blessings of God. How? By obeying His God's Word and His will!

Abraham was one example. God said to Abraham (formerly known as Abram):

"Get out of your country,

From your family

And from your father's house,

To a land that I will show you.

I will make you a great nation;

I will bless you

And make your name great;

And you shall be a blessing.   Genesis 12:1-2

God fulfilled His promise to Abraham when he obeyed:

Abram was very rich in livestock, in silver, and in gold.

Genesis 13:2

Obedience, then, is the key to God's blessings, and we can have the blessings of Abraham:

That the blessing of Abraham might come upon the Gentiles in Christ Jesus, that we might receive the promise of the Spirit through faith.   Galatians 3:14

Another example of God's blessings was His promise of blessings to the children of Israel after they came out of Egypt. He said to them:

And all these blessings shall come upon you and overtake you, because you obey the voice of the LORD your God:

Blessed shall you be in the city, and blessed shall you be in the country.

Blessed shall be the fruit of your body, the produce of your ground and the increase of your herds, the increase of your cattle and the offspring of your flocks.

Blessed shall be your basket and your kneading bowl.

Blessed shall you be when you come in, and blessed shall you be when you go out.

The Lord will cause your enemies who rise against you to be defeated before your face; they shall come out against you one way and flee before you seven ways.

THE BLESSINGS OF CHRISTMAS

The LORD will command the blessing on you in your storehouses and in all to which you set your hand, and He will bless you in the land which the LORD your God is giving you.

Deuteronomy 28:2-8

The birth of Jesus Christ in the New Testament was the ultimate in God's blessings. This was a blessing for all mankind, not just for God's chosen nation or and a select few people. It was the blessing of salvation, if we believe on Him and accept Him as our Lord and Savior. This blessing far exceeds any earthly blessings, which are but temporal. Now, in Jesus Christ, we also get heavenly blessings and for eternity. Hallelujah! Praise God!

Our Lord Jesus commenced His ministry by pronouncing blessings upon the unblessed:

Blessed are the poor in spirit ... ,

Blessed are those who mourn ... ,

Blessed are the meek ... ,

Blessed are those who hunger and thirst for righteousness ... ,

Blessed are the merciful ... ,

Blessed are the pure in heart ... ,

Blessed are the peacemakers,

Blessed are those who are persecuted for righteousness' sake.

Matthew 5:3-10

Paul declared:

451

Blessed be the God and Father of our Lord Jesus Christ, who has blessed us with every spiritual blessing in the heavenly places in Christ. Ephesians 1:3

So, Christian, obey the Lord and be found faithful. Stop wallowing in self-pity, feeling poor and miserable. Instead, start praising and thanking God. Claim and count your many blessings.

The blessing of the Lord makes one rich,
And He adds no sorrow with it. Proverbs 10:22

Merry Christmas and a prosperous new year to everyone.

ᘗ **92** ᕬ

THE ELEVENTH COMMANDMENT
(LOVE SUBLIME)

Text: Mark 12:30-31

Jesus said:

*"And you shall love the Lord your God with all your heart, with
all your soul, with all your mind, and with all your strength."
This is the first commandment. And the second, like it, is this:
"You shall love your neighbor as yourself."*

This divine dictum was the answer of our Lord Jesus Christ to a
question from one of the teachers of religion regarding the most important of all the commandments. This is the highest of all the Christians'
moral imperatives. In it, Jesus quoted the Ten Commandments in a
capsulated compendium plus one. What is the "plus one?" It is the
love of self after loving God and our neighbors. This was not included
in the original Ten Commandments. So, for Christians, there are now,
for all practical purposes, eleven commandments.

453

The question of the teacher of religion relative to this issue was rather interesting. Apparently, he just wanted to follow one of the Ten Commandments, and that was why he asked which one of them was the most important. But the Decalogue is essentially a unit, meaning to say that one commandment cannot be separated from the rest of the commandments. It is integrated, just like the human soul that cannot be separated from the human body even by death (physical death that is).

Now, the big question is: As Christians, are we still obligated to follow or obey the Decalogue? The answer is yes, plus one! The ten commandments have not been abrogated even though we are now under grace and no more under the Law. We are to still follow this divine dictum, not to be saved, because we are already saved through our faith in the Lord Jesus Christ. We follow the Decalogue plus one because this is our code of conduct, our standard of Christian and personal behavior, based on moral principles. It is characteristic of a Christian to love God, his fellow being and himself.

When, why and how do we love God? What is love, by the way? Love is defined as "affection based on admiration or benevolence: a warm attachment, enthusiasm or devotion. The attraction based on sexual desire: the affection and tenderness felt by lovers." It is "an unselfish concern that freely accepts another in loyalty and seeks his good." It is also "the fatherly concern of God for man."

Our love affair with God begins when we are saved and have been born again. We love God because He first loved us. It is a reciprocal and mutual love relationship between God and man, when man is saved.

And how should we love God? Answer: with all of our heart, soul, mind and strength.

The Israelites were reminded by God of this divine dictum. They were to pass this on to their children as a legacy of faith, it was to occupy the majority of their conversations and, as a symbol, it was to be tied on their foreheads and arms (see Deuteronomy 6). The Jewish concept of the heart and mind is that these two are integrated. For example: *"as he [a man] thinks in his heart, so is he"* (Proverbs 23:7). These two can, however, be distinguished by way of rhetorical function. This means that man's love of God must involve his total being, both his abstract and physical elements.

A close look at this divine dictum will reveal that when God gave this to His people, the Israelites, and when Jesus pronounced it, both were in the imperative mode. They were mandates. And when God says something to His people and He repeats it, we'd better pay attention, even more so when He repeats it three times. This means it is something serious, very serious indeed. When we discipline our children as parents over some of their misdemeanors, we warn them by counting (one, two, three), and after three, if they have not listened, then they get punished.

How do we love God with our whole being? The first mention is loving God with all our heart. The human heart is the seat of our emotion. We get emotional when we are in love. It is an exciting, powerful and wonderful feeling, especially when that love is between a man and a woman. Very often a person in love will defy reason, ignore ridicule and suffer all kinds of mistreatment just to be with the object of affection. It is a feeling of "you and me against the world."

Do we love God? Do we get emotional with our love for God? I do! Every time I think of how Jesus Christ suffered on the cross in order to redeem and save me from my sins, I get emotional — very emotional. Tears run down my cheeks as I weep. Every time I remember how God lifted me up from a life of poverty to a life of plenty, I burst into tears because of God's goodness and faithfulness to me and my family. Every time I worship God in church, lifting up my hands and singing songs of praise to Him, I get emotional. This emotion is the expression of my love for God, and I know full well what I am doing because my mind tells me. My love for God is with ardor and fervor, dedication, devotion and obedience to His will.

The next question is: how do we love our fellow being? Besides the profound illustration given by our Lord Jesus Christ in answer to the question by one expert of the Law (*"and who is my neighbor?"* Jesus answered him by telling the story of the Good Samaritan (see Luke 10:30-37). The apostle Paul gave a wonderful exposition and elaboration of this sublime love (see 1 Corinthians 13). This love emanates from God, for God is love.

Love for our neighbor is characterized by patience, kindness, not being envious or proud, and not being rude or selfish. It is not easily angered, keeps no record of wrongs. It does not delight in evil but rejoices with the truth. It always protects, always trusts, always hopes, and always perseveres. Love never fails.

One of the characteristics of love is sacrifice. God loved us so much that He sacrificed His Son. Sacrifice is "the act of offering someone or something precious to God or to someone else." It also means "to surrender or give up at a loss" or "to endure." We all know that Jesus Christ did this when He suffered on the cross. This was a cruel loves, as a matter of fact. Sometimes love can be cruel.

Then, Jesus said, " *"If anyone desires to come after Me, let him deny himself, and take up his cross, and follow Me"* (Matthew 16:24). Does this mean that we have to take up a literal wooden cross and carry it around? I have seen some Christians do this. But I believe that the meaning of what Jesus said is the divine dictum aforementioned. It is our love for God and our fellow being, and when we do this, we deny ourselves. The direction of this act of love is vertical, toward God, and the other is horizontal, toward our fellow being. The image formed in this act is the cross.

Of course, we must not neglect or ignore to love ourselves. This is the eleventh commandment, according to our Lord Jesus Christ. It is human nature that everyone loves himself or herself. I need not elaborate on this matter. But it is very important that the order or sequence of our love must be the following: first, love Jesus, then others, and then yourself. The acronym formed is JOY, which is constant happiness whether the circumstances in our lives are good or bad. Yes, love sublime will bring you joy, joy unspeakable and full of glory! �֍

OUR SWEDISH CONNECTION

Not long after I obeyed the Lord and came back to the Philippines from the U.S., I received a phone call from a man who said that he wanted to serve the Lord in our church the following Sunday. He said he was with two other guys and that they had come from Sweden. The man was working with Star of Hope International, and, according to him, the Lord spoke to him to come to Asia in the midst of his busy schedule in Scandinavia.

When the men arrived in Thailand, he was told by the Lord to go on to the Philippines. He told the Lord that he didn't have any contact in the Philippines, but he was told to go anyway.

The three men arrived in the Philippines and got a room at the Manila Holiday Inn. After praying together the next morning, they went down the lift for a cup of coffee. According to the man who called me, they saw a church directory on the left side of the lift and on it was our phone number, and so he called us. That was on Saturday.

I went to their hotel early Sunday morning to pick them up. These three people from Sweden were big, blonde and tall fellows. The tallest and biggest guy said, "Where is your car, Brother?"

I said, "I don't have a car. I am just a poor pastor."

"Well, then," he said, "go and get a taxi!"

The taxi I got was small, and he could not get into it. As he was trying to get in, he split his pants. It was a rather hilarious scene. He had to go back to his hotel room to change his pants, and I had to find a bigger taxi.

When they arrived at our church, they were surprised to see that it was a rather small church, but a happy one. They saw everybody clapping their hands and joyfully singing to the Lord. The name of our church was Murphy Pentecostal Church near Cubao, Quezon City. The leader of the group, the big guy, destroyed one of our plywood chairs when he sat on it.

They men were moved by the plight of the small children they noted looked malnourished, and they promised to help them through a feeding program. They also promised to help me buy a used car. To be hones, I pretty much ignored their promises. Many promise and never come through. But one month after the men had returned to Sweden, I received the biggest surprise when I opened our mail box to find a check for US $3,000.00 with a note saying, "Get yourself a used car, Brother!"

Praise the Lord! Hallelujah! That had to be from God!

Curious about how this whole thing had come about, Liling (my wife) and I went to the Holiday Inn where our new friends had stayed. We wanted to see the church directory they told us about. None could be found near the elevator, where they told us they had seen it. We asked several hotel workers about the church directory, and they all answered, "What church directory?" One said, "I have been working here for ten years, and

I have not seen that church directory you are talking about. Besides, we don't put church directories in our hotel.

Well, then, who put it there? Surely, God works in many mysterious ways as many say. I choose to call it divine Providence. This was the beginning of our partnership with Star of Hope in Sweden for the work in the Philippines, and it has continued ever since. ✄

ℭ **94** ℬ

TOTAL OBEDIENCE

Text: John 14:15

"If you love Me, keep My commandments."

This is a challenging statement of our Lord Jesus Christ to His disciples, His followers. The challenge was to prove and validate their love for Him by obeying and keeping His commandments.

In the immediate context, there is no mention of what kind of commandments Jesus had in mind, but in chapter 13, verses 34 and 35, He told them about a new commandment that He was giving them. He said:

A new commandment I give to you, that you love one another; as I have loved you, that you also love one another. By this all will know that you are My disciples, if you have love for one another. John 13:34-35

But this was only one commandment, whereas the text referred to "commandments," more than one. So what are these commandments Jesus was referring to? I believe that Jesus was referring to the general commandments and to personal commandments.

What are the general commandments? These are the Ten Commandments and their related ordinances.

What is a personal commandment? It is a commandment from God given to a particular and specific individual.

The Ten Commandments were given by God to His people as part of His covenant with them and served as guidelines for their daily living. Those Ten Commandments are:

1. *You shall have no other gods before Me.*
2. *You shall not make to yourself a carved image ... and bow down to them and serve them.*
3. *You shall not take the name of the LORD your God in vain.*
4. *Remember the Sabbath day to keep it holy.*
5. *Honor your father and your mother that your days may be long upon the land.*
6. *You shall not murder.*
7. *You shall not commit adultery.*
8. *You shall not steal.*
9. *You shall not bear false witness against your neighbour.*
10. *You shall not covet.*   Exodus 20:3-17

Although God gave these Ten Commandments to His people through Moses at Mount Sinai more than three thousand years ago, they are still relevant today. They have an abiding significance, for God's character is unchangeable. These laws originated from God and from His eternal character, therefore their moral values cannot change.

Jesus did not abrogate the Ten Commandments, but rather upheld them. He said:

> *Do not think that I came to destroy the Law or the Prophets. I did not come to destroy but to fulfil.* Matthew 5:17

The Ten Commandments are still relevant today, for the world desperately needs to see the name and character of God displayed in the lives of Christians who still take His Word seriously. These commandments, particularly coupled with the teachings of Christ, are still the best guidelines for practical daily living known to man. They form the heart of the covenant between God and His people. He told them:

> *Now therefore, if you will indeed obey my voice and keep my covenant, then you shall be a special treasure to Me above all people.* Exodus 19:5

And how about a personal commandment? This is best exemplified in the story of the rich young man who came to Jesus. He first asked Jesus a question:

Good Teacher, what good thing shall I do that I may have eternal life?   Matthew 19:16

The initial answer of Jesus was this:

"You shall not murder," "You shall not commit adultery," "You shall not steal," "You shall not bear false witness," "Honor your father and your mother," and, "You shall love your neighbor as yourself."   Matthew 19:18-19

The young man said to Jesus:

All these things I have kept from my youth. What do I still lack?   Matthew 19:20

Jesus said to him:

If you want to be perfect, go, sell what you have and give to the poor, and you will have treasure in heaven; and come, follow Me.   Matthew 19:21

When the young man heard this he went away sorrowful, for he had great possessions.

What were the commands of our Lord Jesus to the rich young man? And why did he not obey them? Jesus gave him three commands. First, he had to sell his possessions. Second, he had to give to the poor. And third, he was invited by Jesus to come and follow

Him. Actually, these three commands of our Lord to the rich young man were a paraphrase of the first two of the Ten Commandments. Do you remember those first commandments?

You shall have no other gods before Me.

You shall not make to yourself carved images and bow down before them.

The rich young man did not obey the Lord's command for the obvious reason that he had great possessions. Those possessions had become his god, his idol. He refused to obey the Lord because he loved his possessions more than he loved God. Thereafter, he was doomed to live an ironic life, being rich but also sorrowful.

God has promised His people that if they will be obedient to His commandments, He will bless them:

And all these blessings shall come upon you and overtake you, if you obey the voice of the LORD your God. Blessed shall you be in the city, and blessed shall you be in the field. Blessed shall be the fruit of your body, and the fruit of your ground, and the fruit of your beasts, the increase of your cattle, and the young of your flock. Blessed shall be your basket and your kneading trough. Blessed shall you be when you come in, and blessed shall you be when you go out. ...

The LORD will command the blessing upon you in your barns, and in all that you undertake; and He will bless you in the land which the Lord your God will gives you. ...

*And the L*ORD *will make you abound in prosperity ... .*

*The L*ORD *will bless all the works of your hands; and you will lend but you shall not borrow.*   Deuteronomy 28:2-12, RSV

The blessing of the Lord makes rich,

    and he adds no sorrow with it.   Proverbs 10:22, RSV

CB **95** BD

WHEN ALL THINGS ARE NEARLY LOST

Text: Job 42:10-12

Mishaps and misfortunes that bring devastation and misery to mankind are beyond our control. It is a painful and pitiful experience when a survivor is practically stripped of everything he has, including the loss of his entire family, when struck by a calamity or catastrophe with immense proportions. When this happens, many people lose hope and commit suicide. But, as Christians, how do should we respond when a great tsunami or a Super-Typhoon-Yolanda-like catastrophe strikes our life?

Maybe a major fire gutted your home and even burned up your entire family. Maybe the company where we are working completely shut down, and you lost your source of income. What should we do when everything is lost except our own life? Who do we turn to? Who can we call on?

The story of Job in the Old Testament is a great comfort and an inspiring challenge to resilience for Christians who face adverse and unpleasant situations in life. But, before we explore this tremendous triumph of a man against the terrible tests and trials

467

that he experienced, let us get acquainted with the cast of this human and divine drama. First, there was Job, of course. He is the main character. Then, there was God, followed by Satan, Job's wife and children, Job's friends and servants, the Sabeans and the Chaldeans, Job's enemies. The story takes place in two locations, a place on Earth called the land of Uz and Heaven.

Job is described by the narrator as a man of moral integrity. He was upright and blameless; he feared God and shunned evil. He was also extremely wealthy and was the greatest man among all the people of the east.

Then, the narrator shifted his focus to the heavenly scene where the angels came to present themselves before the Lord. Interestingly enough, Satan came along with the angels. The Lord asked Satan, *"Where have you come from?"* (Job 1:7).

Satan answered, *"From roaming through the earth and going back and forth in it"* (Job 1:7).

Then the Lord said to Satan, *"Have you considered my servant Job? There is no one on earth like him; he is blameless and upright, a man who fears God and shuns evil"* (Job 1:8).

"Does Job fear God for nothing?" Satan replied. "You protected him and his family and blessed his work so that his flocks became numerous. But strike everything he has, and he will surely curse You to Your face" (see Job 1:9-11).

The Lord said to Satan, "Very well, then, everything he has is in your hands. Just don't touch him" (see Job 1:12).

Now the scene shifts back to Earth. Satan unleashes his destructive power through his influence on human and natural elements, dealing devastating blows to Job's livestock, causing him to lose them all, and killing all his children in a single day. How unlucky can one man be! But, amazingly, instead of cursing God, Job worshipped and praised God.

Back to Heaven again: God repeats His praise of Job's moral integrity before Satan, but Satan answers Him, "Strike his flesh and bones, and he will surely curse You to Your face" (see Job 2:4). Then the gave Satan permission to afflict Job with painful sores throughout his body, but he was not allowed to kill him.

While Job was in pain and in a miserable condition, his wife pressured him to curse God. His friends came along as well, expressing their empathy for a while, but then they became *"miserable comforters"* later (Job 16:2). What a terrible blow of extreme prejudice all of this was on Job!

You and I, as readers of this story, are mere passive participants, and, as such, are privileged to see the broader picture and perspective of the story. For example, Job's understanding that all the bad circumstances and situations in his life came from God. He said, *"The Lord gave and the Lord has taken away"* (Job 1:21). I agree with the first part of his statement: "The Lord gave." But I certainly don't agree with last part and perhaps you don't either. Why? Because clearly, in this story, it was not God who took away everything from Job. It was Satan. It was not God who gave Job the sickness, but Satan.

Oftentimes people blame their misfortunes and sickness on God. Even insurance companies excuse their liability when the things insured are destroyed by calamities by reason of the stipulation in the contract under "Acts of God." Don't blame God for your misfortunes and bad circumstances; blame Satan instead.

Did Job know that it was Satan who brought all these situations into his life? I don't think so. Did he know that he was being used by God as a pawn in a game of chess between God and Satan? Again I don't think so. But, as we continue to read the story of Job, we know that it was Satan who caused all of his troubles, including his sickness. Why? Because we are also spectators of this divine and human drama unfolding before our eyes.

The statement of Jesus concerning Satan, who is also known as the devil, is most appropriate in Job's situation. He said:

> *The thief [referring to the devil] comes not but to steal, kill and destroy.*   John 10:10

Job had no idea that bad things come from the devil, so he assumed everything—good and bad—came from God. He even thought that God might kill him. He said, *"Though he slay me, I will hope in him"* (Job 13:15).

As a general rule, God will not kill people. Neither does He delight in the fact that people are in desperate situations in life or in poverty. Why? Because God is an advocate of life and He is a good God, One who loves to bless His people and give them abundant life. Jesus said:

> *"I am the way, the truth and the LIFE.*
>
>   John 14:6, Emphasis Mine

> *I have come that they may have life, and that they may have it more abundantly.*   John 10:10

God is the Giver of life. In Him, is life (see John 1:4). Therefore it is wrong for Christians to say, when their loved ones have died, that God has taken them. Whether Christian or not, people die because they are humans, and humans are all mortal.

As Christians, therefore, can we say that if we become victims of disasters or calamities that those things were caused by the devil or if we get sick that it's the devil who made us sick? It is possible, especially if Christians live faithfully for God. But sometimes, we have no one else to blame but ourselves, especially in cases of sicknesses like cancer.

Perhaps, before we became Christians, we abused our body through various vices—like smoking cigarettes or excessive drinking of alcohol. Now, after many years, our immune systems have weakened, so that sicknesses occur in our body. Remember, what we sow, we will also reap—even if we are now Christian.

In the end, Job emerged resilient and victorious over all of the tremendous and terrible trials and calamities that he experienced. The Lord made him prosperous again and gave him twice as much as he'd had before. The Lord blessed the latter part of Job's life more than the first. He now had 14,000 sheep, 6,000 camels, a thousand yoke of oxen and a thousand donkeys. And he had also seven sons and three daughters. After all of his suffering, Job lived to be one hundred and forty years old.

How did Job overcome his trials and testing? Well, although his theology was rather imperfect, at least he had a theology, and before God, that was good enough to grant Job the victory. What was Job's imperfect theology? He attributed the misfortunes of his life to God, which was rather inaccurate. What was the otherwise-sound basis of his theology? Job simply believed in God, no matter what happened, and we can emulate Job when similarly situated.

Happy Resurrection Day, everyone! Jesus Christ is alive! He has risen! Hallelujah!   ✼

℃ℬ **96** ℬ

WHEN THE IMMORTAL GOD BECAME MORTAL
(A CHRISTMAS STORY)

Text: John 1:1-3 and 14

Who is God? The Bible reveals that in the beginning God created the heavens and the Earth. God created the whole universe, but the Earth was given particular mention, apart from the rest of the other heavenly bodies and planets in the universe. According to this narrative, the Earth must be a special planet. It is also interesting to note that in Genesis 1:2, after God created the heavens and the Earth, that the Earth was *"formless and empty,"* and *"darkness was over the surface of the deep."*

Some Bible scholars believe that between verses 1 and 2, a cataclysmic event occurred that rendered the Earth empty and in darkness. They speculate that the Earth had once been inhabited by angels who rebelled against God, and that this rebellion resulted in the destruction, emptiness and darkness of the Earth. Could this have been the time when dinosaurs and other giant animals roamed the Earth? These scholars may be speculating, but they have several biblical references to back up their theory. If they are

473

right, then what Genesis 1:3 relays is actually a re-creation of the Earth, not the original one.

Through His word, God spoke into existence all the things in this world, both animate and inanimate. God said, *"Let there be light,"* and there was light (Genesis 1:3). Then God created the sky, the stars, the sun, the moon, the seas and the land that produced vegetation, seed-bearing plants and trees that bore fruit of various kinds. He made the sea to bring forth fish of different varieties and birds to fly the expanse of the Earth.

Then God said, *"Let the land produce living creatures according to their kinds: livestock and wild animals"* (Genesis 1:24). And God saw that it was good.

Finally, God made man according to His *"image and likeness."* The Lord God put man in the Garden of Eden and gave him a command not to eat of the fruit of the forbidden tree. Unfortunately, man disobeyed God, sinning against Him, and the penalty was death, spiritual death and the curse.

Now back to the question: Who is God? God may be described in terms of attributes. An *attribute* is "an inherent characteristic of a person or being." The natural attributes of God are: God is a Spirit. Therefore, He has no body, no physical form. Thus God is invisible, but of His own volition and prerogative, He visibly appears to men on special occasions.

God's visible manifestation is called a theophany. He became visible in human form in the person of Jesus Christ, but His essence is invisible. God is also changeless, immortal, all-powerful, all-knowing, He is everywhere. God is eternal, holy and righteous. He is truth and He is love.

Our knowledge and understanding of God continues to increase as we faithfully serve and search for Him in our daily lives. It will finally be complete in eternity, when we stand in His presence in Heaven, which is His abode.

One of the natural attributes of God aforementioned is that He is immortal. And what does *immortal* mean? It means that He is exempt from death. He has an unending life. So, why did God become mortal? Isn't being immortal absolute? Well, in this case with God, it is not.

Yes, it is a rule for Him, but every rule has its exception. It was His divine prerogative to condescend to mortality. This is the great mystery the apostle Paul referred to:

And without controversy great is the mystery of godliness:

God was manifested in the flesh,

Justified in the Spirit,

Seen by angels,

Preached among the Gentiles,

Believed on in the world,

Received up in glory.   1 Timothy 3:16

So, why did God become mortal? I believe that He chose this for certain reasons, and I would like to offer two reasons from the Bible. The first one was to save mankind from sin and destruction:

For God so loved the world that He gave His only begotten Son, that whoever believes in Him should not perish but have

475

everlasting life. For God did not send His Son into the world to condemn the world, but that the world through Him might be saved. John 3:16-17

The second reason God became mortal was to show people who God was. Before Jesus Christ was born and manifested in the flesh, people didn't know God. They worshipped different and unknown gods. This is one of the reasons there are so many different religions in the world today. In Jesus Christ, we see, know and understand the true and living God because He is God. He is the express image of the invisible God (see Hebrews 1:3).

And how did God become mortal? The Bible says:

The Word became flesh

and made His dwelling among us. John 1:14, NAB(RE)

The secular word for this is *incarnation,* and Mary was instrumental in this divine process. This is the doctrine that the eternal Son of God became human and that He did so without, in any manner or degree, diminishing His divine nature.

This divine condescension is also relative to the first question aforementioned. Where and when did this happen? It happened in the little town of Bethlehem where King David was from because Joseph was of the lineage of David. While Mary and Joseph were there to be registered for the tax, Jesus was born, and Mary wrapped the baby Jesus in swaddling clothes and laid Him in a manger because there was no room for them in the inn. This great and momentous event in the history of mankind happened when

Caesar Augustus issued a decree that a census should be taken of the entire Roman world, and everyone went to his own town to register. Was it a coincidence? Definitely not! It was Divine Providence.

So the fact that God became mortal is part of the Christmas story. Jesus Christ, the Son of God, was born in Bethlehem of Judea and His birth was welcomed by multitudes of angelic hosts who sang in jubilation:

> *Glory to God in the highest,*
> *And on earth peace, goodwill toward men!*   Luke 2:14

However, it was unfortunate that during the first Christmas, only a handful of people welcomed the birth of Jesus Christ and those, of course, were led by Mary and Joseph, the shepherds and the people who heard the news of the shepherds. But most of the people surrounding this great event were indifferent and complacent, despite their knowledge of this great event (see verse 17). For their part, the shepherds did the right thing:

> *Then the shepherds returned, glorifying and praising God for all the things that they had heard and seen, as it was told them., for the shepherds returned glorifying and praising God!*   Luke 2:20

Thank God that He became mortal at Christmas. Let us welcome Jesus Christ this Christmas by receiving Him into our hearts, our homes and families, our churches and communities, with joy and gladness, like Mary and Joseph and the shepherds. Let us know and understand the significance and the true meaning of why God became mortal at Christmas. Yes, Christmas is the greatest blessing the world has ever known because it is the birthday of the Savior of all mankind!

Have a blessed and merry Christmas, everyone, and a happy and prosperous New Year! ✄

THE IMMINENT RETURN OF CHRIST

Text: John 14:1-3

Do not let your hearts be troubled. You believe in God; believe also in me. My Father's house has many rooms; if that were not so, would I have told you that I am going there to prepare a place for you? And if I go and prepare a place for you, I will come back and take you to be with me that you also may be where I am.

These are the words of our Lord Jesus Christ to His disciples, and they contain several comforting promises. First, He said that as His followers, we must not allow our hearts be troubled. Troubles generally affect our heart. The heart, in biblical concept, by the way, is the integrated component of the mind, the emotion and the will of man. This essentially is the soul of man. How can we keep our hearts from being troubled? The answer is: by trusting God and the Lord Jesus Christ.

Then, He said that He would go and prepare for us a place in His Father's house (Heaven) for us. This is indeed a comforting promise for those of His disciples who do not have a place (a house) of their own. Finally, He said that He would come back, for He wanted us, His followers, to be with Him in Heaven. Very comforting promises of Christ indeed!

This promise by Christ was confirmed by the angels who stood with the disciples while they were looking up intently into the sky while Jesus ascended to Heaven. They said:

Men of Galilee, why do you stand gazing up into heaven? This same Jesus, who was taken up from you into heaven, will so come in like manner as you saw Him go into heaven   Acts 1:11

The disciples asked Jesus two questions privately relative to His coming again. They asked:

Tell us, when will these things be? And what will be the sign of Your coming, and of the end of the age?"   Matthew 24:3

In His answer, Jesus warned the disciples to be vigilant because many would come in His name to deceive. They would hear about rumors of wars, nation would rise against nation., and there would be famines and earthquakes in various places. These, He said, were *"the beginning of sorrows"* (Matthew 24:8). Many false prophets would deceive many, and because of the increase of wickedness, the love of many would grow cold. But Jesus told them not to be alarmed by all of this.

The return of Christ is part and parcel of what the Christians call "Eschatology" which simply means "The doctrine of the Last

Things." The Second Coming of Christ will usher in the establishment of His Millennial Kingdom.

Now, there are differing beliefs among Christians regarding this doctrine. Bible Scholars categorized them into three. They are the post-millennialists, the a-mellennialsits and the Pre-millennialsts. The Millennial Kingdom of Christ will also be closely connected with the Tribulation period. It will be a terrible time of unprecedented trouble on Earth, when the wrath of God will be poured out upon sinful humans.

There are also three beliefs regarding the Tribulation period, and they are known as Pre-Trib, Mid-Trib and Post-Trib. These different beliefs on the doctrine of the last things are rather complicated. What is certain, however, is that Christ will come again.

There will be two phases involving the Second Coming of Jesus. The first one was elaborated on by the apostle Paul in 1 Thessalonians 4:16-17:

For the Lord Himself will descend from heaven with a shout, with the voice of an archangel, and with the trumpet of God. And the dead in Christ will rise first. Then we who are alive and remain shall be caught up together with them in the clouds to meet the Lord in the air. And thus we shall always be with the Lord.

The second phase is when our Lord Jesus will descend and set foot on the Mt. of Olives to commence His Millennial Kingdom on Earth.

The events that will transpire between the time of the Rapture and the time of the actual, physical and obvious descent of our Lord Jesus Christ are called the Great Tribulation period. This will be a time of unprecedented trouble when the wrath of God is poured out upon mankind on Earth. This Tribulation period will last for seven years, according to the prophet Daniel and confirmed by the book of Revelation. It will be during this time that the devil and his cohorts will unleash their power of extreme and intense persecution upon God's people, who are remnants of the Rapture. It will also be during this time that the Mark of the Beast will be forced upon people, and once they are marked, they will be already doomed!

Today, we are witnessing the fulfillment of the predictions of Jesus concerning the signs of His return. False Christs and false prophets abound, deceiving many people. There have never been as many earthquakes and natural calamities as we are e experiencing today. Two of the world's greatest wars were fought this past century, killing more than 100 million people. Our generation today is under the dreadful threat of global warming and climate change, which could result in enormous devastation and catastrophe on Earth and among mankind, not to mention the existing nuclear threat.

Our world is not getting better but is getting worse, despite our technological progress and scientific advances. Our only hope, therefore, is the return of Jesus Christ.

The big question is: Are you ready for Christ' return? If not, now is the day of salvation. It is not too late yet. You can be saved and be ready for the soon coming of Jesus.

Please pray like this:

Our heavenly Father, be merciful to me a sinner. Forgive me of my sins and wash me by the blood of Jesus, which was shed on Calvary. I now open my heart, and I receive Jesus Christ as my personal Lord and Savior. I trust that my name is now written in the Book of Life. Guide me by your Holy Spirit, as I commit to follow Jesus for the rest of my life.

I ask this in Jesus' name.

Amen!

Yes! Jesus Christ is coming again, and it is sooner than we think — perhaps today! ✻

Author Contact Page

You may contact the author in the following ways:

Pastor Gani Coruña

P.O. Box 154 G.P.O.

Greenhills Commercial Center

Greenhills, San Juan City, 1502

Metro Manila

Philippines

E-Mail: gani.coruna@starofhope.org

www.ingramcontent.com/pod-product-compliance
Lightning Source LLC
Chambersburg PA
CBHW062354090426
42740CB00010B/1277